Bridge to College Success

Intensive Academic Preparation for Advanced Students

Bridge to College Success

Intensive Academic Preparation for Advanced Students

Heather Robertson

California State University, Los Angeles
American Culture and Language Program

HEINLE & HEINLE PUBLISHERS
A Division of Wadsworth, Inc.
Boston, Massachusetts 02116

Director: Laurie E. Likoff
Production Coordinator: Cynthia Funkhouser
Text and cover design: Caliber/Phoenix Color Corp.
Production and composition: Caliber/Phoenix Color Corp.
Printer and Binder: Malloy Lithographing, Inc.

Bridge to College Success: Intensive Academic Preparation for Advanced Students

ISBN 0-8384-2907-6

Library of Congress Cataloging-in-Publication Data
Robertson, Heather.
    Bridge to college success : intensive academic preparation for
advanced students / Heather Robertson.
        p.   cm.
    Includes bibliographical references and index.

    1. English language—Textbooks for foreign speakers.
2. Interdisciplinary approach in education.   3. Study, Method of.
4. College readers.   I. Title.
PE1417.R578   1991
428.2′4—dc20   90-49682
                                                    CIP

94 93 92 91 9 8 7 6 5 4 3

Contents

Chapter
1

Higher Education in the United States   1

Chapter
2

Culture   19

Chapter
3

Learning and Memory   37

Chapter
4

United States History and Government   59

Chapter

5

Your Health   81

Chapter

6

English Communication   105

Chapter

7

Sociology   127

Chapter

8

Computers and Society   145

Chapter

9

Business   169

Chapter

10

Natural Science   193

Appendix A

Word Roots, Prefixes, and Suffixes   221

Appendix B

Guide to Writing a Research Paper   227

Appendix C

Skills Inventory   243

Preface

Overview

Bridge to College Success provides an intensive preparation for the student who will soon be attending college classes or who is already in college. It is best used with advanced English as a Second or Foreign Language students who have achieved scores of at least 475 on the Test of English as a Foreign Language, (TOEFL), or read at the ninth-grade level or higher.

This book challenges the advanced student to complete authentic college assignments and master college-level material. An integrated approach is used in which students practice reading, writing, listening, and speaking skills. Independent thinking is encouraged through questions for analysis following the lectures and readings. Focus is on the content and extensive practice in the language.

Interesting and *relevant* information is presented to students in a form that challenges their language abilities. The information presented is intentionally *controversial* in order to stimulate discussion. As in college courses, readings and lectures in this text don't always "have the answers"—they may present problems and competing theories or points of view. Students are asked to work with and analyze ideas and to use language as a means of communicating these ideas.

Rationale

As a teacher of students planning to enter college soon (and some already attending college classes), I found that most English as a Second Language textbooks were helpful in developing students' language skills, but not suitable for preparing students for college work. Something was needed to give students the feel of a real college course.

A comparison of what ESL students have learned, how they learn, and what they will be faced with in college can illustrate my reasons for writing this book.

1. In lower-level ESL classes, students are taught to read carefully and study discourse in detail. When they go to college, they are overwhelmed by the workload. No longer is slow, careful reading appropriate, because they cannot read the 100 or so pages they are assigned every week.

2. ESL students are often taught to study new vocabulary as a part of language development. In college the amount of new vocabulary can be frightening, and students need to learn to give priority to the key terms for each course instead of trying to learn every new word.

3. ESL programs tend to include writing as a discrete class or course component. In contrast, most college classes require written work as a way of learning and of evaluating what students have learned about the subject. Students find that they have to write research reports as well as take essay tests and complete smaller writing projects of

various types—not to show their language ability, but to prove they have learned the material.

4. College lectures contain a great deal of information that students must work with, and lecture notes become essential tools for study, yet many ESL students do not take adequate notes.

5. In many classes, participation has an impact on students' final grades, but ESL students are often intimidated and unsure about speaking in class, especially when the questions being discussed seem to have no obvious "right" answer.

6. ESL students are accustomed to having more guidance than American college students in how to complete assignments. This puts them at a disadvantage when college teachers give assignments and assume students will work independently and "figure out" problems for themselves.

To introduce ESL students to the new expectations and tasks college work entails, I prepared *Bridge to College Success*.

Approach

The basic philosophy underlying the book is that, to prepare for college work, students should practice with college material. Each chapter focuses on a general education theme, and contains a wide range of activities and types of assignments, anchored by a lecture, an excerpt from a college textbook, and a writing assignment. There are few "language skill exercises" in the traditional sense. Instead, the focus is on understanding, manipulating, and discussing the content of each chapter. An additional purpose of this text is to aid students in understanding and adapting to United States social and educational systems.

Since many students may be unfamiliar with the approach taken by this book, a preface for the student explains it in terms an ESL student can understand.

Supplementary Materials

Supplementary materials include audio and video cassettes of the lectures and an Instructor's Manual containing lesson tips and sample midterm and final examinations, an answer key, and lecture transcripts.

Acknowledgments

Grateful appreciation is given to the many people who contributed in various ways to this book. I would like to thank colleagues who field-tested and reviewed this material, and those who helped produce the field-test lecture tapes; these people were instrumental in enabling me to revise and polish the material: Priscilla Taylor—Program Coordinator, Joe McVeigh—Materials Coordinator, Dr. Eleanor Wilbon—Instructor, and Nick Zonen—Instructor, California State University, Los Angeles, American Culture and Language Program; Dr. Janet Fisher—Professor, Division of Curriculum and Instruction, California State University, Los Angeles; Young Gee—Instructor, Glendale City College, California; Sherrie Kelly—Instructor, University of California, San Diego; Ralph H. Skov—Instructor, Orange County College, California; Gregory Lee Riffle—Instructor, and Gail Cameron—Instructor, American English Academy, Alhambra, California.

Special acknowledgment goes to the Director of the Cal State L.A. American Culture and Language Program, Sally Gardner, and her staff for giving much appreciated support, encouragement, and flexible teaching assignments while I was writing the book. I would also like to thank my students, who were the "field testers" upon whom I tried out text material and whose feedback was instrumental in developing interesting and challenging lessons. I am also grateful to the Cal State L.A. professors who kindly allowed me to record their lectures on video and audiotape and gave their permission to have them included in this text.

Several people at Newbury House/HarperCollins *Publishers* deserve special recognition. Laurie Likoff, Director of Newbury House, and her assistant, Alida Greydanus, oversaw the book project and showed unending patience with my numerous questions. Cindy Funkhouser, Production Coordinator, and Caliber Design Planning, Inc. did a very professional job of text production, and Jim Donohue and Joana Jebsen handled the marketing.

Finally, a special word of thanks goes to my family. My father was very helpful in reading and commenting on the rough manuscript, and I am grateful to my husband and children for their patience, understanding, and all the dinners they cooked while I was working long hours at the word processor.

Credits

The following authors, publishers and instructors have generously given permission to reprint and adapt their material.

TEXT CREDITS

Chapter 1

Page 3: Sally Gardner, Director, American Culture and Language Program, California State University, Los Angeles. Lecture given 6-14-90. Reproduced by permission.

Page 13: Linda Mathews, "When Being Best Isn't Good Enough," *Los Angeles Times Magazine*, July 19, 1987. Copyright © 1987, *Los Angeles Times*. Reprinted by permission.

Chapter 2

Page 20: Sherrie Kelly, Instructor, Department of International Studies, University of California, San Diego, Extension. Lecture given 5-25-90. Reproduced by permission.

Page 20: Adapted from Peter S. Adler, "Culture Shock and the Cross-Cultural Learning Experience," in Louise F. Luce and Elise C. Smith, eds., *Toward Internationalism*, Second Edition, Cambridge, Mass.: Newbury House Publishers, 1987, pp. 24–35. Reprinted by permission.

Page 29: Alex Thio, *Sociology*, copyright © 1989 by Harper & Row Publishers, Inc., pp. 54–62. Reprinted by permission.

Page 32: Robin M. Williams, Jr., *American Society: A Sociological Interpretation*, Third Edition, New York: Knopf, 1970, pp. 452–502. Reprinted by permission.

Chapter 3

Page 38: Rolando A. Santos, Ph.D., Professor of Education, Division of Educational Foundations, California State University, Los Angeles, lecture given 1-31-89. Reproduced by permission.

Page 47: Carole Wade and Carol Tavris, *Psychology*. Copyright 1987 by Harper & Row Publishers, Inc., pp. 256–265. Reprinted by permission.

Chapter 4

Page 58: Dr. Arthur J. Misner, Professor Emeritus, Political Science, California State University, Los Angeles, lecture given 2-7-89. Reproduced by permission.

Page 70: Richard N. Current, T. Harry Williams, Frank Freidel, and Alan Brinkley, *American History: A Survey*, Volume I, 7th edition. Copyright 1987 by Alfred A. Knopf, Inc., pp. 329–339. Reprinted by permission.

Chapter 5

Page 84: Joan J. Lewis, M.A., Counselor, Student Health Center, California State University, Los Angeles, adapted from a lecture given 5-8-89. Reproduced by permission.

Page 84: "Vulnerability Scale" from the *Stress Audit*, developed by Lyle H. Miller and Alma Dell Smith. Copyright 1983, Biobehavioral Associates, Brookline, MA 02146. Reprinted with permission.

Page 86: *Reading Power and Study Skills For College Work*, adapted from Carl A. Lefeure and Helen E. Lefeure, Second Edition. Copyright © 1983 by Harcourt Brace Jovanovich, Inc., reprinted by permission of the publisher.

Page 94: Carole Wade and Carol Tavris, *Psychology*. Copyright 1987 by Harper & Row Publishers, Inc., pp. 279–282. Reprinted by permission.

Chapter 6

Page 104: Clyde R. Miller, *What Everybody Should Know About Propaganda; How and Why it Works*, New York: Methodist Federation for Social Action, Commission for Propaganda Analysis, 1948. Reprinted by permission.

Page 115: Paul Edward Nelson and Judy Cornelia Pearson, *Confidence in Public Speaking*, Third Edition. Copyright © 1987 Wm. C. Brown Publishers, Dubuque, Iowa. All Rights Reserved. Reprinted by permission.

Chapter 7

Page 128: Dr. Bernard B. Berk, Associate Professor, Department of Sociology, California State University, Los Angeles. Lecture given 5-23-89. Reproduced by permission.

Page 129: Adapted from Graeme Newman, *Comparative Deviance: Perception and Law in Six Cultures*. New York: Elsevier, 1976, pp. 142–143. Reprinted by permission.

Page 131: Allessandra Stanley, "Soul Brother No. 155413", *Time*, Feb. 20, 1989, p. 40. Copyright 1989 The Time Inc. Magazine Company. Reprinted by permission.

Page 137: Alex Thio, *Sociology*, copyright 1989 by Harper & Row Publishers, Inc., pp. 160–169. Reprinted by permission.

Chapter 8

Page 146: Professor Paul C. Blakely, Political Science Dept., California State University, Los Angeles. Lecture given 3-7-89. Reproduced by permission.

Page 157: Reprinted by permission from *The Mind Tool*, Fourth Edition, by Neil Graham. Copyright © 1986 by West Publishing Company. All rights reserved.

Chapter 9

Page 170: Dr. James D. Boulgarides, Professor, Marketing Dept., California State University, Los Angeles. Lecture given 3-14-89. Reproduced by permission.

Page 172: Daniel A. Wren and Don Voich, Jr. *Management*, Third Edition. Copyright © 1984 John Wiley & Sons, Inc., pp. 413–415. Reprinted by permission of John Wiley & Sons, Inc.

Page 175: Adapted from Marla Treece, *Communication for Business and the Professions*, Fourth Edition. Copyright © 1989 by Allyn and Bacon. Reprinted with permission.

Page 180: Leon C. Megginson, Donald C. Mosley, and Paul H. Pietri, Jr., *Management Concepts and Applications*, Third Edition. Copyright © 1989 by Harper & Row Publishers, Inc. Reprinted by permission.

Chapter 10

Page 194: Richard J. Vogl, Professor of Biology, California State University, Los Angeles. Lecture given 3-17-89. Reproduced by permission.

Page 196: Copyright © 1987 by St. Martin's Press, Inc., from *Handbook of Technical Writing*, Third Edition, by Charles Brusaw, Gerald Alred, Walter Oliu. Reprinted by permission of St. Martin's Press, Inc.

Page 206: From *The Message of Ecology*, by Charles J. Krebs. Copyright © 1988 by Charles J. Krebs. Reprinted by permission of Harper & Row, Publishers, Inc.

ART CREDITS

Grateful acknowledgment is made for use of photographs and drawings from the following sources.

Chapter 1

Page xx: California State University, Los Angeles Creative Media Services.

Chapter 2

Page 18: California State University, Los Angeles Public Affairs Office.

Chapter 3

Page 36: Photo by author

Chapter 4

Page 58: California State University, Los Angeles Public Affairs Office.

Chapter 5

Page 80: Photo by author

Chapter 6

Page 104: Courtesy of Foster Parents Plan, Inc.

Chapter 7

Page 126: Los Angeles Times

Chapter 8

Page 144: Photo by A. William LaChasse

Chapter 9

Page 168: Photo by A. William LaChasse

Page 170: "Decision Style Inventory" from James D. Boulgarides, Mary A. Fischer, and Elizabeth Gjelten, *Are You in the Right Job?* New York: Monarch Press, copyright © 1984, p. 34. Reprinted by permission.

To the Student

This material will help you learn to read, write, speak, and listen to English so that you can take courses at college successfully. It contains reading passages taken from actual college textbooks, samples of college lectures, and also has writing and speaking assignments of the kind you will find in college.

You may find this material different from other English textbooks you have used in the past. First, you may feel that the readings and lectures are quite difficult. This is because they are exactly the kind of work you will be expected to do in college. This is your chance to try college-level work in a class where you can learn the skills you need to be successful in college.

Second, there are few actual language exercises in this book. You will "pick up" the language as you go along. By learning to understand and communicate the ideas and information in each chapter as you would in a real college course, you will acquire the language skills you need.

Let's take a closer look at how this works. You will learn new vocabulary from the information given in each of the readings, based on the context. This means that the sentences in which you find new words will give you an idea of the meaning of the new words. If you have problems with vocabulary, you may want to devote extra time to vocabulary study, but for most students this is not necessary.

In addition, your reading speed and comprehension will increase just from the practice you will get in reading and understanding chapters from college textbooks. The same is true for listening to academic lectures. By listening to the lectures for each unit and taking notes, you will be practicing and improving your listening comprehension and notetaking skills.

The questions for discussion and writing topics in each unit will help you practice and develop your speaking and writing skills, and also will introduce you to the kind of thinking and problem solving that is expected in college. With all this practice, you will learn college-level English, even though you will not be doing the kind of vocabulary and grammar exercises that are usually found in English textbooks.

Finally, this material covers all the language skills, including listening, reading, speaking, writing, and thinking independently. This is important because you will need to master all of these skills when you attend college classes.

Chapter

1

Higher Education in the United States

Outline

Note taking for Lectures
Lecture: "Higher Education in the United States"
Observation: A College Class
Reading Speed Pretest
Marking A Text
Reading Exercises: "When Being Best Isn't Good Enough"
Word Parts
Writing: A College Application Essay
"When Being Best Isn't Good Enough"

Objectives

When you finish this chapter, you will be able to do the following:

Language and Study Skills

1. Define general terms related to higher education.
2. Take lecture notes which include key points of a lecture.
3. Find and mark main ideas and important details in a reading passage.
4. Write a college application essay

Content Mastery

1. Describe important elements of higher education in the United States, including the characteristics of a good school, different kinds of public schools, admissions criteria, and typical college courses and assignments.
2. Describe the behavior of students and their professor in a typical college class, based on your own observation.

Many students look forward to college life eagerly but also a little fearfully. There are entrance requirements to meet and, after that, new and difficult work to do. What do colleges require for admission and for graduation? This chapter is a general introduction to higher education in the United States. It will give you not only an idea of the systems and issues of higher education, but also an introduction to the most basic skills needed for taking college classes.

Important Terms

As you listen to the lecture and read the passage for this chapter, note the following important terms and their meanings. When you finish the chapter, you should be able to define each one.

accreditation	liberal arts
affirmative action	lower division
Associate of Arts	Master of Arts
Baccalaureate of Arts	Master of Science
Baccalaureate of Science	objective criteria
bias	post graduate
breadth requirements	prerequisite
college	private school
community college	public school
competitive	quarter
credits	quota
critical thinking	Scholastic Aptitude Test
distribution requirements	semester
Doctor of Philosophy	senior
extracurricular activities	sophomore
freshman	subjective criteria
graduate	undergraduate
grade point average	university
junior	upper division
laureate	valedictorian

NOTE TAKING FOR LECTURES

Most professors expect students to master textbook material on their own, and in lectures they supply new or more up-to-date information that is not in the book. Examinations generally cover both lecture and text material in varying proportions, depending on the professor. A good rule of thumb is to expect tests to be 50% on lectures and 50% on text material. This means that your lecture notes must be good enough to serve as study aids for examinations.

Note taking is a skill that takes a lot of practice to master. In this book, there is a lecture for each chapter, and you should take careful notes for every one in order to develop this important skill.

Basic Guidelines for Taking Notes

1. Always come to class ready to take notes. Keep a notebook with enough paper and carry pens, pencils, erasers and so on to class every day.
2. Have your notebook open and be ready to start taking notes before class starts. If you're not ready, you may miss important announcements while you are taking out your notebook and preparing to take notes.
3. Take down what the professor writes on the board, but also take notes even if the professor doesn't use the board.
4. Write down key words and phrases. It is not necessary to write complete sentences or to include words that are not necessary. See the sample page of notes for an example.

Sample Page of Notes

The numbers in the following list refer to those circled on the sample notes on the next page. These guidelines will help you become an effective note taker.

1. Always label the notes with the class and date.
2. Include important announcements such as exam dates, assignments and meeting times in your notes.

3. a. Leave a very wide left margin when you take notes. You can fold your paper to remind yourself of the margin until you get into the habit.
   b. Later when you study, you can use the margin to make notes or indicate the most important points to remember.
4. Be sure to include important terms that the professor defines. Write definitions but make them brief. Note any examples the professor uses.

Speech 150 Lect 10/13

pizza party 8:00 @ Garfono's tonight

Models of Communication
  Model = representation of a process
    can be object, etc.
      structural models - show diff. components
      functional - show how comp. interrelate
        & Function together

I One-Way Models - 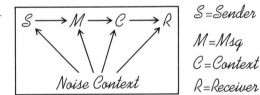 *S = Sender*
                                           M = Msg
                                           C = Context
                                           R = Receiver

Problems: no feedback accounted for
         no pattern - non-sequential (should be)
         role of receiver is too passive
Ex → One-Way Models – radio, TV
    in commun. Non Verb. feedback very important

II Interactional Model - (2 way)

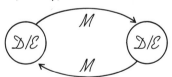 *D = Decode*
                      E = Encode
                      M = Msg.

takes response into account, ongoing Process
problems: time → waiting to Decode & encode
similar ping-pong when people take turns sending msg.

III Transactional M.:   "transceiver" =
    we are simultaneously senders & receivers
    we believe nonverbal over verbal M. -
      "body dosen't lie"

Figure 1.1. Sample Lecture Notes

5. Indicate main subject areas by putting them close to the margin. Indent when you write details about each subject. This way, it will be easy to see which details are related to each main point when you read your notes later.
6. If the professor uses diagrams or graphs, copy them down in your notes. Include any information you need to remind yourself of what the drawing is about.

Common Symbols Used in Notes

In order to write more quickly when taking notes, use abbreviations and symbols. You can develop your own system of abbreviations and symbols. Feel free to be creative, but be sure that you can understand what you wrote when you study your notes later! The following is a list of some examples.

The same as	=	And	&
Not the same or opposite	≠	Number of	#
Increase	↑	At	@
Decrease	↓	Important point	*
Result	→	Therefore	∴
With	w/	Approximately	c. or ~
Without	w/o		

LECTURE: "HIGHER EDUCATION IN THE UNITED STATES"

What is college like in the United States? This lecture introduces a typical public college system, and also explains what kinds of courses and assignments are given in college. It was given at California State University, Los Angeles, by Heather Robertson Gardner to a group of visiting Korean college professors and administrators as an introduction to the system of higher education in the United States. The lecture was adapted for this text by Joe McVeigh, at California State University, Los Angeles. It might be one you would hear as part of an orientation for new college students. Take notes, following the instructions in "Note taking for Lectures." You will need to use them to answer the comprehension questions.

Comprehension Questions

Refer to your notes as needed to answer the following questions.
1. What is the difference between a college and a university?
2. What is the difference between a public and private school?
3. Describe the three California public systems of higher education. What degrees are offered at each level?
4. According to the lecture, what kinds of things make a university a good school?
5. What did the lecturer say about the kinds of courses college students have to take?
6. What kinds of homework should you expect to have in college?

Questions for Analysis

1. How does the U.S. system of higher education differ from the system in your country?
2. How does your own experience with schoolwork compare with typical U.S. college work presented in the lecture?

OBSERVATION: A COLLEGE CLASS

In order to get an idea of what a college class is like, you will visit one and observe a professor in action. If you are already attending a college class, you can use it for your observation. You will not only practice your note-taking skills, but you will also practice your communication skills when you make arrangements for your observation.

Arranging a Class Observation

Choose a nearby college or one you wish to attend in the future. Use the following steps, and be ready to use all your English communication skills! Also, be persistent; don't give up if people are not helpful or don't understand you. Just find someone else to help you. Finally, don't let the college atmosphere intimidate you. Remember, you will be attending college before long, if you haven't already started.

1. The best way to begin is to choose a class in your major. Check a college class schedule to find out when and where the class meets, and who teaches it. Schedules are usually available at department offices. (Don't be shy about asking people for directions to a department office.)
2. After you get the course name, time, room, and instructor from the class schedule, you need to contact the professor to get permission to observe. Ask the department secretary for the professor's office hours, office location, and phone number. Call or visit the professor during these hours.
3. Professors are very busy people and are usually in class teaching, not in offices. This means that it will probably be difficult to get in touch with the professor you want. If you have trouble contacting the professor, leave a written message (with your name, telephone number, and a request to observe a particular class) for him or her at the department office. They will put it in the professor's mailbox.
4. Once you have permission, go to the class on the date that you agreed upon with the professor, and *arrive 10 minutes early*! Sit in the back of the room, and be sure not to talk during class. Remember, you are an observer, not a participant in the class. Follow the directions on the Class Observation Form. Stay until the class finishes, and when it ends, be sure to thank the professor for allowing you to observe.

Discussion

When observations are completed, share and discuss answers on the Class Observation Form with your classmates.

CLASS OBSERVATION FORM

Instructions

1. Take notes for the first 30 minutes of the lecture. You will hand in your notes *as is* to your instructor.
2. For the remainder of the lecture, observe the class and answer the questions that follow. Hand in your observations with your notes.
3. Be prepared to discuss your observations.

Questions

1. How do the students behave in class? Do you get the impression that they are interested, bored, comfortable? Note specifically what behaviors make an impression on you.
2. Are the students in your class taking notes? All the time or only once in a while?
3. Do the students ask questions or disagree with the professor during or after class?
4. Does the professor ask the students questions? Do students volunteer the answer or does the professor call on specific students?

5. What clues does the professor give to let the students know the topic and the main points of the lecture?
6. Does the professor refer to homework assignments? What are they? (Examples: reading, papers, exams, etc.)
7. Write down anything that you particularly noticed or that impressed you about this class.

READING SPEED PRETEST

When your teacher tells you to begin, start reading the following passage. After exactly 1 minute, the teacher will stop you. Mark the word you are reading when the teacher says stop.

15	Yat-pang Au's high school career was, by most measures, triumphant. He graduated first in his
32	class of 432 at San Jose's Gunderson High School with a straight-A average, ran a Junior Achieve-
45	ment company, took home prizes from the countywide science fair, lettered in cross-country and
56	track and was elected a justice on the school's Supreme Court.
71	At the school's honors assembly in May, Yat-pang was summoned so frequently to the stage
87	to accept medals and trophies that he began to duck his head and smile self-consciously whenever
102	his name was called: winner of seven scholarships, including ones from the National Society of
114	Professional Engineers and from Junior Achievement; Bank of America laboratory science laure-
124	ate; runner-up as Santa Clara County's Young Businessman of the Year.
138	Teachers and counselors sang his praises. Robert McPeek, a vice principal, later called the
153	lanky 18-year-old "one of the finest students I've ever encountered and a real gentleman, too."
170	Teacher's pets are often detested by other students, but not Yat-pang. Not only was he elected to
188	student body and club offices, but he was, in his mother's words, a "social animal" who spent too
204	much time chatting on the phone and squired his friend and co-valedictorian, Lisa Hirai, to the
206	senior prom.
224	And yet one goal, the honor he had most coveted to cap his high school years, eluded Yat-pang:
241	He was rejected by the University of California at Berkeley. At least 10 other students from Gun-
270	derson High will be entering Berkeley as freshmen this fall, but not Yat-Pang.
286	Yat-pang was so stunned by the rejection letter from Berkeley that he can still remember, in
304	detail, the February afternoon it arrived. "I read it again and again, because I thought maybe I had
323	misunderstood or that it wasn't addressed to me," he recalled. "I had my mind and my heart set on
324	Berkeley. . ."

GO ON TO THE COMPREHENSION QUESTIONS

Comprehension Questions

Answer the following questions without referring to the passage. Focus on the questions for the lines that you read. You may guess the answers to questions for lines that you didn't have time to read.

1. (15–56) Which of the following best describes Yat-pang's school performance?
   a. He was an average student but he worked hard.
   b. He was a good student and his teachers liked him.
   c. He was the best student in his class.
   d. He was more of a social animal than a student.
2. (71–124) T F Yat-pang received many awards and scholarships.
3. (138–206) T F Yat-pang was not liked by other students.
4. (224–324) Yat-pang was disappointed because
   a. He couldn't take his friend to the senior prom.
   b. He was rejected by Berkeley.
   c. His teachers criticized him.
   d. His school made a mistake.

Your Reading Speed

Find the mark you made when the teacher announced that 1 minute had passed. Count the number of words on the line that you didn't have time to read. Subtract this from the number at the beginning of the line. The result is your reading speed in words per minute.

Example

132   Teachers and counselors sang his praises.

              X   1   2   3

132 − 3 = 129 words per minute.

Understanding Your Test Results

Compare your reading speed to college level: 325–350 words per minute, according to Norman Lewis in *How to Read Better and Faster* (4th ed., New York: Crowell, 1978, 7). If you are already at or close to this speed, good for you! If not, make a speed of about 325 words per minute your goal for the end of this course.

Your reading comprehension score represents only your comprehension of key points in the reading passage. You may feel that there were too many new words. It is important to remember that in college you will probably come across thousands of new words. New vocabulary should not often interfere with your ability to understand the main points, and understanding main points should be your primary goal.

MARKING A TEXT

When you read, it is important to be actively thinking about the material. One way to be an active reader is to mark the text as you read it. Marking the text can increase your reading comprehension because it forces you to think about what the author is saying and to look for the important points. This exercise is designed to help you become a better reader by developing your skill at recognizing and marking main ideas in a text.

Steps in Marking a Text

1. Be prepared to mark the text the *first* time you read it. This will reduce the total time you spend reading. Students with good study skills tend to read the full text once, then study the highlighted parts or their notes when they go through the material again.
2. Have a pen, pencil, or highlighter marker in hand as you read. Highlighter seems to be preferred by most students.
3. While you read, guide the writing implement smoothly and quickly under the sentences you are reading. Don't stop under each word. When you find something you want to mark, just touch the pen or marker to the paper. This will allow you to read without interrupting your pace, and will increase your reading speed.
4. What should you mark?
   a. Mark main ideas.
   b. Mark the most important supporting points.
   c. Mark new vocabulary words for future study.
      (But *don't* stop reading to check your dictionary.)
5. A general rule of thumb is that you should mark at least one main point for each paragraph.
6. Avoid making the mistake of marking too much. If you look at a page and find that you marked more than half, you are probably overdoing it.

How Do You Find the Main Ideas?

At this point, you may be wondering how you can find the main ideas. In the English language, each paragraph of an article or book chapter has a main idea related to the main topic of the article or chapter. It is usually expressed in a sentence that introduces or summarizes the information in a paragraph. In addition to the main idea sentence, a paragraph has information and details that support or explain this main idea.

The first thing to consider is where main ideas are most likely to be placed within a paragraph. In American academic writing, the most likely places are, in this order, (1) the first sentence of the paragraph, (2) the second sentence, (3) the last sentence of the paragraph.

Next, consider the kind of information contained in a main idea. Usually, it is a general statement. Main ideas usually don't contain information such as examples, explanations, statistics, dates, and other details. These are usually support for the main idea, not the main idea itself.

Practice

1. Find the main idea of the first paragraph of the reading "When Being Best Isn't Good Enough" for practice. Check with your classmates and teacher to see if they marked the same thing.
2. Try again with the second paragraph, then check with classmates and teacher as before.
3. If you are having trouble finding the main idea, discuss paragraph 3 with a classmate or your teacher and decide on the main idea. Keep working on one paragraph at a time and check your answers until you are finding the main idea most of the time. Then go on to complete the reading passage according to the instructions in the following exercises.

READING EXERCISES: "WHEN BEING BEST ISN'T GOOD ENOUGH"

Reading Goal   Read to find the main ideas. Although there may be many new vocabulary words, try not to let them interfere with your search for the main points.

The reading passage located at the end of this chapter (4,653 words) is from the *Los Angeles Times Magazine*, July 19, 1987. Before starting, count the number of pages in the passage. At the beginning of the reading selection, write down your guess of how long it will take to read it. Then use the following guidelines as you read the passage. When you finish reading, write down how long it took.

1. As you read, find and mark the main ideas. Remember to run a pencil or highlighter under each line as you read.
2. Underline new vocabulary, but don't puzzle over meanings. Force yourself to keep reading, even if you feel that you don't completely understand. Remember that the important thing is to find the main points and get a general idea of what the reading is about.
3. Use your dictionary only after you finish reading the material. It is important not to break up the reading process by frequently checking the dictionary. Write down the time you took to read the passage *before* using your dictionary.
4. You may want to read the comprehension questions before you start, and keep them in mind as you read.

Reading Comprehension

How long did it take to read the passage? Remember, the time should not include time you spent looking up words in the dictionary. You should have taken about two hours (or less if you are a fast reader).

First, quickly go through the comprehension questions and pencil in answers that you feel you know from memory. You don't have to be too specific. For example, you could say "good" or "bad" for question 1 if you don't remember the exact grades. Don't check the reading passage yet.

After you have answered as many questions as you can from memory, go through the questions again, and refer to the parts you highlighted in the reading passage as a guide to more answers.

1. **a.** Was Yat-pang a good student? How do you know?
   b. Was he accepted at Berkeley?
2. **a.** What is the controversy over Asian-American admissions at Berkeley?
   b. Give some statistics to explain this controversy.
3. What were Berkeley officials' responses to the accusations about their admissions policies?
4. According to the article, what *objective* admissions criteria does the University of California (UC) system use?
5. The UC system also uses other admissions criteria. What other things are considered when making admission decisions?
6. How does the total number of applicants (freshman level) to Berkeley compare to the number accepted? How is this related to controversy over admissions policy?
7. What rules has the California state legislature made in regard to admission of minority students to the UC system? How has this affected admission criteria?
8. In the case of Yat-pang, what did Berkeley say about the reasons for his admission decision?
9. According to the article, is the university system likely to change its admissions policies?

Questions For Analysis

1. From this article, what can you learn about Berkeley's admission requirements? Support your answer with specific references to the article. Do you think they are fair to students? Why or why not? Do you think these requirements are typical of most universities?
2. Compare Berkeley's admission standards to those of universities in your country.
3. If Yat-pang had chosen a different major, would he have had a better chance of being admitted? Why or why not?
4. What might some of the reasons be for the practice of setting aside spaces for minority students (under affirmative action) and admitting them even if they don't meet regular admissions criteria?

WORD PARTS

English words are often made of combinations of word parts. By studying these word parts, you can increase your vocabulary because one part may be used in many words. **Word roots** are basic word parts that can appear in any position within the word. **Prefixes** are used at the beginning of a word. **Suffixes** appear at the end of words.

Match the words in the list of examples with the correct word part, then write your guess for its meaning. Check your answers with your teacher or the list in Appendix A. Make a point of learning any of the word parts that are new to you.

Root	Meaning	Example
1. agr	_____	_____
2. ann, enn	_____	_____
3. anthrop	_____	_____
4. aqua	_____	_____
5. astro, aster	_____	_____
6. audi	_____	_____
7. bibli	_____	_____
8. bio	_____	_____

Prefix

	Meaning	Example
9. a-, an-	_____	_____
10. ab-	_____	_____
11. ante-	_____	_____
12. anti-	_____	_____
13. arch-	_____	_____

Suffix

	Meaning	Example
14. -an, -ian	_____	_____
15. -ant, -ent,	_____	_____
-ar, -ary,		_____
-eer, -er,		_____
-ess, -ist		_____
-or		_____

Examples

abnormal	apolitical	biological
agriculture	aquarium	musketeer
American	architect	revolutionary
annual	astronomy	senator
antebellum	audience	servant
anthropology	bibliography	
antisocial	bigamist	

WRITING: A COLLEGE APPLICATION ESSAY

Many colleges and universities require an essay to be submitted when you apply for admission. Each school has slightly different rules for the content of the essay, so it is important to read the application instructions very carefully. Also, undergraduate application essays are different from graduate essays. In a graduate essay, you must tell about your academic accomplishments and research in more detail. In this exercise, you will write a typical undergraduate application essay. If you are already enrolled in a college, this is a good way to introduce yourself to your teacher.

What Is an Essay?

There are certain common characteristics of academic essays that college students should be familiar with.

1. An essay has at least three paragraphs: introduction, body, and conclusion.
2. The essay introduction includes a thesis sentence, which states the topic and purpose of the essay.
3. The introduction is one-fifth of the total length, the body is three-fifths, and the conclusion is one-fifth.
4. An essay length of five paragraphs seems to be considered ideal by many English composition teachers, but actually there is a wide variation in essay lengths.
5. Each paragraph should be about one-third to one-half of a handwritten or typed double-spaced page in length. (A paragraph longer than one page is most likely too long and should be divided.) This means that the shortest essay (three paragraphs) would be about one page long. A five-paragraph essay would be one and a half to two pages long. Essays can also be longer than this, of course.

Writing Topic

Write an essay about yourself that could be sent to a college with your application. Alternative topic: Write an essay about yourself which could be sent to a company where you would like to work. (Change "major" to "career" and "school" to "company.")

Gathering Information

To prepare for this essay, you will need to think about things you have done and what they show about you. This is called your "track record." Make a list of your past activities, grades, hobbies, work experience, achievements, and so on. Listing your strengths along with things you have done which illustrate these can also be helpful. When you write your essay, choose items from your list to serve as examples.

Planning the Essay

It is extremely important to give *specific* details for each point—names, dates, grades, and so on. Americans value *evidence*, in this case your track record. You may find it difficult to write about yourself in this way because of cultural differences, but mastering the American method of "selling yourself" will open doors for you in this country.

In the first paragraph, answer these questions:

1. Who are you?
2. What is your educational background? What school did you graduate from? What was your major or what were your best/favorite subjects?
3. End the paragraph with a sentence stating your plans for the next step in your education, for example: "Now, I have come to the United States to get a bachelor's degree in economics."

In the second paragraph, answer these questions:

1. Why did you choose your proposed major?
2. What background and experience do you have in this subject? What kind of grades did you get? Any awards or honors? Mention any other pertinent information; for example, experience working in your family's business, volunteer work, and so on.

3. What other skills do you have that make you a good candidate for this school? Be sure to mention any leadership or creative abilities you have demonstrated. For example: captain of a team, president of a club or the school, organizing parties or events, building or making something, and so on.

In the third paragraph, answer these questions:

1. What are you planning to do after you graduate from this school?
2. How will your education at this school help in your future goals?
3. What (if anything) have you already done toward your goals? For example, you may have already lined up a government job or a position you will have in a family business when you finish your education.

In the last paragraph, answer these questions:

1. Why did you choose this school? Give reasons that show you know something about the school. A good answer might be, "It has an excellent computer science department." Answers like the following should be avoided: "It's near my home." "It has a low tuition fee." These do not show that you know about the school and its strengths. They are also not very complimentary to the school.
2. End by stating why you would be a good candidate for admission, and why you think this school is a good choice.

Follow-up Exercise

Give the first draft of your application essay to your teacher. Form groups of three or four. Imagine that you are university admissions officers. (In the case of job-related essays, pretend that you are personnel officers.)

Your teacher will give each of you one essay to read. Read the essay, and decide whether you will admit the "applicant" or not. Base your decision on the content of the essay, not the grammar or other language considerations. Exchange essays within your group until each group member has read all the essays given to your group. If you cannot understand some part of the essay, find the author and ask about it.

1. Discuss your decision for each applicant with the group. Explain the reasons why you would admit or reject each applicant, quoting from the essay to support your points. The group should come to a final decision for each essay.
2. The group should write a brief note to the author of each essay, stating whether the applicant is "accepted" or "not accepted" and the reasons for the decision. The note should be signed with the names of the group members.
3. Return the notes from "admissions officers" and the essays to their authors.
4. Circulate around the room and discuss your "admission decision" with each author. Tell the author what you think are good points and areas needing improvement in the application essay.
5. Taking your classmates' comments into consideration, rewrite your essay. If you have questions about how to improve your essay, consult your teacher.

When Being Best Isn't Good Enough

Why Yat-pang Au Won't Be Going to Berkeley

BY LINDA MATHEWS

YAT-PANG AU'S HIGH SCHOOL career was, by most measures, triumphant. He graduated first in his class of 432 at San Jose's Gunderson High School with a straight-A average, ran a Junior Achievement company, took home prizes from the countywide science fair, lettered in cross-country and track and was elected a justice on the school's Supreme Court.

At the school's honors assembly in May, Yat-pang was summoned so frequently to the stage to accept medals and trophies and certificates that he began to duck his head and smile self-consciously whenever his name was called: winner of seven scholarships, including ones from the National Society of Professional Engineers and from Junior Achievement; Bank of America laboratory science laureate; runner-up as Santa Clara County's Young Businessman of the Year.

Teachers and counselors sang his praises. Robert McPeek, a vice principal, later called the lanky 18-year-old "one of the finest students I've ever encountered and a real gentleman, too."

Teachers' pets are often detested by other students, but not Yat-pang. Not only was he elected to student body and club offices, but he was, in his mother's words, a "social animal" who spent too much time chatting on the phone and squired his friend and co-valedictorian, Lisa Hirai, to the senior prom.

And yet one goal, the honor he had most coveted to cap his high school years, eluded Yat-pang: He was rejected by the University of California at Berkeley. At least 10 other students from Gunderson High will be entering Berkeley as freshmen this fall, but not Yat-pang.

Yat-pang was so stunned by the rejection letter from Berkeley that he can still remember, in detail, the February afternoon it arrived. "I read it again and again, because I thought maybe I had misunderstood or that it wasn't addressed to me," he recalled. "I had my mind and my heart set on Berkeley. I'd thought about Berkeley for years; I'd worked hard in high school to get into Berkeley. I couldn't believe I'd been turned down."

Then he called his father, Sik-kee Au, a Berkeley alumnus who owns a small security-alarm business in the Silicon Valley. "I thought my son was joking," said Sik-kee. "I couldn't imagine how he could be rejected. Then I thought it was a mistake."

Since then, both Yat-pang Au and his father have discovered there was no mistake. In the process, they have become embroiled in a fierce controversy that touches not only Berkeley but also the other campuses of the University of California and competitive universities across the country. The issue, say the Aus and other Asian-Americans, is whether institutions of higher learning have imposed quotas on Asian-American students, whether Asian-Americans are being kept out to preserve Caucasian majorities.

There may be a parallel between what is happening to

Linda Mathews is a Times assistant foreign editor, and a former correspondent in Hong Kong and Beijing.

Asian-Americans now and what happened to Jews in the 1920s and 1930s at some Ivy League schools. As the historian Samuel Eliot Morison wrote, "the bright . . . Jewish lads from the Boston public schools" became so successful at gaining entrance to Harvard and other institutions that administrators began to complain of what was discreetly called "the Jewish problem." To keep a lid on the number of Jewish students—denounced as "damned curve raisers" by less-talented classmates—the universities imposed quotas, sometimes overt, sometimes covert. As Harvard President Abbott Lawrence Lowell solemnly explained, admitting too many Jews might have inspired further anti-Semitism.

Today's "damned curve raisers" are Asian-Americans, who are winning academic prizes and qualifying for prestigious universities in numbers all out of proportion to their percentage of the population. And, like Jews before them, the members of the new model minority contend that they have begun to bump up against artificial barriers to their advancement.

CASUAL INSPECTION OF the Berkeley campus, 60 miles away from the Aus' home, makes any suggestion of anti-Asian bias seem implausible. Asians represent 6.7% of California's population, but they account for 25.5% of the Berkeley student body. In Sproul Hall, a visitor can eavesdrop on conversations in three Chinese dialects as well as Vietnamese, Korean and Tagalog, the official language of the Philippines. The fast-food shops on Telegraph Avenue, outside the university's main gate, sell not only hamburgers but sushi and *bulgogi* and *soba* noodles. If anything, Asian-Americans seem overrepresented.

But, to those challenging the fairness of the university's admissions system, the numbers are misleading; the percentage of Asians in the student body might be even higher, the critics contend, if admissions were still based strictly on merit. Since the mid-1970s, both Americans of Asian descent and immigrants from Asia have so outperformed Caucasian, black and Latino students in high schools that universities have manipulated admissions criteria to hold back the Asian influx, say the critics.

"As soon as the percentages of Asian students began reaching double digits at some universities, suddenly a red light went on," said Ling-Chi Wang, a peppery Chinese-born professor of ethnic studies at Berkeley and one of the university's severest critics. "Since then, Asian-American admissions rates have either stabilized or declined. . . . I don't want to say there's a conspiracy, but university officials see the prevalence of Asians as a problem, and they have begun to look for ways to slow down Asian-American admissions. Are they scared of Berkeley's becoming an Asian university? They're shaking in their socks."

"Berkeley's own projections a few years ago suggested that, before long, Asians were going to constitute at least 30% of the student body," said Henry Der, executive director of Chinese for Affirmative Action, a San Francisco-based civil rights group.

"That realization caused uneasiness, a sense that the university might lose some of its support in white communities. That's why the university has instituted practices to put a lid on the number of Asians."

"Asian-Americans, in essence, have become victims of their own academic success," declared Don T. Nakanishi, an assistant professor of education at UCLA. "They're viewed as a threat. We now have university administrators worrying about Caucasians becoming 'underrepresented' and about how to curb the decline of white students in the UC system."

UC President David P. Gardner stirred up a storm last December when, in an interview with the San Diego Union, he expressed concern that "the overrepresentation" of Asian-Americans in the UC system made it difficult to increase black and Latino enrollment and might cause unrest among other racial groups, including whites. Later, in a meeting with angry Asian-American leaders, Gardner said his remarks had been misinterpreted and promised that all qualified students would be accommodated somewhere in the UC system.

Alameda County Superior Court Judge Ken M. Kawaichi, co-chairman of the Asian-American task force that has led the challenge to Berkeley's admissions system, was among those who met with Gardner. Unconvinced by the UC president's explanations, Kawaichi speculated recently that "administrators and admissions officers have some idealized picture of what a university campus should look like. It should be predominantly white, maybe 70%, with a sprinkling of Asians and as many blacks and Hispanics as can be found."

BUD TRAVERS, SITTING in his high-ceilinged office in Berkeley's Sproul Hall, was having trouble controlling his temper as a reporter reeled off a litany of Asian-American complaints against the university. "I am exasperated that I'm constantly responding to criticism of this kind, to wild charges that are never backed up with facts," said Travers, assistant vice chancellor for undergraduate affairs on the Berkeley campus. "Instead we should be applauded for our success. We have more Asian-American students at this campus than at any other university in the country except the University of Hawaii at Manoa. And we never get any credit for it."

Travers, a former intercollegiate tennis champion, has been Berkeley's point man in the battle over Asian-American admissions. He has drafted countless reports in response to Asian-American organizations, dug through vast computer printouts to find the statistics to explain the university's position, met with disappointed applicants and their angry parents. And he's a little weary of it all.

"We have a real success story here," said Travers. "Our Asian-American students . . . do everything: Eight of our student senators are Asians, the No. 1 player on the women's tennis team is Asian, the co-president of the graduate student government is Asian, as are many of the debaters on our national champion team. It is ridiculous to suggest that Asian-Americans are denied opportunities here."

W. M. Laetsch, vice chancellor for undergraduate affairs and Travers' boss, is even more emphatic. "There have never been quotas here; there will never be quotas here," he said. "We get hammered mercilessly on this when we're doing better than anyone else in the country. It's so ludicrous that I don't know whether to laugh or cry."

Laetsch noted that the proportion of whites in Berkeley's student population has fallen from 68.1% in 1975 to 55% in 1986, "so if there is a conspiracy to perpetuate white control, we're not doing very well." In the same period, Asian enrollment has jumped from 16.8% of the total to 25.5%, black from 4.1% to 5.5% and Latino from 3.2% to 7.8%.

"You could make a case that it is whites who are underrepresented, but we very rarely get complaints from white parents or

white students," said Travers.

Yet the controversy will not go away. Yat-pang and his parents, as well as several other Asian-American families, have complained to the U.S. Justice Department, claiming that the UC admissions system discriminates against them. Nathaniel Douglas, an official with the department's civil rights division, said the charges are being investigated but no decision has been made on whether to file a formal complaint against the university.

The state Legislature also has been drawn into the debate. At the request of California Senate President Pro Tem David A. Roberti, the state auditor's office is reviewing several years' worth of university applications as well as a report on Asian-American admissions released by Travers' office last January. The Assembly Subcommittee on Higher Education has held hearings on the issue.

SIK-KEE AU AND HIS WIFE, Mandy, don't need reports and studies to confirm their gut feelings that their son was rejected because of his race. "There's no doubt in my mind," said Mandy, 41, whose life revolves around the family business and her five thriving sons. "I appealed after Yat-pang's rejection letter came, and I was told, 'Your son is good but he's not good enough.' Yet we know of other students, with lower test scores and grades, who were admitted to Berkeley."

Mandy is, like her husband, an immigrant from Hong Kong who was educated in the United States and is now a naturalized U.S. citizen. "We've felt discrimination before," she said, "but I really hate to see it affecting education. Education is special; every child should have an equal chance. I worry not only about my children but about other people's children."

The Aus say anti-Asian sentiment lies submerged not very far below the surface of California life. The family has been made to feel unwelcome in their posh neighborhood of brand-new houses, on expansive and lushly landscaped lots, that sell for $500,000 and up. "People have come by and yelled, 'Chinaman, go home,' " said Sik-kee, 45.

And then there was the terrifying incident one morning in May, when, just before dawn, someone hurled a large stone Chinese lion from the Aus' front porch through the leaded glass window of their living room. "At first I thought it was random violence," said Sik-kee. "Then I began to think, 'Why did they choose the stone lion instead of a brick or a stone?' Maybe it was an anti-Asian gesture."

The vandalism, which prompted Mandy to buy a gun and take shooting lessons, happened just after the San Francisco press reported Yat-pang's complaint against Berkeley. The Aus summoned the Los Gatos police, but the officers, Sik-kee said in disgust, "didn't seem interested. They didn't even take fingerprints."

Yat-pang is less certain than his parents that Berkeley has discriminated against him. "I am keeping an open mind," he said, with the easy confidence that makes him seem older than 18. "Berkeley has promised to let me and my parents look at the records of people who were admitted. I felt my scores and grade point average qualified me for Berkeley, but maybe other people *were* better."

His father glanced at him sharply and said, "Don't blame yourself."

ASIAN-AMERICAN ORGANIZATIONS focus their complaints on the growing reliance, particularly at Berkeley and UCLA, on subjective admissions criteria and the greater latitude given admissions officers. Such groups say that it is no coincidence that the two campuses have begun to emphasize such intangibles as the applicant's extracurricular activities and his character as the number of Asian-American applicants has mounted.

"In the 1960s, admission to UC was based on high school

grade point averages," explained Der of Chinese for Affirmative Action. "In the 1970s, UC began to take into consideration SAT scores. We could live with that. . . . But, in the 1980s, we've seen UC start paying attention to so-called supplemental criteria, which means subjective criteria. That change works to the detriment of Asian-American applicants, so it's very valid to raise the question of whether admissions criteria are being manipulated to keep our numbers down."

Asian-American students often lead their high school classes and, nationally, score higher than whites on the mathematics portion of the Scholastic Aptitude Test, though below whites on the verbal part of the test. So, under a system that emphasizes these quantifiable matters, Asian-Americans do well. But such students, especially immigrants, come from homes that emphasize school work over extracurricular activities, or they hold down part-time jobs that preclude such activities; when the intangibles are added to the admissions equation, say Berkeley's critics, the Asian-Americans suffer.

Der, a founder of the Asian-American Task Force on University Admissions, noted that over the past three years, the Berkeley admissions office has systematically de-emphasized objective admissions criteria.

Sixty percent of the freshman class that entered Berkeley in the fall of 1985 were admitted on the basis of what Berkeley calls its Academic Index—a formula that calls for the applicant's high school grade point average to be multiplied by 1,000, then added to the sum of his scores on the verbal and math portions of the SAT and his scores on three College Board Achievement tests. The maximum score on each test is 800, so the maximum Academic Index is 8,000.

For the class that entered Berkeley in 1986, the portion admitted on the basis of the Academic Index was slashed to 50%. Of this fall's freshmen, only 40% were judged by their Academic Index scores. Of the remainder, 30% will be athletes, or blacks, Latinos and American Indians admitted under affirmative action programs, or those with special talents and interests. The other 30% were selected by weighing supplemental criteria, ranging from such subjective matters as their character, as revealed by their application essays, to such open-and-shut matters as to whether they had studied four years of foreign language.

The trouble with this new admissions system, said Der, is that "it gives the university a tremendous amount of latitude." He and the task force, chaired by Judge Kawaichi and Judge Lillian K. Sing of the San Francisco Municipal Court, also object that the

> 'There have never been quotas here; there will never be quotas here. It's so ludicrous that I don't know whether to laugh or cry.'
> —W. M. LAETSCH,
> UC BERKELEY
> VICE CHANCELLOR

> 'Admissions officers have some idealized picture of what a university campus should look like. It should be predominantly white, maybe 70%.'
> —KEN M. KAWAICHI,
> ALAMEDA COUNTY
> SUPERIOR COURT JUDGE

criteria have been changed yearly, without advance notice to the state's high school students and without consulting Asian-American students, professors or civil rights organizations.

"If the university as a public institution is to fulfill its long-held commitment to competitive academic excellence and equal opportunity . . . it cannot erect artificial barriers, which on the surface appear to be neutral and color-blind, but which in effect cause an adverse impact on otherwise highly qualified and motivated Asian-American students," said a task force study of Berkeley. "Neither can the university continue to make admission policy decisions behind closed doors."

Nonsense, retort Berkeley's administrators; they say there is no proof that Asian-Americans fare badly when judged by subjective criteria and that, as the applicant pool has expanded in recent years, the looser criteria have become a necessity to make informed judgments among applicants.

"The usual complaint about the supplemental criteria was that we were going to admit a class of student body presidents," said Travers, the assistant vice chancellor. "But we use the criteria not just to pick student leaders. We also give extra points to the kids who open up computer software businesses in their garages, or have to work after school in their parents' grocery stores, or those who lost their parents and live with their grandparents. We see all those attributes as advantages, as adding to the diversity of the class."

The supplemental criteria add "some necessary human element" to the admissions process, said Laetsch, the Berkeley vice chancellor and a biologist. "If we had a system based purely on the Academic Index, we'd get a very homogenous student body. And we'd be putting our faith in standardized tests whose value is often in dispute. We'd be rejecting some students whose test scores were only a few points lower than those who were admitted; the system would be based on very fine and meaningless gradations. Using the supplemental criteria, we think we get the better, more interesting students—not just the good test-takers."

The task force leans heavily on statistics to make its case that Berkeley put the brake on Asian-American admissions. Through the 1970s, more than 70% of all applicants—Asians and whites alike—were admitted. But, as the Asian pool increased with the influx of immigrants in the early 1980s, admission rates for Asians began to drop below those for whites. By 1984, only 34.4% of Asian applicants were admitted, contrasted with 48.1% of whites, and the actual number of Asians on campus plummeted. That's when the task force organized and demanded an explanation from the university.

'Asian-Americans have become victims of their own success. They're viewed as a threat.'

—Don T. Nakanishi, UCLA Assistant Professor of Education

The task force argued that, if anything, Asians should be admitted in larger proportions than whites. Only 15% of California's white high school graduates even meet UC's eligibility requirements, the task force said, contrasted with 26% of Asians—testimony to the higher grade point averages and test scores of Asians.

In the past year, the admission rates for Asians and whites have begun to converge. For the class entering Berkeley this fall, the Asian admission rate almost perfectly matched that of whites—30.1% of Asians versus 30.9% of whites.

Travers, the Berkeley assistant vice chancellor, insisted that the university made no attempt to fix the rates but task force members scoff. Wang, the Berkeley professor, says the university has clearly yielded to political pressure. "There is a greater awareness on the part of university officials that the Asian-American community isn't going to put up with discrimination any more," he said.

LAETSCH AND TRAVERS ATTRIBUTE much of the agony over Berkeley's admissions process to the skyrocketing demand for places in the university's 3,500-member freshman class. More than 21,000 high school seniors applied to Berkeley this past year, a record, and more than twice the number who applied just five years ago. About 7,000 were admitted, and university officials assume that about half of those will enroll in September.

Once Berkeley and UCLA were considered "safety schools," where the state's best high school seniors could count on being admitted even if they were rejected by Stanford, Pomona or an Ivy League school. Nearly everyone who met the university's eligibility standard—based chiefly on finishing in the top 12.5% of a graduating class—knew he would be admitted.

"That's just not true anymore," said Laetsch. "Today we turn down people who would have been admitted easily 10 or even five years ago. . . . We turn down at least 2,000 kids each year with 4.0 grade point averages."

Word of the sharply upgraded admissions standards at Berkeley and UCLA, the most sought after and most competitive UC campuses, is only just beginning to reach the public. "The kids know this, the teachers know, and the guidance counselors know," said Rae Lee Siporin, director of undergraduate admissions at UCLA. "But the mommies and daddies don't. . . . Parents are shocked when I tell them, 'Yes indeed, your kid can get rejected even with a 4.0.' Asian-American kids with 4.0s get turned down, and so do Anglo kids with 4.0s."

Admission to UCLA, where Asians will account for 27% of the freshmen expected to register this fall, has become more competitive than that at many elite private colleges. The average Asian student admitted to the College of Letters and Sciences comes with a 3.97 grade point average, and the average white student is just a step behind with a 3.91 average. SAT scores for both groups top 1,200.

Another pressure in the admissions process comes from 1974 state Legislature resolutions ordering the UC campuses to make the racial compositions of their student bodies match the racial compositions of each year's high school graduating class. Despite a decade's efforts, blacks and Latinos remain underrepresented in the UC system, so both Berkeley and UCLA have set aside a growing number of places in their freshmen classes for these minority groups; that means that, under affirmative action programs, both campuses accept minority students who do not meet ordinary eligibility standards.

'What's the real difference between a middle-class black student and a middle-class white student? Or a middle-class white and a middle-class Asian?'

—John H. Bunzel, former President, San Jose State University

At Berkeley, the number of members of these minorities has leaped from 285 in the 1975 freshman class to 728 in the class that entered last September. UCLA has done even better; more than 25% of last year's freshmen were members of these minority groups.

It is inevitable, say UC administrators, that as the number of blacks and Latinos is increased to meet the legislative mandate, the Asian and white populations on campus will be squeezed. "We have a limited pie," said Thomas E. Lifka, assistant vice chancellor for student and academic services at UCLA. "Our enrollment cannot grow. So our problem is how to be as balanced and fair as we know how to be in meeting the needs of all our constituents. Not everyone is going to be satisfied."

WHEN MANDY and Sik-kee Au began to probe Berkeley's reasons for rejecting their eldest son, the university pulled no punches. Yat-pang, said Vice Chancellor Laetsch, "is a good but not an exceptional student." His mistake, said Laetsch, was that he applied to Berkeley's College of Engineering, which "turns down hundreds of students just like him." Yat-pang made it even more difficult for himself by pursuing a spot in a specialized double major—electrical engineering, and computer and material sciences—that admitted only 31 of 184 applicants.

"You play in that sandbox, you have to understand you're taking a chance," said Laetsch.

The College of Engineering, following standard university practice, selected the top 40% of its Class of '91 on the basis of the Academic Index; the cutoff for that group was 7,550 points. Yat-pang, whose SAT scores were solid but not as outstanding as his grades, had an Academic Index of 7,210: 4,000 for his perfect grade point average, 620 on the verbal SAT, 720 on the math, as well as 700 on the advanced math achievement test, 620 on the physics and 550 on the English composition.

Even if he couldn't make it on academic credentials alone, Yat-pang felt he should have been admitted once more subjective criteria were considered. "I am not a nerd," he declared, and his mother backed him up, saying, "Many Asian students have reputations as bookworms, but not Yat-pang."

In high school, Yat-pang ran the Math and Science Clubs, dominated science fairs and joined the Academic Decathlon team, the activities usually associated with valedictorians. But he also ventured beyond these brainy pursuits—running track, teaching economics to fifth-graders in a special program, showing such profits for his Junior Achievement company that he was a finalist for Santa Clara County's Young Businessman of the Year award. Although he intends to study engineering at DeAnza Community College this fall, Yat-pang yearns to be a businessman or, more precisely, an entrepreneur.

For years, he's had a taste of business at his father's firm, where all the Au sons work part time. Like the others, Yat-pang started out cleaning up the shop and assembling circuits. Since then, he's become the company's crack technician and installer, going on jobs as far away as Florida. In his spare time, he has written a software manual for the computer-run alarm system used by, among other clients of Au Electric, Los Angeles City Hall.

Yat-pang shows no signs of teen-age surliness. Like a dutiful Chinese son, he has always accepted the rules laid down by his parents: No television unless they're home to supervise. Everyone must appear on time for dinner. And, in the absence of the parents, the younger brothers—aged 12 to 17—must obey Yat-pang. "I tell the others that, even if they think Yat-pang is wrong, they must do as he says until I come home," said Sik-kee. "Then they can complain to me." Asked whether her eldest has any faults, Mandy thought for a while and said, "Sometimes he talks too long on the phone."

Perhaps because he has always played by the rules, racked up one semester after another of straight A's, Yat-pang says he sometimes has trouble understanding why he failed to achieve the single most important goal he ever set for himself. "I wonder what I should have done differently," he said. He plans to try to transfer to Berkeley after two years at DeAnza, whose engineering program is said to be very good. "The important thing, I guess, is not to be discouraged by what has happened so far," he concluded.

P LENTY OF OTHER ASIAN-AMERICAN kids are discouraged, however. "Of course, they're upset when they work their heads off, finish first or second in the class and then are rejected by Berkeley or UCLA," said Karen Chang Eubanks, college adviser at Roosevelt High School in East Los Angeles. "It's especially hard if they turn around and see someone from our school with a 2.69 grade point average and much lower scores admitted because he's Hispanic. I favor affirmative action, but I don't know how the UC system can make a rational distinction between Asian kids and Hispanic kids at a school like ours. They all come out of the same neighborhood; they're all equally disadvantaged."

Other educators are also concerned that race has become an entrenched part of university admissions. "I buy the argument that universities should have diverse student bodies," said John H. Bunzel, a former president of San Jose State University and a former member of the U.S. Civil Rights Commission. "The problem is that when race becomes a factor in admissions, too often it becomes the determining factor. What's the real difference between a middle-class black student and a middle-class white student? Or a middle-class white student and a middle-class Asian? Perhaps it makes sense, for the sake of diversity, to make sure the poor and disadvantaged are represented. But we ought to move away from race-conscious admissions policies."

UC administrators call Bunzel's ideas noble if impractical for a university like theirs, still struggling to meet the affirmative action guidelines set by the Legislature. "Everyone would like to get to the point where admissions can be truly race-blind, where affirmative action isn't needed," said Laetsch of Berkeley, just a bit wistfully. "But that's a long way off."

Rae Lee Siporin, UCLA's admissions director, says she, too, has fantasies about eliminating all racial considerations from admissions. "I was feeling perverse one day, and I said, let's take the names off all our computer printouts and just use numbers to identify students," she recalled. "That way, we wouldn't know who was Asian and who was white. Problem is, it would be just my luck that our admission rate for Asians would drop 10% that year—and how would I ever explain that?" □

Chapter
2

Culture

Outline

Lecture: "Culture Shock"
Field Study: Reactions to Norm Violations
The Language of Gestures
Guessing Meaning from Context
Outlining a Reading Assignment
Reading Exercises: "Culture"
Word Parts
Writing: Illustrating Concepts
"Culture"

Objectives

When you finish this chapter, you will be able to do the following:

Language and Study Skills

1. Guess meaning from context.
2. Make an outline of a reading passage.
3. Use an outline to write an essay.
4. Write an essay explaining and illustrating concepts.

Content Mastery

1. Describe culture shock, its symptoms and stages.
2. Show how gestures differ from one culture to another.
3. Explain what culture is and how it affects communication.
4. Define key terms relating to culture.
5. Conduct a sociological research study on norm violations.

In this chapter we look at cultural factors that affect us. What is culture? What happens to us when we begin to live in a new culture? As people who are or will someday be living in a different culture (even a different part of the United States could have a different culture!), it is important to know what it is and how it affects us.

Important Terms

As you listen to the lecture and read the passage for this chapter, note the following important terms and their meanings. When you finish the chapter, you should be able to define each one.

adjustment phase
beliefs
closed symbolic system

cross cultural learning experience
cultural awareness
culture

culture shock
defense mechanism
folkway
honeymoon phase
interpersonal skills
isolation
knowledge
law
material culture
mores

nonmaterial culture
norms
open symbolic system
recovery phase
regression
rejection
repression
sanction
self-awareness
symbol
values

LECTURE: "CULTURE SHOCK"

What happens when we start to live in a culture different from the one in which we grew up? This lecture will discuss the effects in detail. It is excerpted from a presentation given by a graduate student in a sociolinguistics class at California State University, Los Angeles. The assignment was to read and critique a book (Louise F. Luce and Elise C. Smith, eds., *Toward Internationalism*, 2nd ed., Cambridge, Mass.: Newbury House, 1987). This excerpt is about a chapter by Peter Adler, "Culture Shock and the Cross-Cultural Learning Experience." Take careful notes, paying special attention to the relationships between main ideas and supporting points. Remember to indent details under their corresponding main ideas.

Comprehension Questions

Refer to your notes as needed to answer the following questions.

1. What are the causes of culture shock?
2. List and describe four defense mechanisms.
3. Describe six symptoms of culture shock.
4. List and describe the four stages of culture shock.
5. What did the lecturer suggest to help relieve culture shock?
6. What do we learn from living in another culture?
7. What is the main message, or thesis, of this lecture?

Questions for Analysis

1. What things do you especially like or dislike about American culture?
2. What is a key difference between your culture and U.S. culture?
3. Have you ever experienced culture shock? If so, explain how you felt and how you coped with it. If not, find someone who has experienced culture shock and ask how it felt and how he or she coped with it.

FIELD STUDY: REACTIONS TO NORM VIOLATIONS

A scientific field that involves the study of modern cultures is sociology. In this activity, you will have a chance to see how a sociological research project might be conducted.

Discussion. What are some norms?

1. If you act normally according to your culture, could any of your actions break norms in the United States? Generate examples of actions that are norms in one culture and not in another.
2. Do Americans have any behaviors, any norms, that bother you? If so, what?

3. What kinds of actions do you think would break the norms in every culture represented in this room?

4. How would you react to someone who wasn't behaving normally? Have you had this experience?

Objective of the Field Study

The object of this study is to find out how people react to norm violations, and what social actions they might have that could stop people from breaking norms.

Procedure

You will need to perform some unusual action that violates a norm. The first thing you need to do is decide what action you would be willing to perform. You may choose an action that requires one or two people. Another student will be the observer, and will take notes on people's reactions.

Some examples are:

1. Do something that is customary in your country but not in the United States.

2. Face the wrong way (toward the back) in a crowded elevator.

3. Talk to a tree (or a wall, etc.).

Next, get together with one or two classmates. Decide who will be an actor and who will be an observer. Then agree on which unusual act will be performed.

Forming Hypotheses

The teacher will write the proposed actions of each group on the board. Discuss the following questions

1. What reactions do you expect to get?

2. How do you think the actors might feel?

The Study

Go out onto the school campus and perform the action you have chosen. Be sure to choose a location where there are a lot of people, so that their reactions can be observed.

Actors   Perform the action. Pay special attention to how you feel as you are violating the norm. Why do you feel this way? Notice people's reactions to you.

Observers   Try not to be noticed. Watch people carefully and take notes on how they react to the actors. Even things such as where a person looks, a smile, or a change of direction are important to note.

Presentation of the Results

Each group will report orally at the next class meeting on the results of the study.

Analysis of the Results

1. Did people react as predicted? If not, can you figure out why?

2. How did you feel (actors)? Have you ever felt this way before? When?

3. Did the observers experience any feelings or reactions?

4. What kinds of subtle social controls can you infer from this study?

5. Do you think that sometimes an international student might violate a norm because he or she doesn't know exactly how to act in this culture? Can you think of any examples?
6. How will you be able to tell if you violate a norm? What could you do to "fix" the situation if that happens?

THE LANGUAGE OF GESTURES

Culture affects not only the way we communicate with words, but also the way we communicate with movements such as gestures and body language. This exercise will explore some of the ways that such movements differ from culture to culture.

1. Your teacher will assign each student one of the words or expressions from the following list.
2. Think of how the word you were assigned can be expressed using gestures or movements instead of spoken language.
   a. In your country, what gesture would you use to express this idea?
   b. In the U.S., what is the appropriate gesture?
3. One by one, each student will demonstrate the gesture used in his or her own country. (Some countries may not have gestures for some of the concepts.) The class will try to guess the meaning of the gesture. Next, the student will show what the corresponding gesture is in the United States. The teacher can demonstrate the gesture if students don't know it.

Word List

be quiet	I'm disappointed! (darn it!)
come here	I'm joking.
crazy	I promise (Scout's honor)
excellent	me (I, myself)
five (5)	money
go away	nine (9)
good luck (for the person making the sign)	one (1)
	Shame on you!
good-bye	so-so (OK, wishy-washy)
Hi!	ten (10)
I don't know.	two (2)
I don't like it.	victory
I forgot!	write
I have an idea!	you

Discussion   Can you give examples of how other kinds of body language, such as speaking distance, eye contact, handshakes, and so on, differ in other cultures?

GUESSING MEANING FROM CONTEXT

In the following paragraphs from the reading passage, guess the meanings of the underlined words from the context. You may feel uncomfortable about guessing, but give it a try. It is not unusual for American teachers to ask students to guess the answer to a problem. We call this guess a "hypothesis" and expect it to be revised and corrected when more information becomes available.

Notice that familiar words may take on special meanings from their context. Write your guesses next to each word below the paragraph. You will discuss your answers in the next exercise.

Paragraph 1

Culture helps us develop certain knowledge and beliefs about what goes on around us. <u>Knowledge</u> is a collection of ideas and facts about our physical and social worlds that are relatively objective, <u>reliable</u>, and <u>verifiable</u>. Knowledge can be turned into technology, and as such it can be used for controlling the natural <u>environment</u> and dealing with social problems. The high <u>standard of living</u> in modern societies may be <u>attributed</u> to their advanced knowledge and <u>sophisticated</u> technology.

knowledge _____

reliable _____

verifiable _____

environment _____

standard of living _____

attributed _____

sophisticated _____

Paragraph 2

Each culture has its own idea not only about what is important in the world but also about how people should act. This is the <u>normative component</u> of a culture, made up of its norms and values. <u>Values</u> are socially shared ideas about what is good, desirable, or important. These shared ideas are usually the basis of a society's <u>norms</u>, rules that specify how people should behave. While norms are specific rules <u>dictating</u> how people should act in a particular situation, values are the general ideas that support the norms.

normative component _____

values _____

norms _____

dictating _____

Guessing Meaning from Context: Discussion

Small Groups   Form groups of three to five students. Group members will have these duties:

Discussion leader   This student will make sure that everyone in the group has a chance to speak.

Secretary   This person will take notes on the definitions that members of the group agree upon. The secretary will also write definitions on the board of words the teacher assigns to the group.

Reporter   The reporter will tell the class how members of the group decided on the definitions of the assigned words.

Compare your guesses for the meanings of the words.

1. Do you agree on the meanings?
2. Choose two or three of the words and explain to the group how you decided upon the meaning for each word.
3. Your teacher will assign some of the words to your group. Decide on definitions for each and have the secretary write them on the board.

Class Read the definitions written on the board by each group.

1. Did your group arrive at similar ones?
2. The reporter should tell the class some of the ways members of the group arrived at their definitions.

OUTLINING A READING ASSIGNMENT

This exercise is designed to help you see the organizational pattern of a chapter and to understand the relationship between its various sections.

Guidelines for Outlining

1. The most important ideas are listed closest to the left margin.
2. Subordinate ideas and details are indented under their corresponding main idea.
3. Roman numerals, numbers and letters can be used to indicate each level of importance, but are not necessary.

Example

I. Important idea
   A. key point in support of the idea
      1. details about the key point
      2. more details about the key point
   B. second key point in support of the idea
II. Next important idea

Exercise

From the reading passage for this chapter, make an outline using only the headings, subheadings, highlighted material, and boldface or italicized words. *It is not necessary to read the passage to complete this exercise.* In fact, it is better *not* to read it yet. Leave several spaces between each item in the outline. You will fill in the spaces later when you read the passage. The first part is done for you:

I. (Introduction)
   culture
   material culture
   nonmaterial culture
II. The Cognitive Component
   knowledge
   beliefs

READING EXERCISES: "CULTURE"

Reading Goal   Read quickly to find information to use in filling in the outline you prepared.

The reading material at the end of this chapter (6,580 words) is taken from a freshman-level sociology textbook, *Sociology: An Introduction*, by Alex Thio. The complete chapter is 24 pages long; the book has 23 chapters. To calculate the reading homework load for this course, divide the number of chapters by the number of weeks in a school session. For example, in a 10-week quarter the reading load would be 2.3 chapters or about 56 pages a week.

1. Mark main ideas and important details as you did in Chapter 1, but this time, add them to the outline that you made in the "Outlining a Reading" exercise. This will help you mentally organize the items you mark, increasing your reading comprehension.
2. Whenever possible, try to guess the meanings of new words from their context. Remember to use your dictionary only after you finish reading the entire material.
3. Note how long it takes you to finish the reading passage. It should take approximately two to three hours (less than two hours if you are a fast reader).

Group Discussion

1. After reading the passage, form groups of three or four. Use your outlines to decide upon the most important points of the reading passage—those that you might be tested on if you were really taking a sociology course.
2. Make five "test questions" about these points.
3. One member of the group should write the questions on the board.

Class Discussion

Compare the questions that each group has written on the board.

1. Are there any differences?
2. About which points did most groups write questions?
3. What clues can be used as a guide to important points?
4. Are the questions similar to the reading comprehension questions that follow? Discuss any differences.

Reading Comprehension

1. How is culture defined in the text?
2. **a.** What is the difference between material and nonmaterial culture?
   b. Which is more important to sociologists?
3. What elements form the cognitive component of culture?
4. What is the relationship between values and norms?
5. What are two types of norms?
6. Is a sanction a norm? Explain your answer.
7. What are some major American values mentioned by Williams, and what are some values he omitted?
8. What is a symbol?
9. How does human communication differ from that of animals?

QUESTIONS FOR ANALYSIS

1. Describe some norms from your culture that are different from norms in the area where you live now. What values might underlie these norms?
2. During the field study conducted earlier in the chapter, did you experience sanctions? If so, describe them.
3. Do you think the American values mentioned in the reading are accurate? Give examples from your own experience to support your answer.

WORD PARTS

Match the words in the list of examples with the correct word part, then write your guess for its meaning. Check your answers with your teacher or the list in Appendix A. Make a point of learning any of the word parts that are new to you.

Root	Meaning	Example
1. capit	_____	_____
2. celer	_____	_____
3. chron	_____	_____
4. clud, clus	_____	_____
5. cosm	_____	_____
6. crat	_____	_____
7. cred	_____	_____
8. cur, course	_____	_____

Prefix

9. auto-	_____	_____
10. bene-	_____	_____
11. bi-	_____	_____
12. circum-	_____	_____

Suffix

13. -ance, -ence	_____	_____
14. -ancy, -ency	_____	_____
15. -ary, -arium	_____	_____
-ory, -orium		_____

Examples

autocrat	circumnavigate	incredible
automatic	cosmos	independence
aviary	cursive	infancy
benefit	decapitate	laboratory
bicycle	decelerate	
chronological	exclude	

WRITING: ILLUSTRATING CONCEPTS

Thesis and Focus

What is a Thesis?   A thesis (theses = plural form) is a sentence that tells the reader what you will be discussing in your essay. Theses vary depending on the assignment. The simplest thesis just restates the essay topic. For example: "In this essay, I will describe a norm and a value from the Korean culture."

More complex theses ask or answer a question, or make an original statement that is supported in the essay.

What is a Focus?   Every essay must have a focus, a specific area of the subject that it addresses. Most essay topics are broad, and students can narrow or limit the topics and focus on whatever area of the subject they like.

For instance, in the assignment for this chapter you may wish to focus on a norm and a value related to family life; even more specifically, perhaps a norm and value for the relationship between a father and his children.

It would be incorrect to choose a norm about one subject and a value about another. For example, do not make the mistake of writing about a norm related to dating and a value related to working. An essay like that would lack focus.

Putting the Thesis and Focus Together   Usually, the thesis and focus are stated in the same sentence. For example: "In this essay I will describe a norm and value found in father-child relationships in Korea."

Exercise   Practice writing a thesis and focus for this chapter's writing topic.

Writing Topic

Write about your own culture or one that you know something about. What is a norm and a value of this culture?

Gathering Information

Think of several norms and values of your culture. Discuss them with a classmate, telling stories from your experience to illustrate each one.

Narrowing the Topic

The writing topic is quite broad, so the first thing you will need to do is narrow the focus for your essay. You could choose from the norms and values in regard to the family, for example, or in regard to business negotiations, friendships, eating, or any other area of the culture.

Planning the Essay

You used an outline to organize the information in a reading passage; now you will use an outline to organize a writing assignment. Make an outline for your essay, using the following guide.

     I. Introduction
        Things generally covered in the introduction include: general background information; definitions of important terms ("norm," "value"); statement of *thesis* and *focus*

II. Body

The body consists of one or more paragraphs. It is usually divided into parts in some logical way: according to subdivisions of the topic, similarities and differences, and so on. These parts are called main points.

A. first main point
  1. detail about this subject
  2. another detail
    details include facts, examples, explanations, stories from your experience, etc.
B. second main point
  details. . .
C. third main point
  details. . .

III. Conclusion

A. summary: restate your main points, and indicate how these main points support or prove your thesis.
B. If you wish, you can also add some comments. You should not introduce a new subject in the conclusion, however. Your comments must refer to the thesis and the information in the body of the essay.

Follow-up Exercise

Work in groups of three or four. Your teacher will collect the essay drafts and redistribute them.

1. Read the essay your teacher gives you, and find the thesis and focus.
2. Exchange essays within your group until every member has read each essay and found the thesis and focus.
3. Discuss which essay has the best thesis and focus statement, and why you think so.
4. Write the best thesis and focus statement on the board.
5. Tell the class why your group felt it was the best.
6. When you rewrite your essay, improve your own thesis and focus based on what you learned from this exercise.

Culture

Not long ago a social scientist received this rejection letter from an economics journal in China:

> We have read your manuscript with boundless delight. If we were to publish your paper it would be impossible for us to publish any work of a lower standard. And as it is unimaginable that, in the next thousand years, we shall see its equal, we are, to our regret, compelled to return your divine composition, and to beg you a thousand times to overlook our short sight and timidity (Moskin, 1980).

As Westerners, we may find this letter puzzling. If they think the paper is so great, why won't they publish it? Why would they publish inferior ones instead? Unable to find a satisfying answer, we may end up saying, "Ah, the inscrutable Chinese!" To the Chinese, however, the letter is not strange at all. It merely represents a proper way of being polite.

Not only the Americans and the Chinese but also other people around the world tend to see things differently. Obesity may seem unsightly to most Westerners, yet it might appear beautiful to Tonga islanders in the South Pacific. Chopping off a convicted murderer's head may seem barbaric to Westerners but only just and proper to Saudi Arabia's devout Moslems. What lies behind this variation in human perception? To a large extent, it is culture. A **culture** is a design for living or, more precisely, "that complex whole which includes knowledge, belief, art, moral, law, custom, and any other capabilities and habits acquired by [the human being] as a member of society" (Tylor, 1871).

It is obvious from this definition that when sociologists talk about cultures, they are not talking about sophistication nor about knowledge of the opera, literature, or other fine arts. Only a small portion of a population is sophisticated, but all members of a society possess a culture. Neither is culture the same as society, although the two terms are often used interchangeably. *Society* consists of people interacting with one another in a patterned, predictable way. But *culture* consists of (1) abstract ideas that influence people and (2) tangible, human-made objects that reflect those ideas (Velo, 1983). The tangible objects make up what is called the **material culture.** It includes all conceivable kinds of physical objects produced by humans, from spears and plows to cooking pots and houses. The objects reflect the nature of the society in which they were made. If archaeologists find that an ancient society made many

elaborate, finely worked weapons, then they have reason to believe that warfare was important to that society. In their study of contemporary societies, however, sociologists are more interested in **nonmaterial culture,** which consists of knowledge and beliefs (its cognitive component), norms and values (normative component), and signs and language (symbolic component).

In this chapter we will begin by examining those three components of culture. Then we will discuss why culture is essential to our survival, what is common to all cultures, and how cultures vary. Finally, we will see how variations in human cultures have been explained.

THE COGNITIVE COMPONENT

Culture helps us develop certain knowledge and beliefs about what goes on around us. **Knowledge** is a collection of ideas and facts about our physical and social worlds that are relatively objective, reliable, or verifiable. Knowledge can be turned into technology, and as such it can be used for controlling the natural environment and dealing with social problems. The high standard of living in modern societies may be attributed to their advanced knowledge and sophisticated technology. Knowledge is best exemplified by science, which we discuss more extensively in Chapter 19 (Science and Technology). On the other hand, **beliefs** are ideas that are more subjective, unreliable, or unverifiable. They may include, for example, the idea that God controls our lives. Beliefs seem to play a greater role in traditional societies. The best example of beliefs is religion, which we discuss in Chapter 15 (Religion).

THE NORMATIVE COMPONENT

Each culture has its own idea not only about what is important in the world but also about how people should act. This is the normative component of a culture, made up of its norms and values. **Values** are socially shared ideas about what is good, desirable, or important. These shared ideas are usually the basis of a society's **norms,** rules that specify how people should behave. While norms are specific rules dictating how people should act in a particular situation, values are the general ideas that support the norms. Thus the specific American norm against imprisoning people without a trial is based on the general American value of democracy. Parents are required by a norm to send their children to school because society places a high value on mass education. We are allowed to criticize our government because we value freedom of speech. Even a norm as mundane as that against pushing to the head of a line is derived from a general value, one that emphasizes fairness and equal treatment for all.

Values and norms also vary together from culture to culture. Since they are subjective in nature, a value and its norms that may be considered good in one society may appear bad in another. As you know, American teachers are relatively inclined to encourage their pupils to think for themselves because we put a high value on individualism. To the Soviets, however, the American norm of self-reliance is dangerous because it encourages antisocial behavior; to them, the American value of individualism means rampant selfishness—the no-holds-barred pursuit of one's own interests, the attitude of "the hell with others." On the other hand, Soviet teachers are more apt to encourage their students to be selfless and serve the state because they believe in socialist collectivism. As Americans see it, though, the Soviet teachers seem to be promoting total obedience to authority, championing a socialist collectivism that amounts to individual enslavement. Consider also one difference between American and Chinese cultures. If someone says to us, "You have done an excellent job!" an American norm requires that we say "Thank you." This may be traced to the value our society places on fair exchange: you scratch my back and I'll scratch yours, so if you praise me I'll thank you for it. In China, however, the same praise will elicit a self-effacing response like "Oh no, not at all" or "No, I've done poorly." The reason is that humility ranks high in the Chinese value system. Thus the Americans might consider the Chinese weird for being unappreciative and the Chinese might regard the Americans as uncivilized for being immodest.

Values and norms also change together over time. In the past most Americans supported the norm of school segregation because they valued racial inequality. Today the norm has given way to school integration because the value has shifted to racial equality. In China before the late 1970s, ideological purity ("We would rather have a poor country under socialism than a rich one under capitalism") was the country's reigning value. One of its resulting norms was to send professors, students, scientists, and other intellectuals to the farm to learn equality from the peasants. After the late 1970s, the new value of pragmatism ("It doesn't matter if the cat is white or black as long as it catches mice") took over, and one of its accompanying norms has been to send many of the intellectuals abroad to learn modernization from the West.

Norms

Day in and day out, we conform to norms. They affect all aspects of our lives. As a result, we are usually not aware of them. If someone asked why we say "Hi" when greeting a friend, we might be inclined to answer, "How else?" or "What a silly question!" We hardly recognize that we are following an American norm. This fact will dawn on us if we discover that people in other societies follow quite different customs. Tibetans and Bhutanese, for example, greet their friends by sticking out their tongues. They are simply following their own norms.

These norms are rather trivial; they reflect one type of norm called a **folkway.** They are relatively "weak," only expecting us to behave properly in our everyday lives. It's no big deal if we violate them; nobody would punish us severely. The worst we would get is that people might consider us uncouth, peculiar, or eccentric—not immoral, wicked, or criminal. Often society turns a blind eye to violations of folkways. Suppose we go to a wedding reception; we are expected to bring a gift, dress formally, remain silent and attentive during the ceremony, and so on. If we violate any of these folkways, people may raise their eyebrows, but they are not going to ship us off to jail.

Much stronger norms than folkways are **mores** (pronounced *mor-ayz*). They absolutely insist that we behave morally, and violations of such norms will be severely punished. Fighting with the bridegroom, beating some guests, burning down the house, and kidnapping the bride are violations of mores, and the offender will be harshly dealt with. Less shocking but still serious misbehaviors, such as car theft, shoplifting, vandalism, and prostitution, also represent violations of mores. In modern societies most mores are formalized into **laws,** which are explicit, written codes of conduct designed and enforced by the state in order to control its citizens' behavior. Hence violations of these mores are also considered illegal or criminal acts, punishable by law. Some folkways—such as driving safely, mowing the lawn, or no liquor sale on Sundays—may also be turned into laws. Laws are usually effective in controlling our behavior if they have strong backing from norms. If there is not enough normative support, the laws are hard to enforce, as in the case of legal prohibitions against prostitution, gambling, teenage drinking, and other victimless crimes.

In fact, all kinds of norms play an important role in controlling behavior, and society has various methods of enforcing them. These enforcement measures are called **sanctions.** They may be positive, rewarding conformity to norms, or negative, punishing violations. Positive sanctions range from a word of approval for helping a child across a street to public adulation for rescuing someone trapped in a burning building. Negative sanctions can be as mild as a dirty look for heckling a speaker or as severe as execution for murder. Some sanctions are applied by formal agents of social control such as the police, but most often sanctions are applied informally by parents, neighbors, strangers, and so on.

Be regularly rewarding us for good actions and punishing us for bad ones, the agents of social control seek to condition us to obey society's norms. If they are successful, obedience becomes habitual and automatic. We obey the norms even when no one is around to reward or punish us, even when we are not thinking of possible rewards and punishments. But human beings are very complicated; we cannot be easily conditioned, as dogs are, by rewards and punishments alone. Thus sanctions by themselves could not produce the widespread, day-to-day conformity to norms that occurs in societies all over the world. To obtain this conformity, something more is needed: the values of the culture.

Values

Since norms are derived from values, we are likely to abide by a society's norms if we believe in its underlying values. If we believe in the value our society places on freedom of religion, we are likely to follow the norm against religious intolerance. If we take to heart the American achievement values, we would accept the norm of studying and working hard. If employers still cling to the traditional belief that a woman's place is in the home, they would violate the norm against job discrimination by not hiring married women. In developing countries parents often carry on the norm of producing many babies because they continue to hang on to the traditional value of big extended families. Why do values have such power over behavior? There are at least three reasons: (1) Our parents, teachers, and other socializing agents (see Chapter 6: Socialization) teach us our society's values so that we will feel it is right and natural to obey its norms. (2) Values contain an element of moral persuasion. The achievement value, for example, in effect says, "It's good to be a winner; it's bad to be a loser." (3) Values carry implied sanctions against people who reject them (Spates, 1983).

People are not always conscious of the values instilled in them, nor do they always know why they obey norms. Sometimes norms persist even after the values

from which they are derived have changed. Do you know, for example, why we shower a bride and groom with rice after a wedding? We may feel it is the proper thing to do, or a pleasant thing to do, or in a vague way a sign of wishing the newlyweds well. In fact, the norm is derived from the high value our ancestors placed on fertility, which was symbolized by rice. Thus, over time, a norm can become separated from the value that inspired it. It comes to be valued in itself, and we may follow the norm simply because it seems the right thing to do.

We can easily determine a society's norms by seeing how people behave, but values are not directly observable. We can infer values from the way people carry out norms. When we see that the Japanese treat their old people with respect, we can safely infer that they put great value on old age. When we learn that the Comanche Indians were expected to save their mothers-in-law during a raid by an enemy before trying to save their own lives, then we conclude that the Comanche placed a high value on mothers-in-law. When we see that most American women are dieting, some to the point of becoming anorexic, we know that our culture places an enormous value on slenderness as the model for feminine beauty (Mazur, 1986).

Often, values are not easy to identify. Why is casino gambling illegal in most states, while many of these same states run lotteries? Why do most Americans consider pornography a source of sexual violence but favor the continued sale of pornographic movies and magazines (Press, 1985)? Assessing values in a society is such a complex procedure that sociologists often come up with different, even conflicting, interpretations. But well-reasoned and well-supported analyses can give us insight into a culture. Consider, for example, sociologist Robin Williams's (1970) influential analysis of American values. In his analysis there are fifteen basic values that dominate American culture: success, hard work, efficiency, material comfort, morality, humanitarianism, progress, science, external conformity, individualism, in-group superiority, equality, freedom, patriotism, and democracy (see Table 3.1).

This list does seem to capture something of what is recognizably "American" and to make some of our behavior more understandable. The idea that Americans value freedom and individualism makes more understandable the tendency of politicians to speak out against taxing Americans to support those on welfare. The notion that Americans value equality is consistent with our relative lack of norms governing interactions between people of different social classes. The idea that Americans value hard work and success explains why athletes work themselves to exhaustion in hope of making it to the Olympics. The American value of efficiency

Table 3.1 Major American Values

Economic Values
1. *Success:* achievement of wealth, power, or fame
2. *Hard work:* readiness to put in long hours if necessary
3. *Efficiency:* the ability to get things done and to do a good job
4. *Material comfort:* a high standard of living, the "good life"

Religious Values
5. *Morality:* the tendency to judge people on the basis of whether they are good or bad, right or wrong
6. *Humanitarianism:* being kind and helpful, providing aid and comfort, contributing time or money to the unfortunate as well as to charitable organizations

Social Values
7. *Progress:* the belief that change is for the good, that the future will be better
8. *Science:* mastery over the external world of things and events as opposed to inner experience of meaning and emotion
9. *External conformity:* emphasizing agreement and avoiding disagreement (hence the dictum, "Never argue about religion")
10. *Individualism:* self-reliance, independence, and the right of each person to develop his or her own personality because each individual has intrinsic worth
11. *In-group superiority:* measuring each person's worth by his or her racial, ethnic, class, or religious background

Political Values
12. *Equality:* treating all people as equals and advocating equal opportunity for everyone
13. *Freedom:* freedom from government controls and freedom to run one's own affairs
14. *Patriotism:* pride in being American and in "the American way of life"
15. *Democracy:* faith in "the people" and their right to govern themselves

Source: From Robin M. Williams, Jr., *American Society: A Sociological Interpretation,* 3rd ed. New York: Knopf, 1970, pp. 452–502.

can also explain why we are living in an increasingly impersonal society: we attend very large lecture classes, receive computer letters, seek help from God through pray-TV, work on assembly lines, and eat in fast food restaurants (Ritzer, 1983).

Williams's list further points to some of the areas of conflict in American culture. When external conformity, freedom, and individualism are all highly valued, it is difficult to resolve clashes over whether homosexu-

ality, pornography, or abortion should be prohibited by law. In the business world, the value given to efficiency and success often clashes with considerations of morality: Should companies in pursuing efficiency and success sell adulterated foods and other unsafe products, engage in deceptive advertising, or violate price-fixing laws? Or should they resist these immoralities and risk losing out to competitors? Cultures are basically integrated; they form coherent wholes. But as the inconsistencies among American values demonstrate, that integration is never perfect. This is not surprising because the cultures of large, modern industrial societies are generally less integrated than those of small, traditional ones (Archer, 1985).

Williams's list, however, does not fully reflect the complexity of American culture. It omits the important value of romantic love. It also fails to include three other values in American culture: (1) sociability—the importance of getting along well with others and being able to make friends easily; (2) honesty—the belief that keeping contracts is moral, good for business, or the "best policy"; and (3) optimism—the feeling that the future is hopeful and things will work out for the best (Spindler and Spindler, 1983).

Moreover, some of the values Williams identified have been changing. For one thing, many writers argue that Americans no longer value hard work. According to Daniel Yankelovich (1981), the "ethic of self-denial" (hard work) began to give way to the "ethic of self-fulfillment" ("I've got to love me, enjoy myself, explore myself") in the 1960s and early 1970s, and by the early 1980s as many as 80 percent of all adult Americans had become "self-fulfillers." Marvin Harris (1981) describes the value shift this way:

Americans have lost their forefathers' work ethic and puritan sense of discipline. In former years Americans worked and saved up for their pleasures. Now young people say they owe it to themselves to have a good life, to get everything that is coming to them—booze, drugs, food, travel, multiple orgasm—right away with no personal entanglements, marriage, or children to worry about.

Actually there is no real abandonment of hard work for easy living. Most Americans still work hard, but they also try to enjoy themselves more—on the job and off. In fact, their work ethic has heavily influenced their pursuit of leisure, so that the harder they work on the job the harder they work at their leisure. In a content analysis of *Fortune* magazine from 1957 through 1979, sociologist Lionel Lewis (1982) found that business leaders, like many other Americans, strive to succeed in their leisure pursuits as well as in their work. As one avid jogger explains, "Running, like business, is full of drudgery. But inherent in our philosophy is the belief that physical fitness gives us a headstart over a less fit competitor" (Lewis, 1982). In short, Americans have not given up the work ethic but have merely added the leisure ethic.

Other values that have also changed in American life include optimism about the future, tolerance of nonconformity, and the importance of material success. In the 1950s there was more optimism, less tolerance of nonconformity, and greater interest in individual success. Between the early 1960s and early 1980s there was less optimism, more tolerance, and greater concern for other people. Today there is a swing back to the values of the early 1950s (Spindler and Spindler, 1983).

However, Americans have also been pursuing their personal ambition so relentlessly that they have little or no time left for their families, friends, and communities. This leaves them "suspended in glorious, but terrifying, isolation." (For more discussion on this and other negative consequences of individualism, see box, p. 59.) Consequently, there is an attempt to move beyond the isolated self by spending more time with the family, seeking meaningful rather than casual relationships, and working to improve community life (Bellah et al., 1986). This tension between concern for oneself and concern for others is an enduring part of American culture. As sociologist Amitai Etzioni tells his interviewer (Kidder, 1987),

[We have] a continuous, unending conflict where on the one hand the community keeps saying, "There's too much individualism: Listen to me, don't abort, don't smoke, gayness is bad," and on the other hand people saying, "No, I have a need," and feeling inside themselves a tug-of-war. This kind of tug-of-war has been going on in America since "the founding days." We have it today, and we're going to have it in the 21st century.

Studies of American culture have further shown that some of its core values have exhibited remarkable stability and continuity through time. These include equality, honesty, hard work, self-reliance, and sociability (Spindler and Spindler, 1983).

QUESTIONS FOR DISCUSSION AND REVIEW

1. Why is sociology's definition of "culture" different from popular uses of that word?
2. What are cultural values and norms, and how do they combine with sanctions to control people's behavior?
3. How do folkways differ from mores?
4. To what extent do your personal values agree with the list of cultural views identified by Williams?

THE SYMBOLIC COMPONENT

The components of culture that we have discussed so far—norms and values as well as knowledge and beliefs—cannot exist without symbols. A **symbol** is a language, gesture, sound, or anything that stands for some other thing. Symbols enable us to create, communicate and share, and transmit to the next generation the other components of culture. It is through symbols that we get immersed in culture and, in the process, become fully human. We can better appreciate the importance of symbols, and particularly language, from Helen Keller's (1954) account of her first step into the humanizing world of culture. Blind and deaf, she had been cut off from that world until, at the age of seven, she entered it through a word:

> Someone was drawing water and my teacher placed my hand under the spout. As the cool stream gushed over one hand she spelled into the other the word water, first slowly, than rapidly. I stood still, my whole attention fixed upon the motion of her fingers. Suddenly I felt a misty consciousness as of something forgotton—a thrill of returning thought; and somehow the mystery of language was revealed to me. I knew then that "w-a-t-e-r" meant the wonderful cool something that was flowing over my hand. The living word awakened my soul, gave it light, hope, joy, set it free! There were barriers still, it is true, but barriers that could in time be swept away.

Once Helen Keller understood that her teacher's hand sign meant water, once she understood what a word is, she could share her world with others and enter into their world, because she could communicate through symbols. All words are symbols; they have meaning only when people agree on what they mean. Communication succeeds or fails depending on whether people agree or disagree on what their words or signs mean. Helen Keller's experience is a vivid example of the general truth that almost all communication occurs through the use of symbols.

Animal and Human Communication

Animals, too, communicate. If you try to catch a seagull, it will call out "hahaha! hahaha!" to signal its friends to watch out for an intruder. A squirrel may cry out to warn other squirrels to flee from danger. A chimp may greet its fellows by making the "pant hoot" sound, and it threatens them by breaking off and waving branches. When an ant dies, it releases a chemical to induce the surviving ants to carry it to a compost heap. Certain fish signal their presence by sending electric impulses from their muscles. But these signal systems differ in very fundamental ways from human communication.

First of all, our symbols are *arbitrary*. If you do not speak Chinese, you would not know what a *gou* is. *Gou* is the Chinese word for dog. There is no inherent connection between the word and the thing itself. The Spaniards, after all, call the same animal *perro* and the French call it *chien*. Even "dingdong" is an arbitrary symbol: a bell may sound like "dingdong" to us, but not to the Germans, to whom a bell sounds like "bimbam." The meaning of a word is not determined by any inherent quality of the thing itself. It is instead arbitrary: a word may mean *whatever* a group of humans have agreed it is supposed to mean. It is no wonder that there are a great many different symbols in human communication to represent the same thing (Poog and Bates, 1980). On the other hand, animals are not free to arbitrarily produce different symbols to indicate the same thing because their behavior is to a large extent biologically determined. This is why, for example, all seagulls throughout the world make the same sound to indicate the presence of danger.

Second, animal communication is a *closed system*, whereas human language is an *open system*. Each animal species can communicate only a limited set of messages, and the meaning of these signals is fixed. Animals can use only one signal at a time—they cannot combine two or more to produce a new and more complex message. A bird can signal "worms" to other birds but not "worms" and "cats" together. Animal communication is also closed in the sense of being stimulus-bound; it is tied to what is immediately present in the environment. The bird can signal "worms" only because it sees them. It is impossible for an animal to use a symbol to represent some invisible, abstract, or imaginary thing. As philosopher Bertrand Russell said, "No matter how eloquently a dog can bark, he cannot tell you that his parents are poor but honest." In contrast, we can blend and combine symbols to express whatever ideas come into our heads. We can create new messages, and the potential number of messages that we can send is infinite. Thus we can talk about abstractions such as good and evil, truth and beauty, for which there is no physical thing that is being signaled. It is this creative character of language that leads many people to believe that language is unique to humans. Although several chimpanzees have been taught sign language, it is doubtful that they have created *novel* sentences of their own (Terrace et al., 1979).

Chapter
3

Learning and Memory

Outline

Objectives

When you finish this chapter, you will be able to do the following:

Language and Study Skills

1. Define important terms from the field of psychology.
2. Write a complete definition.
3. Use the SQ3R reading method.
4. Take an active role in a class discussion.
5. Write an essay of comparison and contrast using concepts from reading and lecture material.
6. Use vocabulary cards to study new words.

Content Mastery

1. List and explain four ways we learn.
2. Conduct an experiment using conditioning to teach a new behavior.
3. Discuss the use of punishment in schools.
4. Explain how our memory works and how to improve it.

Would you like to have a better memory? Would you like to be able to learn more in less time? In this chapter, you are introduced to the field of psychology, which is the study of the behavior of organisms. We explore the area of psychology devoted to the human mind, focusing on learning and memory. The information can be especially helpful to students who want to understand the learning process and who want to improve their memories.

Important Terms and People

As you listen to the lecture and read the passage for this chapter, note the following important terms and their meanings. When you finish the chapter, you should be able to define each one.

Aristotle   conceptual category
chunk   conditioning

corporal punishment
déjà vu
echo
encoding
episodic memories
equilibrium
feral child
fixed reinforcement
icon
imitation
innate
instruction
long-term memory (LTM)
mnemonic device
motivation
multistore model of memory
negative reinforcement
overlearning
Jean Piaget
Plato

positive reinforcement
primacy effect
procedural memories
recall test
recency effect
recognition test
rehearsal
relearning method
retrieval
scheme
semantic memories
sensory register
serial position effect
short-term memory (STM)
SQ3R
storage
tabula rasa
tip-of-the-tongue (TOT)
trial and error
variable reinforcement

LECTURE: "HOW WE LEARN"

How do humans learn? Children and adults learn in a variety of ways, and a few of them are described in this lecture. It was a guest lecture given to a group of international students by Rolando A. Santos, Ph.D., Professor of Education, California State University, Los Angeles. This is an example of a lecture you might hear in a basic psychology course. In your notes, be sure to write brief definitions of key terms, because the professor gives specialized definitions that may not be found in a standard dictionary.

Comprehension Questions

Refer to your notes as needed to answer the following questions.

1. Describe Plato and Aristotle's debate about human learning. Which viewpoint is emphasized in modern psychology?
2. Based on the professor's description of feral children, can you infer what kinds of things we learn from our environment when growing up?
3. Briefly explain each of the following key terms defined in the lecture:
   a. tabula rasa
   b. imitation
   c. instruction
   d. trial and error
   e. conditioning
4. Use examples to show the differences among positive reinforcement, negative reinforcement and punishment.
5. Describe two methods of positive reinforcement described in the lecture.
6. Does the professor feel that conditioning can be used appropriately by teachers in the classroom. Explain.
7. According to Piaget, the human mind seeks equilibrium. What does he mean?

Questions for Analysis

1. Think of some of the best teachers that you have had, either in the United States or in another country. Describe some of the teaching methods they used and if possible identify them based on the methods discussed in the lecture.

2. How would you apply the lecture information in raising your own children?
3. Based on the information about conditioning, can you form a hypothesis about why some people become compulsive gamblers?

USING CONDITIONING TO SHAPE BEHAVIOR

In this activity, you will try out some of the concepts discussed in the lecture. Your goal will be to have an experimental subject "learn" a predetermined action.

1. One student in the class should volunteer or be chosen to be the experimental subject. This person must leave the room and wait until called back in. While waiting, the subject can read the rest of these instructions and study the lecture notes if there is time.
2. After the subject leaves the room, the class should decide what action the subject will "learn." Some examples are: write his or her name on the board, turn off the lights, open a window. If time allows, a series of actions can be performed.
3. Decide on what kind of reinforcement to use. Generally in this situation something like saying "right" or cheering or clapping would be appropriate. The whole class should join in giving the reinforcement at the appropriate time. It is important that reinforcement be given immediately after an action is performed.
4. Call the subject back in and begin. Avoid telling the subject what to do. Instead, use reinforcement.

Questions for Analysis

1. Did you find that you changed your planned procedure in any way? For example, was reinforcement used as planned? If there were changes, do you think they were an improvement over the original plan?
2. Was your reinforcement effective? Explain why or why not.
3. At this point the subject should tell the class how it felt to be in this situation. Did the subject feel encouraged and motivated to perform? What things seemed to help the learning process and what things, if any, slowed the learning process?

DISCUSSION: THE USE OF PUNISHMENT IN SCHOOLS

Activity One—Small Groups

Work with a group of four or five students and share your answers to the following questions. Choose one student to be discussion leader and ask the questions. Choose another student to be secretary and note down answers. Choose a third student to be reporter. The reporter will use the secretary's notes to tell the class the results of your group's discussion.

1. When you were in school, what kinds of actions were punished? Give examples from elementary, junior high, and high school levels.
2. What types of punishment were used?
3. Were parents ever contacted when students misbehaved in school? What usually happened if they were contacted?
4. Did teachers or school officials ever administer corporal (physical) punishment such as hitting or spanking a student? If so, what exactly was the punishment?
5. If you know, explain how the use of punishment has changed since your parents were in school.

Activity Two—Whole Class

The reporters present their groups' answers to the rest of the class. If students have questions for the group, they can be addressed to the reporter at this time.

1. Compare the answers of different groups. Does any pattern emerge?
2. Students are often punished for "cheating," but different cultures define cheating differently. Give specific examples of cheating to illustrate what it means in your culture.
3. In your opinion, what types of punishment, if any, are appropriate in school? Be prepared to explain the reasons for your answer.
4. If you were a teacher at your high school, would you punish the following? If so, what punishment would you use, and why?
   a. A student copied a friend's test answers for the college entrance examination.
   b. A student copied a friend's homework.
   c. A student is caught smoking in school.
   d. A student is disrespectful to a teacher (The student called the teacher a bad name.)
   e. A student is caught passing a note to another student during class.
   f. A student didn't do his or her homework.

Defining Terms

In this chapter you will be asked to define key terms from the lecture and reading passage. Defining terms is a skill that is often required in college. Students usually have a general idea of how to go about defining a term, but certain basic guidelines should be followed in order to give a complete definition.

Three Basic Components of a Good Definition

1. When defining a term, the first thing you should do is to make a brief statement of the meaning.

   Example
   A computer is an electronic device that processes data.

   Be careful that your definition is not too general. For example, "A computer is an electronic device" is too general because there are many other electronic devices such as radios, video cameras, and so on.
2. The second thing you should do is describe the key elements of the thing you are defining by breaking the meaning into parts, such as uses, materials, components, and so on. Here is one for our definition of a computer.

   Example
   The main parts of a computer are the central processing unit, the peripherals, and the memory.

   At this point in the definition, it would be appropriate to explain the specialized terms "central processing unit" and "peripherals" before going on.
   Sometimes a term cannot be broken down into key elements. In this situation, step 2 can be omitted.
3. The third part of a definition is an example. You need to give an example to show that you understand the definition and description that you have given. This allows teachers to distinguish between students who merely memorized the definition and students who really understood it.

Example

One kind of simple computer is a pocket calculator. It has a tiny chip that is programmed to do mathematics. This is the central processing unit. It has a little display screen and number keys. These are like peripherals. And it has a small memory that you can use to store the results of some calculations while you do other ones.

Notice that this example doesn't stop after the first sentence. It is a good example because it explains exactly how it is related to the definition.

Oral Practice

Work in groups. Give a one-sentence definition for one of the terms in the following list. Don't tell members of your group which term you are defining; if you have given a good definition, they should be able to guess the word. If your group has trouble guessing, add a description of the key parts of your term. If necessary, give an example. At the end of the exercise, each group should share some good definitions with the class.

animal	happiness	planet
art	heat	plant
atom	history	pronunciation
beauty	house	revolution
bicycle	human	rocket
boat	influenza	run
book	intelligence	satellite
car	language	swim
diet	lock	think
door	love	velocity
eat	mathematics	war
economy	molecule	writing
family	music	
food	pet	

Written Practice

Write a complete definition for one of the words in the list. Remember to include the three basic components of a good definition.

STUDYING VOCABULARY

Most students want to increase the number of words they know. One way is to study word parts. Here is a way to memorize new vocabulary that you find in your school assignments. This method works best with words that you will need to know for tests. Work with new words from the reading assignments and lectures. Study several words each day, using **vocabulary cards**. Look at them several times until you can read one side of the card and remember the opposite side.

Sample Vocabulary Card:

FRONT:

> New Word
> Sample sentence using word

BACK:

> Definition of Word
> Other related words

With this method, you can memorize a large number of new words. One drawback is that unless you see and use these new words often, you will soon forget them. If you want to remember new words for a long time, you must be exposed to them often, so you must read and listen to them as well as memorize them.

The amount of new vocabulary you find may be discouraging, but you can improve your vocabulary not only by actively studying vocabulary cards and word parts, but also by simply absorbing the language around you. Expose yourself to English whenever you can, in as many ways as you can, through reading, TV, radio, and conversation. By surrounding yourself with the language, you will develop vocabulary and other language skills, even though you are not actually studying.

Practice

Make vocabulary cards for the important terms from the lecture. They are included in the list at the beginning of the chapter. Practice reading the word and saying the definition before looking at the back of the card. You may want to work with a friend who can ask you for definitions of each word and check the back of the card to see if you are correct.

Discussion

Each person has a special way of studying vocabulary. What is your method? Perhaps other students have developed methods that you will find useful. Discuss methods of studying vocabulary with your classmates and your teacher, and make a point of trying some of the methods discussed to see if they are helpful for you.

THE SQ3R STUDY-READING METHOD

SQ3R is a method of study-reading your homework assignments. It is more efficient than simply reading and marking the chapter, because you will understand and remember more information. You can combine this technique with the outlining method you learned in Chapter 2. This will help you focus your notes on key points.

Follow these steps when reading the text in this unit:

1. *Survey.* Look through the assigned reading material. Mentally note headings, subheadings, pictures, charts and graphs, and how many pages you must read. Try to get an idea of the general content of the material by reading introductory and summary paragraphs.

2. *Question.* After your initial survey, start at the beginning of the material. When you read each heading or title, make it into a question. This will give your reading a purpose. When making questions, use question words such as *what, who, when, where, why,* and *how.*

   Example for this page: "What does SQ3R stand for?"

3. *Read.* Read the material under each heading to find the answer to your question. If you find that the material is not what you expected, feel free to change to a more appropriate question.

4. *Record.* Record the questions and their answers on a piece of paper. Title the paper with the class, chapter, and date. Follow the same format as for lecture notes. Include any details that you feel are especially important. Also include any italicized or boldface words and their definitions. The questions and answers are your notes on this reading assignment. They should contain the most important information from the text.

5. *Review.* A week or two later, review your notes on the chapter. Feel free to add more information that you feel is important, or write questions in the margins if you are not sure about something. Then check your text or ask your teacher to get answers to any questions you might have.

Suggestions

Be a questioning reader and critically evaluate the author's purpose. What is the author trying to say? Is he or she presenting facts or giving opinions? If several different positions or theories are presented for the same topic, which one does the author favor, if any?

Adjust your reading to fit your needs. If a reading is especially difficult, you may need to read it more carefully by slowing down or rereading parts. Don't hesitate to ask the teacher or a classmate for help if you need it.

READING EXERCISES: "MEMORY"

Reading Goal   Use the SQ3R method to read the material, concentrating on the key points. Write notes for your SQ3R questions and their answers.

The reading passage for this chapter (6,035 words) is from a freshman-level psychology textbook, *Psychology*, by Carole Wade and Carol Tavris. The complete chapter is 30 pages long. The book has 18 chapters, and most of them would be required reading homework in a typical psychology course. To find out what the reading homework load would be, divide the number of chapters by the number of weeks in one school term.

1. Use the SQ3R study-reading technique. Write your notes in outline form.
2. Set a time limit based on your reading speed. Keeping track of how much time you spend on reading assignments can help you improve your study efficiency.

Note: The SQ3R technique tends to take longer at first than just marking a text or outlining, so allow some extra time when using this method. Although it takes longer initially, in the long run SQ3R saves time because you remember the material better and don't need to spend as much time reviewing later.

Reading Comprehension Questions

1. What is the multistore model of memory? Include brief descriptions of three important memory systems in this model.
2. Give an example of a recall type classroom test and an example of a recognition type test.
3. How many items can we keep in short-term memory at one time? How can we extend the retention time and capacity of short-term memory?
4. A student studies a list of 25 vocabulary words. A few moments later, he can remember the first three words and the last four words, but has forgotten the rest. How do psychologists explain this phenomenon?
5. How is information stored and organized in long-term memory?
6. Explain the expression "It's on the tip of my tongue."
7. What are three types of long-term memories?
8. What are some important steps you can take to improve your own memory?

Questions for Analysis

1. What methods have you used to memorize new vocabulary? Have you found any particular method to be more effective? Does the information in the reading passage support your experience?

2. If you stare at a picture for a few seconds and then look at a blank sheet of paper, you may still see the image of the picture. This is called an "afterimage." Explain afterimages based on what is known about the sensory register.

3. Would you prefer to take an essay or a multiple-choice exam? Explain the reasons for your choice.

WORD PARTS

Match the words in the list of examples with the correct word part, then write your guess for its meaning. Check your answers with your teacher or the list in Appendix A. Make a point of learning any of the word parts that are new to you.

Root	Meaning	Example
1. demo	_____	_____
2. dict	_____	_____
3. duc	_____	_____
4. fac, fic, fect	_____	_____
5. flect, flex	_____	_____
6. frater	_____	_____
7. fund, fus	_____	_____
8. gen	_____	_____
9. geo	_____	_____

Prefix

10. co-, con-,	_____	_____
col-, cor-		_____
11. contra-, counter-	_____	_____
12. de-	_____	_____
13. dis-, di-, dif-	_____	_____

Suffix

14. -ation	_____	_____
15. -cide	_____	_____

Examples

college	disagree	homicide
conductor	factory	nullification
congress	fraternity	reflection
counterclockwise	genetic	refund
democracy	geography	valedictorian
descend		

WRITING: COMPARISON AND CONTRAST

Defining Terms in Academic Essays

When you write for a class assignment, you must define all the important terms that you use. This is because the teacher wants to see whether you know the course material. Use the method for defining terms that was discussed on page 40. Definitions are often given in the essay introduction; however, you can also define terms as they are needed later in the essay.

Writing Topic

Write an essay comparing and contrasting the teaching methods used in schools in your country with those used in the United States.

Gathering Information

You may need to do a little research in order to get enough information for this assignment. You can use your experience studying English here, your observation of a college class from Chapter 1, information from the lecture and reading for this chapter, and any other sources of information such as friends or family members who have studied here. If you have only recently come to the United States and your present class is your only experience with U.S. teaching methods, you may need to focus on comparisons from this course in your essay.

Narrowing the Topic

The writing question is quite broad, so you will need to decide upon a focus for your essay. You could choose two or three methods of getting a new response as described in the lecture and discuss how they are used in your country and in the United States. You might decide to write only about a certain level of the educational system, such as elementary school, high school, or college. Or, you could focus on another type of teaching behavior, such as reward or punishment. There are many possibilities for a focus. A good choice would be to compare English teaching methods in your country and the United States, because you probably have relatively more experience in this area.

Planning the Essay

There are various ways to organize an essay of comparison and contrast. The following is a general outline for one way to organize this type of essay. Make an outline for your essay by using the following one as a guide.

I. Introduction
   Introduce what you will compare and contrast, and state your focus (examples of focus: teaching methods in high school, in English class, in regard to tests, homework, punishment, etc.). State what you will show with your comparison and contrast; this is your main point or thesis. For example, will you show that the teaching methods are quite different? Will you emphasize cooperation versus competition?

II. Body
   A. First main point of comparison/contrast
      description: in your country and in the United States
      examples
   B. Second main point of comparison/contrast
      description: in your country and in the United States
      examples
   C. Third main point of comparison/contrast
      description: in your country and in the United States
      examples

III. Conclusion
   When you summarize, you may include comments on one or more of the following points:

Generally speaking, what can you conclude about your comparison and contrast?
Are the teaching methods mostly similar or quite different?
Are there any particular effects of these methods?
Can you make any judgments about the advantages or disadvantages of the methods you discussed?

Follow-up Exercise

Your teacher will pass out copies of several students' paragraphs that include definitions of terms (or you can exchange essays with a classmate).

First, read the paragraphs and underline each definition. Then, as a class, compare definitions.

1. Which definitions are better? In what ways?
2. Where in the essay were the definitions included? In the introduction? The body? Did any particular location seem better?

When you rewrite your essay, work on improving the definitions you wrote based on information from this class discussion.

Memory

All information processing theorists agree that *encoding*, *storage*, and *retrieval* are the basic processes of memory. But just how do these processes take place? According to the *multistore model of memory* (sometimes informally called the "three-box theory,") information must pass through at least three memory levels, or systems, before it achieves any sort of permanence (Atkinson & Shiffrin, 1968, 1971). Each system is presumed to have its own unique characteristics. This model has been extremely influential for the past two decades, and has inspired a great deal of productive research.

encoding (in memory) *The conversion of information into a form that can be stored and retrieved.*

What's Ahead

- *Fleeting impressions*
- *The "leaky bucket" of short-term memory*
- *Organizing memories for the long term*
- *Creative remembering: How we reconstruct the past*

THE MULTISTORE MODEL OF MEMORY: THREE ROOMS IN THE MIND'S LIBRARY

Most of us, when we say we have "a good memory" or "a poor memory," are thinking of memory as a single "place" or system. However, according to the **multistore model of memory,** we do not have one, but three separate, interacting memories: a *sensory register* (or *sensory memory*), for the immediate retention of incoming signals; a *short-term memory (STM)*, for the initial encoding and temporary use of information; and a *long-term memory (LTM)* for the more-or-less permanent storage of information (see Figure 7.1).

To encode the multistore model in your own memory, you might think of memory as a library building that contains a front hallway, a waiting room, and the "stacks." At the first two stages, decisions must be made about whether the "visitor" (piece of information) should be allowed to go deeper into the building. This analogy does not imply that there are actually three separate "places" in the brain corresponding to the three memory storehouses. Talking about memory systems as places is merely a convenience. The three systems are really clusters of mental processes that occur at different stages.

multistore model of memory *The model that portrays the encoding, storage, and retrieval of information as involving three separate though interacting memory systems: a sensory register, a short-term memory, and a long-term memory.*

sensory register *The memory system that momentarily preserves literal images of sensory information. Also called* sensory memory.

First stop: The sensory register

According to the multistore model, all incoming sensory information makes a brief stop in the **sensory register,** the "front hallway" of memory. (Actually, there may be as many sensory registers as there are senses, but to keep things simple, we will speak of one.) Information in the sensory register is short-lived. Visual images, or *icons* [EYE-cons], remain for a quarter to a half a second. Auditory images, or *echos*, remain for a slightly longer time, by most estimates up to two seconds or so. According to the multistore model, the sensory register gives us a little time to analyze the features of a stimulus and to pick out what we need from incoming information for transfer to the

—— *FIGURE 7.1* ——

Information from environment →	**Sensory register** 1. Large capacity 2. Contains sensory information 3. Very brief retention of images (up to 1/2 second for visual; 2 seconds for auditory)	Transferred →	**Short-term memory (STM)** 1. Limited capacity 2. Contents typically encoded acoustically, but other types of encoding possible 3. Brief storage of items (up to 30 seconds if no rehearsal) 4. Involved in conscious processing of information	Transferred → ← Retrieved	**Long-term memory (LTM)** 1. Unlimited capacity 2. Contents typically encoded semantically as well as in other ways 3. Storage thought by some to be permanent 4. Information highly organized and indexed
	↓ Forgotten		↓ Forgotten		

The multistore model of memory

According to this model, there are three separate, interacting memory systems. Information that does not transfer from the sensory register to short-term memory decays or is displaced by new information and is forgotten. The same is true for information that does not transfer from short-term memory to long-term memory. When information is needed from long-term memory, it is transferred back into short-term memory.

recognition *The ability to identify previously encountered material.*

recall *The ability to retrieve and reproduce from memory previously encountered material.*

relearning method *A method to measure retention that compares the time required to relearn material with the time used in initial learning of the material.*

déjà vu [**day-zhah voo**] *The feeling that something happening at the present moment has happened before in exactly the same way. From the French for "already seen."*

next stage of memory. Information that does not go on to the next stage apparently vanishes forever, like a message written in disappearing ink.

You can demonstrate the reality of the sensory register for yourself. Wave a pencil back and forth in front of your eyes while you stare straight ahead. You may see a shadowy image trailing behind the moving object. You will find that it takes about ten cycles every five seconds to maintain the continuity of this afterimage. Since the pencil passes in front of your eyes 20 times in five seconds, or 4 times per second, under these conditions the visual image of the pencil in the sensory register lasts a quarter of a second (Lindsay & Norman, 1977).

We speculate that the sensory register could be involved in the curious phenomenon of **déjà vu.** This is the feeling that something happening at the present moment has happened before in *exactly* the same way. Déjà vu can be quite disorienting, even though it lasts only a few seconds. Perhaps it occurs when information entering the sensory register "short-circuits" or fails to complete its normal route, and must therefore be reprocessed. The feeling of familiarity would result from the fact that you *did* experience exactly the same situation before—though only a fraction of a second before. If you were unable to distinguish when the initial processing occurred, you might mistakenly feel that the experience had occurred in the more distant past. Unfortunately, however, this and other psychological explanations of déjà vu are as difficult to prove as more exotic ones that assume reincarnation or dreams that predict the future.

In normal processing, too, the sensory register needs to clear quickly to prevent sensory "double exposures." It also acts as a filter, keeping out extraneous and unimportant information. Our brains store trillions of bits of information during our lifetimes. Processing everything detected by our senses, including irrelevancies, would lead to inefficiency and frustration.

A Closer Look

MEASURING MEMORY

If you had a choice, which would you rather take, a multiple-choice exam, an essay exam, or an exam that asked you to fill in the blanks? Students often have definite preferences in such matters. They realize that the ability to remember previously learned information depends in part on what kind of performance is called for. Psychologists know this too, and use different kinds of memory tests for different purposes.

Recognition tests tap the ability to identify information to which you were previously exposed. The information is given to you, and you simply say whether it is old or new, or perhaps correct or incorrect, or pick it out of a set of alternatives. In other words, you match a current stimulus with what you have stored in memory. In the classroom, true-false and multiple-choice tests use the recognition method. In contrast, **recall** tests tap the ability to retrieve from memory information that is not currently present. Examples from outside the laboratory are essay exams and memory games such as "Trivial Pursuit." Under most circumstances, recall is more difficult than recognition, but exceptions do occur—for example, when the distractors (false items) on a recognition test are extremely similar to the correct items.

The gap between recognition and recall performance was demonstrated in a study of the ability to remember one's high-school classmates (Bahrick, Bahrick, & Wittlinger, 1974, 1975). People aged 17 to 74 were first asked to write down as many names of classmates as they could remember. Most could recall only a few dozen names, even when they had only recently graduated from high school. Those out of school for 40 years or more recalled on average only 19 names. Even when they were prompted with pictures of their classmates, the youngest subjects failed to name almost 30 percent and the oldest ones failed to name over 80 percent.

Recognition, though, was a different story. The researchers showed each subject ten cards, each with five photographs on it. The subject's task was to say which picture on each card was that of a classmate. (The four distractors on each card were from other yearbooks.) Recent high school graduates recognized 90 percent of their classmates' pictures. More important, so did people who had graduated 35 years earlier. Even those who had finished high school more than 40 years earlier

were able to identify the faces of three-fourths of their classmates. The ability to recognize *names* was almost as impressive. The gap between recognition and recall, therefore, could not be explained solely by the fact that one tapped verbal memory and another visual.

Such results show that tests of recall may underestimate the amount of information people retain over long periods of time. However, this does not imply that recall tests in college courses should be replaced by recognition tests! Recall tests are usually a more stringent measure of memory than recognition tests. If you do well on a recall examination, the instructor can have confidence that you really know the material well.

Another method used in research on memory is the **relearning** (or *savings*) **method**. It requires people to relearn information or a task that was learned earlier. If they learn more quickly the second time, that means they must have remembered something from the first experience, whether or not they realized it. The relearning method is the most sensitive measure of memory; it detects extremely small amounts of remembering. Relearning effects are encouraging to all of us who feel that we have forgotten much of what we have learned. Though we may not recall or recognize much about a topic, should we ever have occasion to relearn it (for example, by taking a refresher course) we will probably learn more rapidly than we did the first time.

Now, how well do you remember what you have just read? Find out by answering the following questions. Then see if you can tell which kind of memory each question is measuring.

1. What is the advantage of using the relearning method to measure memory?

2. Which method may underestimate the amount of information retained over long periods of time: (a) recognition, (b) recall, or (c) relearning.

3. True or false: Recognition tests require you to match a current stimulus with information stored in memory.

ANSWERS:

[Question 1 measures recall; questions 2 and 3 measure recognition.]

1. The relearning method is sensitive to small amounts of remembering. **2.** b **3.** true

Second stop: Short-term memory

According to the multistore model, once an item of information makes it past the sensory register, it enters **short-term memory (STM),** the "waiting room" of our mental library. Like the sensory register, short-term memory retains information only temporarily, for up to about 30 seconds by most estimates (Atkinson & Shiffrin, 1968, 1971; Shiffrin & Atkinson, 1969), though some think the maximum interval may extend to a few minutes (Melton, 1963). In short-term memory, the material is no longer an exact sensory image, but an encoding of one, such as a word or a number. This material either transfers into long-term memory, or decays and is lost forever.

Apparently, any type of information may be stored in short-term memory, but most people (or at least most hearing people) seem to prefer encoding information in STM by sound. When you ask people to memorize a long list of items and then recall them immediately, they are apt to make auditory mistakes, saying, for example, that they heard "beer" when they really heard "bear." In contrast, if you let people study the list for some time and then test them a week or two later, they are apt to make semantic, or meaning, errors, such as reporting that they heard "grizzly" rather than "bear." In long-term memory, information is usually encoded semantically rather than acoustically.

Cases of brain injury dramatically demonstrate the importance of transferring information out of short-term and into long-term memory. You may recall the case of H. M., described in Chapter 3. Surgical removal of his hippocampus did not interfere with H. M.'s ability to store information on a short-term basis. He could hold a conversation, appearing normal when you first met him. The operation also left intact memories that were already encoded in long-term memory; H. M. could recall most of what happened before the surgery. However, he could not retain new information for longer than a few minutes. Many psychologists attribute the memory deficits of people like H. M. to a problem in transferring material out of short-term memory and into long-term storage.

Besides holding incoming information for a brief period, short-term memory also holds material that has been retrieved from long-term memory for temporary use. For this reason, STM is sometimes called *active* or *working memory.* When you need to use already stored information, you pull something like a photocopy into short-term memory, leaving the original still in long-term memory. For instance, if you have to solve an arithmetic problem, you bring a "copy" of the names of the numbers and the instructions for doing the necessary operations into short-term memory, where the operations are actually carried out. The flow of information from long-term memory into working memory is *not* disrupted in patients like H. M. They retain the ability to do arithmetic, use language, and perform all the other tasks that require a working memory.

Chunks of experience. When you look up a telephone number, dial it, and get a busy signal, you are apt to find that when you try to redial you have already forgotten the number. It has disappeared from short-term memory. The same thing happens when you are introduced to someone, address the person by name, and only two minutes later find you've forgotten the name. No wonder short-term memory has been called a "leaky bucket." According to the multistore model, however, if the bucket were not leaky, it would soon overflow. At any given time, the number of items STM can hold is, as one psychologist put it, "the magical number 7 plus or minus 2" (Miller, 1956). Five-number zip codes and seven-number telephone numbers are in this range.

short-term memory (STM)
According to the multistore model of memory, the limited capacity memory system involved in the retention of unrehearsed information for brief periods. It is used to store recently perceived information and information retrieved from long-term memory for temporary use.

If short-term memory is limited to seven (plus or minus two) items, how can we remember the beginning of a sentence spoken to us until the speaker gets to the end? After all, most sentences are far longer than seven words. According to the multistore model, we overcome this problem by grouping small bits of information into larger units, or **chunks.** The capacity of STM is not seven bits of information, but seven chunks. A chunk may be a word, a phrase, a sentence, or a visual image. The date "1492" is one chunk, not four. The acronym "FBI" is also one chunk. In contrast, 9214 is four chunks, and IBF is three—unless your address is 9214 or your initials are IBF!

Even chunking, though, cannot keep short-term memory from eventually filling up. According to the multistore model, the "waiting room" has only five to nine chairs in it. Those chairs can bear a lot of weight, but sooner or later some items must leave so others can enter. An item may either exit entirely, to be lost forever, or go on to long-term memory. Much of the information we encounter during the day is needed for only a few

chunk *A meaningful unit of information; may be comprised of smaller units.*

Retention in short-term memory: Going, going, gone

Subjects heard a set of items consisting of three consonants read aloud. After various intervals of time, they tried to recall the items. During the intervals, they were prevented from rehearsing the items by a distracting task. The longer the interval, the poorer the recall; after only 18 seconds, recall fell to almost zero.

———— *FIGURE 7.3* ————

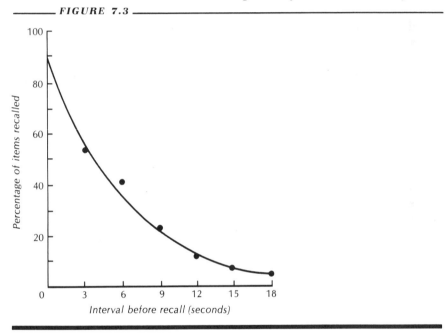

moments. If you are multiplying two numbers, you need to remember which ones they are only until you have the answer. If you are talking to someone, you need to keep their words in mind only until you have understood them. Other information is needed for longer periods and must be transferred to long-term memory. Items that are particularly meaningful, have an emotional impact, or link up to something already in long-term memory may enter long-term storage easily, with only a brief stay in STM. The destiny of other items depends on how soon new information replaces them. The longer information remains in short-term memory, the more likely it is to pass into long-term memory.

rehearsal *The repetition of information for the purpose of improving subsequent retention.*

Rehearsal. One technique for keeping items of information in short-term memory is **rehearsal.** In a classic study, people were given meaningless groups of letters to memorize. After the last item, they had to start counting backwards by threes from an arbitrary number. After only 18 seconds, they could recall few of the original letter groups (see Figure 7.3).

Counting backwards by threes had prevented them from rehearsing. When they were not given the counting task, they had much better recall (Peterson & Peterson, 1959). Thus, if you repeat a telephone number over and over, you may remember it the next day. But if you look up a number and then converse with someone, you are apt to forget the number almost immediately.

serial position effect *The tendency for recall of the first and last items on a list to surpass recall of items in the middle of the list.*
primacy effect *The tendency for items at the beginning of a list to be well recalled.*

The serial position curve. The assumption of a short-term memory distinct from long-term memory has been used to explain a phenomenon called the **serial position effect.** When a person is asked to recall a list of words in any order immediately after the list is presented, the retention of an item depends on its position in the list (Glanzer & Cunitz, 1966). Recall is best for words at the beginning of the list (the **primacy effect**) and at the

The serial position effect

If you try to recall a list of similar items immediately after learning it, you will tend to remember the first and last items on the list best, and the ones in the middle worst. This effect occurs with all sorts of materials.

FIGURE 7.4

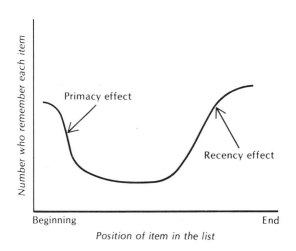

Position of item in the list

end of the list (the **recency effect**). When errors are plotted, the result is a curve with a characteristic shape (Figure 7.4). According to the multistore model, the first few words are remembered well because they were well rehearsed. Since short-term memory was relatively "empty" when they entered, there was little competition among items for rehearsal time, and so the items made it into long-term memory. The last few words are remembered well for a different reason: At the time of recall, they are still sitting in STM and can simply be "dumped." (If there is a 30-second delay after presentation of the list, and people are prevented from rehearsing, the recency effect disappears, presumably because the items in STM have decayed.) The items in the middle are not well retained, because by the time they get into short-term memory, it is "crowded" and individual items get less rehearsal. Therefore, many of them drop out of short-term memory before they can be stored in long-term memory.

recency effect *The tendency for items at the end of a list to be well recalled.*

Quick Quiz

Answer the following, based on the findings discussed so far.

1. STM can usually hold _____ items of information, plus or minus _____.
2. A good way to keep information in STM is to _____ it.
3. In short-term memory, the abbreviation *U.S.A.* probably consists of _____ informational "chunk(s)."
4. The _____ _____ holds images for a fraction of a second.
5. If a child is trying to memorize the alphabet, which sequence should present the greatest difficulty: *abcdefg, klmnopq* or *tuvwxyz?*

ANSWERS:

1. seven, two 2. rehearse 3. one 4. sensory register 5. klmnopq (because of the serial position effect).

Final destination: Long-term memory

Just as the heart of a library is the stacks, the heart of the mental storage system is **long-term memory (LTM).** The multistore model assumes that the capacity of long-term memory has no practical limits. The vast amount of information stored there enables us to learn, get around in the environment, and build a sense of identity and a personal history.

Organization in long-term memory. Because there is so much information in long-term memory, we cannot search it exhaustively, as we can short-term memory. The information must be organized and indexed, just as items in a library are organized and indexed in a card catalog. One way we index words (or the concepts they represent) is by grouping them into categories on the basis of meaning. In a well-known study, people had to memorize 60 words that came from four conceptual categories: animals, vegetables, names, and professions. The words were presented in random order and could be recalled in any order a person wished. People tended to recall the words in clusters corresponding to the four categories (Bousfield, 1953).

More recent evidence on the storage of information by conceptual category comes from a case study of a stroke victim called "M. D." (Hart, Berndt, & Caramazza, 1985). Two years after suffering several strokes, M. D. appeared to have made a complete recovery, except for one puzzling problem: He had trouble remembering the names of fruits and vegetables. M. D. could easily name a picture of an abacus or a sphinx, but not a picture of an orange or a peach. He could sort pictures of animals, vehicles, and food products into their appropriate categories, but had difficulty doing the same with pictures of fruits and vegetables. On the other hand, when M. D. was *given* the names of fruits and vegetables, he immediately pointed to the corresponding pictures. Apparently, M. D. still had a store of information about fruits and vegetables, but his brain lesion prevented him from using their names to get to the information when he needed it, unless the names were provided by someone else. Though this evidence comes from only one patient, it provides support for the idea that information about a particular concept (such as *peach*) is indexed by the concept's semantic category (such as *fruit*).

long-term memory (LTM)
According to the multistore model of memory, the memory system involved in the long-term retention of information; theoretically, it has an unlimited capacity.

The fact that some information is indexed by semantic category, however, does not mean that the mind is limited to that system. We may also index words in terms of the way they sound or look. Have you ever tried to recall some word that was on the "tip of your tongue"? Researchers were able to reproduce this frustrating state by presenting people with definitions of uncommon words and asking them to supply the words. When **tip-of-the-tongue (TOT) states** occurred, people often came up with words that were similar in meaning to the right word before they finally recalled it. For example, if given the definition "a navigational instrument used in measuring angular distances, especially the altitude of the sun, moon, and stars at sea," they might guess *astrolabe*, *compass*, or *protractor*, before recalling the correct answer, *sextant*. However, they might also guess *secant*, *sextet*, or *sexton*, words that are similar in sound and form. Often the incorrect guesses had the correct number of syllables, started with the correct letter, or had the correct prefix or suffix (Brown & McNeill, 1966).

tip-of-the-tongue (TOT) state
The subjective certainty that information is available in long-term memory even though one is having difficulty retrieving it.

Three types of memories
According to one proposal, long-term memory consists of procedural memories (stimulus-response connections that enable us to perform specific acts); semantic memories (general knowledge); and episodic memories (personal recollections). Here are some examples. See if you can come up with three of your own.

_____ *FIGURE 7.5* _____

Procedural memory   Semantic memory   Episodic memory

What is stored in long-term memory?   Researchers are currently investigating other ways in which we organize items of information in long-term memory, such as by their familiarity, personal relevance, or association with other information. The method used in any given instance probably depends on the nature of the memory. For example, information about the capitals of the 50 U. S. states is probably organized quite differently than information about your first date.

To understand the organization of long-term memory, then, we need to understand what kinds of information can be stored there. Endel Tulving (1985) has proposed that there are three general types of long-term memories, as illustrated in Figure 7.5:

1. **Procedural memories** are internal representations of stimulus-response connections. They prescribe a particular action and account for much of the operant learning described in Chapter 6. You have procedural memories of how to brush your teeth, use a pencil, and swim.

2. **Semantic memories** are internal representations of the world, independent of any particular context. Semantic memories include facts, rules, and concepts. With a semantic memory of the concept *cat*, you can say that a cat is a small furry mammal that typically spends its time eating, sleeping, and staring into space, even though a cat may not be present when you give this description and you probably don't know how or when you learned it.

procedural memories
Memories for the performance of particular types of action.
semantic memories *Memories that reveal general knowledge, including facts, rules, concepts, and propositions.*

3. Episodic memories are internal representations of personally experienced events. They allow you to "travel back" in time. When you remember how Tam-Tam, your dear kitty, once surprised you in the middle of the night by pouncing on your face as you slept, you are retrieving an episodic memory.

Other theorists have proposed slightly different ways of describing the contents of long-term memory. Most, however, distinguish skills or habits ("knowing how") from abstract or representational knowledge ("knowing that"). This distinction is supported by recent evidence that skill learning and the acquisition of knowledge are handled by different areas of the brain (Herbert, 1983; Oakley, 1981).

episodic memories *Memories for personally experienced events, including the contexts in which they occurred.*

_____ *Taking Psychology With You* _____

MEMORY SHORTCUTS

Some years ago a team of researchers reported that they could speed up learning in flatworms by feeding them a ground-up mash of fellow worms that had already learned the task in question (the conditioned response of cringing to a flashing light) (McConnell, 1962). Everyone got very excited. If worms could learn by ingesting the "memory molecules" of already-trained worms, could memory pills be far behind? Students joked about grinding up professors, professors about doing brain transplants in students. However, not everyone who tried to replicate the study got the same results, and talk of memory pills faded away.

Today, neuropsychologists continue to explore biological avenues to better memory. Several are experimenting with injections of hormones and neurotransmitters in animals. Scientists are learning more and more about the molecular changes that occur in learning and memory. Eventually, drugs may help people with memory deficiencies and increase the performance of those with normal memories (Rosenzweig, 1984).

For the time being, however, those of us who hope to improve our memories must rely on mental strategies. Formal memory techniques are known as **mnemonic** [neh-MON-ik] **devices**. Some mnemonic devices use easily memorized rhymes ("Thirty days hath September/April, June, and November . . . "). Others use formulas ("Every good boy does fine" for remembering which notes are on the lines of the treble clef in musical notation). Still others use visual images or verbal associations. These tricks work for a variety of reasons. Some force you to encode the material actively and thoroughly. Some make the information meaningful and therefore easier to retrieve. Still others reduce the amount of information to be stored by "chunking" it. The phone number 466–3293, for example, is better remembered in terms of the corresponding letters, which form a meaningful chunk: GOOD-BYE (appropriate, perhaps, for a travel agency).

Books on how to improve your memory often suggest elaborate mnemonics that take time to learn. A favorite is to remember a list of items by taking a mental stroll through your house, forming a visual image of each item at a particular location (the "method of Loci"). Later you repeat the tour, picking off each item as you go. Such aids can help those who must learn lists of relatively meaningless material or remember long speeches. They are also tricks-of-the-trade for stage performers with apparently amazing memories. Most of us, however, do not wish to learn complicated tricks. Why bother to memorize a grocery list with the "mental stroll" method when you can simply write down what you plan to buy? We can

mnemonic [neh-MON-ik] device *A strategy or technique for improving memory.*

benefit more by following some general guidelines, based on the principles in this chapter. They include the following:

■ *Pay attention!* It seems obvious, but often we fail to remember because we never actually encoded information in the first place. For example, which of the following is similar to a real Lincoln penny?

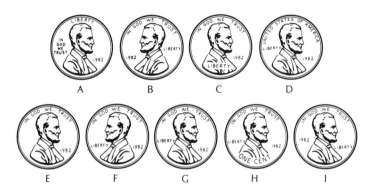

Most people have trouble recognizing the real penny, because they have never attended carefully to the details of a penny's design (Nickerson & Adams, 1979). We are not advising you to do so, unless you happen to be a coin collector or a counterfeiting expert. Just keep in mind that when you do have something to remember, you will do better if you encode it well.

■ *Encode information in more than one way.* As we have seen, the more elaborate the encoding of information, the more memorable it will be. Elaboration can take many forms. In addition to remembering a telephone number by the sound of the individual digits, you might note the spatial pattern they make as you punch them in on a push-button phone.

■ *Add meaning.* The more meaningful material is, the more likely it is to link up with information already in long-term memory. Meaningfulness also reduces the number of chunks of information you have to learn. Thus, if your license plate is 236MPL, you might think of 236 maples.

■ *Use visual imagery.* Memory for pictures is often better than memory for words (Paivio, 1969). You can make up your own mental "pictures" when you have to memorize verbal information. If you are in the import-export business and need to remember the main exports of several different countries, instead of trying to store, say, "Brazil: coffee" you might imagine a map of Brazil with a big coffee mug superimposed on it. Some people find that the odder the image, the better.

■ *Take your time.* If you must remember large amounts of verbal material, leisurely learning, spread out over several sessions, will probably produce better results than harried cramming. (*Reviewing* material right before you are tested on it, however, can be helpful, since it places the information at the top of your "cognitive deck.") In terms of hours spent, spaced or "distributed" learning sessions are more efficient than "massed" ones. Thus you may find that you retain information better after three separate one-hour sessions than after one session of three hours.

Whatever strategies you use, you will find that active learning results in more retention than merely reading or listening passively. The mind does not gobble up information automatically; you must take some pains to make the material digestible. Even then, you should not expect to remember everything you read or hear. Nor should you want to! Piling up facts without distinguishing the important ones from the trivial may merely clutter your mind. It is what you do with what you know that counts. Books on memory written by reputable scientists may help you boost your recall, but books or courses that promise a "perfect," "photographic," or "instant" memory fly in the face of what psychology knows about the workings of the mind. Our advice: Forget them.

GREATER EASTSIDE VOTER REGISTRATION
EDUCATION PROJECT

REGISTER
TO VOTE

★ ★ ★ HERE ★ ★ ★

Chapter
4

United States History and Government

Outline

Lecture: "United States Government"
Understanding and Using Organization Charts
Preparing and Giving an Oral Presentation
Summarizing
Reading Speed Check
Reading Exercises: "The 'Peculiar Institution'"
Word Parts
Writing: Evaluating Evidence
"The 'Peculiar Institution'"

Objectives

When you finish this chapter, you will be able to do the following:

Language and Study Skills

1. Summarize reading material in your own words.
2. Understand, draw, and use organization charts.
3. Give a brief descriptive oral presentation.
4. Write an essay evaluating evidence.

Content Mastery

1. Describe the key characteristics of the U.S. system of government.
2. Describe what slavery was like and how slaves viewed their situation.
3. Explain how slavery influenced the development of black culture.

A person who plans to live in the United States for any length of time needs to know a little about the background of this country. Two key areas that can help us understand the United States are its history and government. In this chapter you learn the basics of the United States government system, and how the states are related to the national government. In addition, we take a look at one period of history, the Civil War, focusing on slavery in the Southern United States.

Important Terms

As you listen to the lecture and read the passage for this chapter, note the following important terms and their meanings. When you finish the chapter, you should be able to define each one.

abolition
Articles of Confederation

cavalier
checks and balances

Congress
Constitution of the U.S.
Constitutional Convention
constitutional amendment
delegate
delegated powers
division of powers
emancipation
Executive Branch
federal system, federalism
gang system
House of Representatives
impeach
institutionalized racism
Jim Crow laws
Judicial Branch, judiciary
kinship network, kinship ties
Legislative Branch, legislature
liberal
lower house
manumission
nullification

parliamentary system
ratify
representation
representative democracy
reserved powers
right to leave the union
"Sambo"
segregation
Senate
separation of powers
Supreme Court
task system
the "National Supremacy Clause"
the "peculiar institution"
the "three-fifths compromise"
tyranny
underground railroad
upper house
veto
vote of confidence
yankee

LECTURE: "UNITED STATES GOVERNMENT"

How is the United States government organized? This lecture covers the basics and also includes some of the reasons why the U.S. system developed as it did. It was an introduction to U.S. government given to a class of international students by guest lecturer Dr. Arthur J. Misner, Professor Emeritus of Political Science, California State University, Los Angeles. This lecture is an example of one you might hear in a course on United States history and government.

Since American students study this subject for several years in elementary and secondary schools, the professors tend to assume the audience has some basic knowledge about the subject. For this reason, you may find the vocabulary in this lecture especially difficult.

Comprehension Questions

Refer to your notes as needed to answer the following questions.

1. Describe the American government system in existence before the Constitution. Why did the framers decide to write the Constitution?
2. Define:
   a. separation of powers
   b. checks and balances
3. How does the parliamentary system differ from the "independent elected" system of the United States?
4. Explain the term "representative democracy" as it applies to the United States.
5. In the federal system of the United States, how is power divided between the states and the national government?
6. What kinds of disputes were there between the states during the Constitutional Convention?
7. Aside from slavery, what were two other important points of disagreement between the Southern and the Northern states?

Questions for Analysis

1. What kind of government do you have in your country? Are there any divisions to your country, such as states or provinces? If so, what is their relationship to the national government?
2. With your teacher, discuss what the U.S. political parties are and their role in U.S. politics. Tell the class about political parties in your country.

UNDERSTANDING AND USING ORGANIZATION CHARTS

Every group in a society has its own pattern of organization based on the relationships among the group members and which ones have more power or authority. Organization charts are visual representations of the way a group is organized, and are often used to show government and business organizational structure.

Use the Organization Charts on the next page to answer the following questions.

1. Look at the Traditional organization chart.
   a. What is the meaning of each box in the chart?
   b. What do the lines mean?
   c. What is the relationship between rows of boxes that are one above the other?
2. What do the five boxes at the top of the Russian chart indicate?
3. What does the encircling line on the American chart mean?
4. Why does the OPEC chart have no lines?
5. What is the distinctive characteristic of the Chinese chart?
6. What do the symbols on the Women's Movement chart mean?
7. Are any of the boxes more important than the others on the United Nations chart?
8. What do the X's on the Latin American chart represent?
9. Explain the Antebellum South chart.

Questions for Analysis

1. Do these charts express facts or opinions?
2. Do you agree or disagree with any of the charts?
   Discuss.

Making an Organization Chart

Draw an organization chart for your country. It can be a factual representation, or can represent your opinion. Share your chart with a classmate. Explain what each box represents and summarize the meaning of the complete chart.

PREPARING AND GIVING AN ORAL PRESENTATION

Preparation

1. On a large piece of posterboard (about 24" by 36" is a good size), redraw the organization chart that you prepared in the previous lesson. Use a wide black felt marker and make the chart big enough to be seen easily by the audience. Give your chart a title, and label the most important boxes.
2. Plan a 3-minute speech by making an outline of the things you will discuss. This outline can be used as notes when you actually give your presentation:

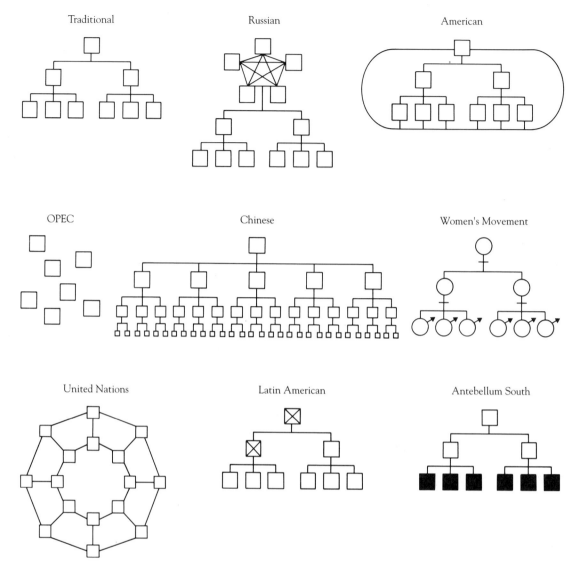

Figure 4.1. Organization Charts

> I. Introduction. Tell specifically what the chart represents. For example, does the chart represent the government, the family, or a typical business organization? For which country?
>
> II. Explain the most important aspects of your chart. These include any distinctive characteristics of the chart, and the most important boxes or divisions of boxes. If the chart represents your opinion, explain your opinion and why you drew the chart as it is.
>
> III. Conclude with a short summary of your points.

3. Practice your speech at home.
    a. Avoid "talking to your chart." Make sure that you look at the entire room/audience as you speak.
    b. Raise the volume of your voice. You need to be heard by everyone in the class, so you cannot use the same volume that you would when speaking to just one person face-to-face. Practice speaking loudly.

    c. Give your speech in front of a mirror and/or tape-record your voice so that you can see and hear yourself.

    d. Ask a friend or family member to listen and comment on your speech.

    e. Time your speech. It should be 3 minutes long.

Giving the Speech

Follow the guidelines you used when practicing. Remember to look at your audience and speak loudly and clearly. Ask if there are any questions when you finish your presentation.

SUMMARIZING

In this exercise you will practice using your own words to summarize. This important academic skill is often used in writing essays about reading material.

The paragraphs for this exercise are excerpted from an American college student's senior-level history class take-home essay final exam answer. The exam question was: "What *one term* comes to mind as the lowest common denominator of American intellectual development?" The student's thesis was that "identity" was the common denominator.

Summarizing paragraphs involves finding the key points and restating them briefly. Follow these steps to summarize a paragraph.

    1. Read the material, marking key words and ideas.

    2. In one or two sentences, restate in your own words the main point of the paragraph, including key words or definitions, if any.

Practice 1   Summarize the paragraph on the lines provided.

The United States covers a vast amount of land area, and in the 1800s, as the land was settled, regional identities began to develop, especially in the South and North. In the South, perhaps a good example of identity would be the cavalier. This stereotype of a kind of wealthy Southerner became a symbol for the South. The cavalier was a gentleman, worldly, educated, proud, and bon vivant. He was anything but practical, preferring to gamble, have fun, and back worthy causes in the name of honor, even if the cause was obviously doomed. Money was no object to him—it was taken for granted. He had a strong sense of place, of roots, perhaps because Southerners owned their plantations for generations. In the North, the yankee became the symbol of regional identity. In contrast to the cavalier, the yankee stereotype was very practical and materialistic. "Yankee ingenuity" became famous. This was the Northerner's habit of inventing gadgets and machines to make life better. Not only was the yankee a tinkerer, but he was also a capitalist, interested in business, industry, and making money. In fact, most of the banking and industry in the United States was controlled by the North.

_____

_____

_____

Summarizing longer passages requires putting different points together into a comprehensive statement.

    1. Read and mark material as before.

    2. Combine the key points of each paragraph into a summary of one or more sentences. Be sure to connect the points in some logical way by using transitional words or phrases.

Practice 2   Summarize the following paragraphs on the lines provided at the end.

The black identity was very different from the white. How did the slaves see themselves? Did they really believe that they were inferior, and accept their position, a stereotype symbolized by the "Sambo," a shuffling, childlike, dependent personality, or did they see their position as one of putting on an elaborate charade, "puttin' on ol' massah' "? In an attempt to answer this question, and the related one of the black identity after the Civil War when prejudice and discrimination still kept them at the bottom of society, historians have looked at modern analogies.

One analogy which has been used is that of the Jews in Nazi concentration camps. Some of them took on the identity of their captors in various ways, imitating their dress, actions, and so on. Some exhibited childlike behavior, such as giggling, lying, cheating, and needing constant supervision and direction. The slaves exhibited many of the same characteristics. The Jews were in camps for only a few years, yet in this time the behavior of many changed dramatically, and it was not a charade. They actually changed some aspects of their identity while in prison camps. In slavery for hundreds of years, blacks had even more time to develop an identity based on their own inferior status and the superior status of whites. Many developed the "Sambo" attitude. They did have an identity, but it was a twisted one, because they were in a closed system, slavery, with little possibility of escape, and whites controlled everything essential to their existence.

_____

_____

_____

_____

_____

_____

Practice 3   Summarize the following paragraphs on the lines provided.

When the slaves were emancipated, Southern whites moved quickly to set up systems to keep blacks at the bottom of the social scale. One of the reasons for this was that the poor whites had a very strong desire not to be associated with blacks. Many poor Southern whites lived in conditions that were similar to or worse than blacks'. They were uneducated and worked at menial jobs. The only distinction that they could make during the slave era was that they were free and blacks were not. This helped poor whites develop an identity that gave them a measure of self-respect, since in their minds, at least they were better than slaves. When slavery was abolished, this distinction was erased, and whites rushed to make a new one to maintain identity and self-respect. Skin color became the defining characteristic, and Jim Crow laws were passed to segregate blacks and whites.

The passing of Jim Crow laws resulted in institutionalized racism; the superior social status of whites to blacks was written into law. Institutionalized racism developed not only because of the identity problems of poor whites. There were also economic reasons. Whites did not want blacks competing for their jobs, and blacks could easily have underbid whites and taken those jobs. This was both because all the slaves were now free and on the open labor market and because they were used to not being paid at all, and therefore might accept lower wages. For these reasons, whites wanted to believe that blacks were inferior and therefore should be segregated. There was reinforcement for these beliefs. The fact that blacks had been slaves was a disadvantage for them, just as an ex-convict carries a stigma, or an ex-asylum inmate. Because of the long period of slavery, black culture had developed differently from white, resulting in differences in speech, values, and behavior. These served to highlight the distinction between black and white. Also, blacks had been in slavery so long that some actually believed they were inferior. This created a self-fulfilling prophesy. In other words, blacks behaved in certain ways because they felt inferior, and therefore whites believed they were inferior, so finally the result was inferior status sanctioned by law.

The effect of Jim Crow laws on black identity was to reinforce their feelings of inferiority, which caused blacks in general not to try to elevate their status. Some sociologists contend that a culture of poverty developed, with values, ideas, and lifestyles that perpetuated low status for blacks even after Jim Crow laws were abolished. The black identity was tied to poverty and hopelessness. The civil rights movement of the mid-twentieth century had to contend with blacks' self-image. In order to really establish equal rights, blacks themselves had to forge a new identity.

_____

_____

_____

_____

_____

_____

_____

READING SPEED CHECK

You will have one minute to read the following passage. Mark the word that you are reading at the end of that time.

15   White Southerners often referred to slavery as the "peculiar institution." By that, they meant not
32   that the institution was odd but that it was distinctive, special. The description was an apt one,
46   for American slavery was indeed distinctive. The South in the mid-nineteenth century was the
63   only area in the entire Western world—except for Brazil and Cuba—where slavery still existed; and
76   Southern slavery differed even from its Caribbean and Latin American counterparts. Slavery, more
93   than any other single factor, isolated the South from the rest of American society. And as that iso-
106 lation increased, so did the commitment of Southerners to defend the institution. William
122 Harper, a prominent South Carolina politician in the 1840s, wrote: "The judgment is made up. We
141 can have no hearing before the tribunal of the civilized world. Yet, on this very account, it is more
157 important that we, the inhabitants of the slave-holding States, insulated as we are by this institu-
174 tion, and cut off, in some degree, from the communion and sympathies of the world by which we
185 are surrounded... and exposed continually to their animadversions and attacks, should
198 thoroughly understand this subject, and our strength and weakness in relation to it."
213   Within the South itself, the institution of slavery had paradoxical results. On the one hand,
230 it isolated blacks from whites, drawing a sharp and inviolable line between the races. As a result,
248 blacks under slavery began to develop a society and culture of their own, one that was in many
264 ways unrelated to the white civilization around them. On the other hand, slavery created a unique
280 bond between blacks and whites—masters and slaves—in the South. The two races may have
294 maintained separate spheres, but each sphere was deeply influenced by, indeed dependent on,
295 the other.
311   Slavery was an institution established by law and regulated in detail by law. The slave codes
326 of the Southern states forbade slaves to hold property, to leave their masters' premises without per-
343 mission, to be out after dark, to congregate with other slaves except at church, to carry firearms,
359 or to strike a white person even in self-defense. The codes prohibited whites from teaching slaves
378 to read or write, and they denied to slaves the right to testify in court against white people. They
394 contained no provisions to legalize slave marriages or divorces. If an owner killed a slave while
409 punishing him, the act was generally not considered a crime. Slaves, however, faced the death
426 penalty for killing or even resisting a white person and for inciting to revolt. The codes also con-
441 tained extraordinarily rigid provisions for defining a person's race. Anyone with even a trace of
455 African ancestry was considered black. And anyone thought to possess any such trace was pre-
466 sumed to be black unless he or she could prove otherwise.

GO ON TO THE COMPREHENSION QUESTIONS

Comprehension Questions

Answer the questions without referring to the passage. Focus on the questions for the lines that you read. You may guess the answers of questions for lines that you didn't have time to read.

1. (15–76) The "peculiar institution" refers to
   a. the distinctive system of slavery in the American South.
   b. the odd system of slavery in the American South.
   c. an unusual system that existed in the mid-nineteenth century.
   d. the prison system in the American South.
2. (93–198)   T   F   Slavery's effect was to isolate the South from the rest of American society.
3. (213–295)   T   F   Black culture developed in a different way from white culture.
4. (311–466) Which of the following was *not* mentioned by the slave codes:
   a. holding property
   b. being out after dark
   c. meeting with other slaves
   d. marrying or divorcing

Your Reading Speed

Find the mark you made when the teacher announced that one minute had passed. Count the number of words on the line that you didn't have time to read. Subtract this from the number at the beginning of the line. The result is your reading speed in words per minute.

Check your comprehension answers. If you made more than one mistake, you may be reading too quickly to adequately understand the material.

READING EXERCISES: "THE 'PECULIAR INSTITUTION' "

Reading Goal   Use SQ3R and summarizing skills together to read and take notes on the material.

The reading passage for this chapter (5,712 words) is from a college United States history textbook, *American History: A Survey*, by Richard N. Current, T. Harry Williams, Frank Freidel and Alan Brinkley. The complete chapter is 38 pages long. There are 15 chapters in the book.

1. Use the SQ3R study technique to guide your notetaking.
2. Summarize paragraphs or the section in order to answer each SQ3R question.

Reading Comprehension Questions

Use your skill at summarizing to answer the following questions about each section of the reading. You can refer to your notes and the reading passage to find the answers to each question. If you used the SQ3R method correctly, you may already have written the answers in your reading notes.

1. List and describe four varieties of slavery. Give the advantages and disadvantages for the slaves for each one.
2. What was the slave trade like during the time just before the Civil War?
3. In what ways did slaves resist whites? Include two typical personality types.
4. On what points do historians disagree about the nature of plantation slavery?
5. How did slavery affect black religion and families?

Questions for Analysis

1. Have you noticed any differences between American blacks and whites (aside from skin color)? If so, describe the differences you have observed. Using the information from the reading, can you propose an explanation about why these differences exist?

2. Why do you suppose there were almost no slaves in the North? What kind of economic and social conditions could have made slavery impractical in the North? What kind of social and economic conditions might have made a favorable environment for the development of slavery in the South?

WORD PARTS

Match the words in the list of examples with the correct word part, then write your guess for its meaning. Check your answers with your teacher or the list in Appendix A. Make a point of learning any of the word parts that are new to you.

Root	Meaning	Example
1. gloss, glot	_____	_____
2. gram, graph	_____	_____
3. gress, grad	_____	_____
4. hydr	_____	_____
5. jac, ject	_____	_____
6. jud	_____	_____

Prefix

7. e-, ex-	_____	_____
8. extra-	_____	_____
9. hetero-	_____	_____
10. homo-, hom-	_____	_____
11. hyper-	_____	_____
12. hypo-	_____	_____

Suffix

13. -dom	_____	_____
14. -ee	_____	_____
15. -hood, -ness	_____	_____

Examples

dehydrate	glossary	homonym
employee	graduate	hypertension
exhale	grammar	hypodermic
extracurricular	hardiness	judiciary
freedom	heterosexual	reject

WRITING: EVALUATING EVIDENCE

Topic Sentences

You have learned to find main idea sentences when you read paragraphs. You also need to use main idea sentences, called topic sentences, when you write. Each paragraph should have one. A topic sentence is a general statement of the key point of your paragraph. The other sentences should contain details, evidence that supports the topic sentence. You will practice writing topic sentences when you plan your essay.

Writing Topic

Slaveowners argued that slaves were happy with their condition. From the reading material, what evidence can you find to support or disprove this claim? Based on your evaluation of the evidence, do you feel that the claim is valid?

Gathering Information

Check the reading passage carefully to find evidence that shows slaves were happy or unhappy. After you check the passage, the class will go through the reading passage together. Be prepared to tell the class the page, paragraph, and line numbers for important evidence that you found. Give a brief summary of the evidence.

Narrowing the Topic

This topic is already quite narrow. Your main job now is to select which evidence you will use, since you don't need to mention every piece of evidence.

In groups or as a class, discuss the evidence. Is it reliable? What was the original source of the information? Some evidence carries more weight than other evidence because it is from a better source. What could make one source better than another? Which evidence would you be more likely to believe? Why?

Planning the Essay

Make an outline for your essay, using the following pattern. Compose sentences to introduce each main point. These will become the topic sentences for your paragraphs.

    I. Introduction
       Your thesis should address the essay topic directly. Let the reader know whether or not you think the slaveowner's claim is valid.
   II. Body
      A. Summarize the evidence supporting the claim
         topic sentence
      B. Summarize the evidence disproving the claim
         (*Note*: The order of paragraphs A and B can be reversed.)
         topic sentence
      C. Evaluate the evidence: Is there more evidence to support or disprove? How good is the quality of the evidence?
         topic sentence
 III. Conclusion
       Summarize your points. Your summary should point out specifically why you feel the claim is valid or not.

Follow-up Exercise

Work in groups of three or four. Your teacher will collect the essay drafts and redistribute them, one essay per group member. Check to be sure that none of the essays your group receives has been written by a group member. Read each essay, exchanging with group members until each member has read all the essays given to the group. Then discuss the following questions.

1. Which of the essays presents the evidence in the most convincing way? Why do you think it is convincing?
2. As a group, choose the essay that you feel is the best, and be prepared to explain the reasons for your choice to the class. Base your decision on the *content* and *organization* of the essay, not the grammar or other language considerations.

Each group will read the topic sentences from their choice of best essay to the class. Then group members will give a brief explanation of why they felt it was the best one. Use ideas that you get from group discussions and presentations to improve your own essay when you rewrite.

The "Peculiar Institution"

White Southerners often referred to slavery as the "peculiar institution." By that, they meant not that the institution was odd but that it was distinctive, special. The description was an apt one, for American slavery was indeed distinctive. The South in the mid-nineteenth century was the only area in the entire Western world—except for Brazil and Cuba—where slavery still existed; and Southern slavery differed even from its Caribbean and Latin American counterparts. Slavery, more than any other single factor, isolated the South from the rest of American society. And as that isolation increased, so did the commitment of Southerners to defend the institution. William Harper, a prominent South Carolina politician in the 1840s, wrote: "The judgment is made up. We can have no hearing before the tribunal of the civilized world. Yet, on this very account, it is more important that we, the inhabitants of the slave-holding States, insulated as we are by this institution, and cut off, in some degree, from the communion and sympathies of the world by which we are surrounded, . . . and exposed continually to their animadversions and attacks, should thoroughly understand this subject, and our strength and weakness in relation to it."

Within the South itself, the institution of slavery had paradoxical results. On the one hand, it isolated blacks from whites, drawing a sharp and inviolable line between the races. As a result, blacks under slavery began to develop a society and culture of their own, one that was in many ways unrelated to the white civilization around them. On the other hand, slavery created a unique bond between blacks and whites—masters and slaves—in the South. The two races may have maintained separate spheres, but each sphere was deeply influenced by, indeed dependent on, the other.

Varieties of Slavery

Slavery was an institution established by law and regulated in detail by law. The slave codes of the Southern states forbade slaves to hold property, to leave their masters' premises without permission, to be out after dark, to congregate with other slaves except at church, to carry firearms, or to strike a white person even in self-defense. The codes prohibited whites from teaching slaves to read or write, and they denied to slaves the right to testify in court against white people. They contained no provisions to legalize slave marriages or divorces. If an owner killed a slave while punishing him, the act was generally not considered a crime. Slaves, however, faced the death penalty for killing or even resisting a white person and for inciting to revolt. The codes also contained extraordinarily rigid provisions for defining a person's race. Anyone with even a trace of African ancestry was considered black. And anyone thought to possess any such trace was presumed to be black unless he or she could prove otherwise.

These and dozens of other restrictions and impositions indicate that the slaves lived under a uniformly harsh and dismal regime. Had the laws been rigidly enforced, that might have been the case. In fact, however, they were applied unevenly. Sometimes slaves did acquire property, were taught to read and write, and did assemble with other slaves, in spite of laws to the contrary. Although major slave offenses were generally referred to the courts (and thus to the jurisdiction of the slave codes), most transgressions were handled by the master, who might inflict punishments ranging from some mild disciplinary action to flogging or branding for running away. In other words, despite the rigid provisions of law, there was in reality considerable variety within the slave system. Some blacks lived in almost prisonlike conditions, rigidly and harshly controlled by their masters. Many (probably most) others enjoyed a certain flexibility and (at least in comparison to the regimen prescribed by law) a striking degree of autonomy.

The nature of the the relationship between masters and slaves depended in part on the size of the plantation. Thus the typical master had a different image of slavery from that of the typical slave. Most masters possessed very few slaves, and their experience with (and image of) slavery was therefore shaped by the special nature of slavery on the small farm. Small farmers generally supervised their workers directly and often worked closely alongside them. On such farms, blacks and whites developed a form of intimacy unknown on larger plantations. The paternal relationship between such masters and their slaves

Richard N. Current, T. Harry Williams, Frank Freidel, and Alan Brinkley, *American History* 7th ed., vol. 1 (New York: Alfred A. Knopf, 1987). Reprinted by permission.

could, like relationships between fathers and children, be warm and in many ways benevolent. It could also be tyrannical and cruel. In general, the evidence suggests, blacks themselves preferred to live on larger plantations, where they had more opportunities for privacy and for a social world of their own.

Although the majority of slaveowners were small farmers, the majority of slaves lived on plantations of medium or large size, with sizable slave work forces. There the relationship between master and slave was usually far less intimate. Substantial planters often hired overseers and even assistant overseers to represent them. "Head drivers," trusted and responsible slaves often assisted by several subdrivers, acted under the overseer as foremen. Larger planters generally used one of two methods of assigning slave labor. One was the task system, most widely used in rice culture, under which slaves were assigned a particular task in the morning, for example, hoeing one acre; after completing the job, they were free for the rest of the day. The other, far more common, was the gang system, employed on the cotton, sugar, and tobacco plantations, under which slaves were simply divided into groups, each of them directed by a driver, and worked for as many hours as the overseer considered a reasonable workday.

Slaves were provided with at least enough necessities to enable them to live and work. They were furnished with an adequate if rough diet, consisting mainly of corn meal, salt pork, and molasses. Many were allowed to raise gardens for their own use and were issued fresh meat on special occasions. They received issues of cheap clothing and shoes. They lived in rude cabins, called slave quarters, usually clustered together in a complex near the master's house. Medical care was provided by the plantation mistress or by a doctor retained by the owner. Slaves worked hard, beginning with light tasks as children; and their workday was longest at harvest time. Slave women worked particularly hard. They generally shared the labor in the fields with the men, and they assumed as well the traditional women's chores of cooking, cleaning, and child rearing in the slave family.

Some historians have argued that the material conditions of slavery were, in fact, superior to those of Northern industrial workers. Whether or not that is true (and the evidence for this conclusion is at least debatable), the conditions of American slavery were undoubtedly less severe than those of slavery in the Caribbean and South America. There the slave supply was constantly replenished well into the nine-

teenth century by the African slave trade, giving owners less incentive to protect their existing laborers. Working and living conditions there were arduous, and masters at times literally worked their slaves to death. In the United States, in contrast, there were strong economic incentives to maintain a healthy slave population. One result of this was that America became the only country where a slave population actually increased through natural reproduction.

One example of the solicitude with which masters often treated their slaves was the frequent practice of using hired labor, when available, for the most unhealthy or dangerous tasks. A traveler in Louisiana noted, for example, that Irishmen were employed to clear malarial swamps and to handle cotton bales at the bottom of chutes extending from the river bluff down to a boat landing. If an Irishman died of disease or was killed in an accident, the master could hire another for a dollar a day or less. But he would lose perhaps $1,000 or more if he lost a prime field hand. Still, cruel masters might forget their pocketbooks in the heat of momentary anger. And slaves were often left to the discipline of overseers, who had no pecuniary stake in their well-being; overseers were paid in proportion to the amount of work they could get out of the slaves they supervised.

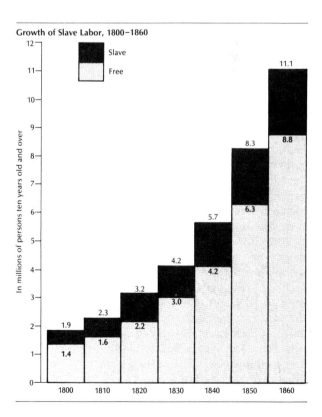

Growth of Slave Labor, 1800–1860

Household servants had a somewhat easier life—physically at least—than did field hands. On a small plantation, the same slaves might do both field work and house work; but on a large one, there would generally be a separate domestic staff: nursemaids, housemaids, cooks, butlers, coachmen. These people lived close to the master and his family, eating the leftovers from the family table and in some cases even sleeping in the "big house." Between the blacks and whites of such households affectionate, almost familial relationships might develop. More often, however, house servants resented their isolation from their fellow slaves and the lack of privacy that came with living in such close proximity to the family of the master. When emancipation came after the Civil War, it was often the house servants who were the first to leave the plantations of their former owners.

Slavery in the cities differed significantly from slavery in the country. On the relatively isolated plantations, slaves had little contact with free blacks and lower-class whites, and masters maintained a fairly direct and effective control; a deep and unbridgeable chasm yawned between slavery and freedom. In the city, however, a master often could not supervise his slaves closely and at the same time use them profitably. Even if they slept at night in carefully watched backyard barracks, they went about by day on errands of various kinds. Others—particularly skilled workers such as blacksmiths or carpenters—were hired out; and after hours they often fended for themselves, neither their owners nor their employers bothering to supervise them. Thus urban slaves gained numerous opportunities to mingle with free blacks and with whites. In the cities, the line between slavery and freedom remained, but it became less and less distinct.

Indeed, white Southerners generally considered slavery to be incompatible with city life; and as Southern cities grew, the number of slaves in them declined, relatively if not absolutely. The reasons were social rather than economic. Fearing conspiracies and insurrections, urban slaveowners sold off much of their male property to the countryside. The cities were left with an excess of black women while they continued to have an excess of white men (a situation that helped to account for the birth of many mulattoes). While slavery in the cities declined, segregation of blacks both free and slave increased. Segregation was a means of social control intended to make up for the loosening of the discipline of slavery itself.

The Continuing Slave Trade

The transfer of slaves from one part of the South to another was one of the most important demographic consequences of the development of the Southwest. Sometimes slaves moved to the new cotton lands in the company of their original owners, who were migrating themselves. More often, however, the transfer occurred through the medium of professional slave traders. Traders transported slaves over long distances on trains or on river or ocean steamers. On shorter journeys, the slaves moved on foot, trudging in coffles of hundreds along dusty highways. Eventually they arrived at some central market such as Natchez, New Orleans, Mobile, or Galveston, where purchasers collected to bid for them. At the auction, the bidders checked the slaves like livestock, watching them as they were made to walk or trot, inspecting their teeth, feeling their arms and legs, looking for signs of infirmity or age. It paid to be careful, for traders were known to deceive buyers by blacking gray hair, oiling withered skin, and concealing physical defects in other ways. A sound young field hand would fetch a price that, during the 1840s and 1850s, varied from $500 to $1,700, depending mainly on fluctuations in the price of cotton. The average figure was about $800, a substantial sum given the value of the dollar at the time. An attractive woman, desirable as a concubine, might bring several times that much.

The domestic slave trade was essential to the growth and prosperity of the whole system. It was also one of the most horrible aspects of it. The trade dehumanized all who were involved in it. It separated children from parents, and parents from each other. Even families kept together by scrupulous masters might be broken up in the division of the estate after the master's death. Planters condoned the trade and eased their consciences by holding the traders in contempt and assigning them a low social position.

The foreign slave trade was as bad or worse. Although federal law had prohibited the importation of slaves from 1808 on, they continued to be smuggled in as late as the 1850s. The numbers can only be guessed at. There were not enough such imports to satisfy all planters, and the Southern commercial conventions, which met annually to consider means of making the South economically independent, began to discuss the legal reopening of the trade. "If it is right to buy slaves in Virginia and carry them to New Orleans," William L. Yancey of Alabama asked his fellow delegates at the 1858 meeting, "why is it

Slave Ownership in the South and Border States, 1860

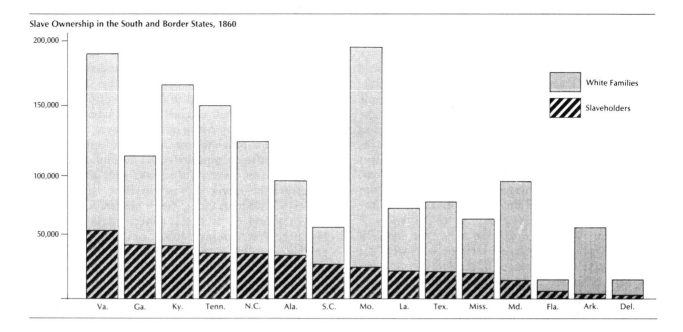

not right to buy them in Cuba, Brazil, or Africa and carry them there?" The convention that year voted to recommend the repeal of all laws against slave imports. Only the delegates from the states of the upper South, which profited from the domestic trade, opposed the foreign competition.

Slave Resistance

Few issues have sparked as much debate among historians as the effects of slavery on the blacks themselves. Slaveowners, and many white Americans for generations to come, liked to argue that the slaves were generally content, "happy with their lot." That may well have been true in some cases. But it is clear that the vast majority of Southern blacks were not content with being slaves, that they yearned for freedom even though most realized there was little they could do to secure it. Evidence for that conclusion comes, if from nowhere else, from the reaction of slaves when emancipation finally came. Virtually all

Southern blacks reacted to freedom with joy and celebration; relatively few chose to remain in the service of the whites who had owned them before the Civil War (although most blacks, of course, remained for many years subservient to whites in one way or another).

Rather than contented acceptance, the dominant response of blacks to slavery was a complex one: a combination of adaptation and resistance. At the extremes, slavery could produce two opposite reactions—each of which served as the basis for a powerful stereotype in white society. One extreme was what became known as the "Sambo"—the shuffling, grinning, head-scratching, deferential slave who acted out the role that he recognized the white expected of him. More often than not, the "Sambo" pattern of behavior was a charade, a façade assumed in the presence of whites. In some cases, however, it might have represented more than that—the tragic distortion of personality that the rigors of slavery inflicted on its victims. The other extreme was the slave rebel—the black who could not bring himself or herself to either acceptance or accommodation but harbored an

─────────── WHERE HISTORIANS DISAGREE ───────────

The Nature of Plantation Slavery

Few subjects have produced so rich a historical literature in recent years as the nature of American slavery. And in that literature is lodged one of the liveliest of all scholarly debates. Even more vividly than other historical controversies, the argument over slavery illustrates the extent to which historians are influenced by the times in which they write. Popular attitudes about race have always found reflection in historical examinations of slavery. Never has that been more true than in the past two decades.

The first accounts of slavery, written before the Civil War by contemporaries of the institution, were usually stark expressions of the political beliefs of their authors. Southern chroniclers emphasized the benevolent features of the system, the paternalism with which masters cared for their slaves (a stark contrast, they implied, to the brutal impersonality of Northern factory owners and their "wage slaves"), and the carefree, happy demeanor of the slaves themselves. From Northern writers (many of them abolitionists) came a picture of slavery as a brutal, savage institution that dehumanized all who were touched by it. Theodore Dwight Weld's *American Slavery as It Is* (1839), for many years a widely cited book, depicted a system so horrible in its impact, it was little wonder the book inspired many of its readers to political action.

By the end of the nineteenth century, however, the political climate had changed. White Americans were now eager to foster a spirit of sectional reconciliation; and in both North and South, there was emerging—in popular literature, in folktales and myths, and increasingly in scholarship—a romantic vision of the Old South as a graceful and serene civilization. It was a receptive climate for the publication in 1918 of the most influential study of slavery of the time (and for many years there-

after): Ulrich B. Phillips's *American Negro Slavery*. Phillips portrayed slavery as an essentially benign institution, in which kindly masters looked after submissive, childlike, and generally contented blacks. Black people, he suggested, were for the most part lazy and irresponsible; and the occasional harshness of the slave system was simply a necessary part of supervising a backward labor force. The book was, in effect, an apology for the Southern slaveowner; and for nearly thirty years, it remained the authoritative work on the subject.

Beginning in the 1940s, when the nation began finally to confront forthrightly its legacy of racial injustice, new approaches to slavery started to emerge. As early as 1941, Melville J. Herskovits was challenging one of Phillips's assumptions: that slaves had retained little if any of their African cultural inheritance. In fact, Herskovits argued, many Africanisms survived in slave culture for generations. Two years later, Herbert Aptheker attacked another of Phillips's claims: that slaves were submissive and content. "Discontent and rebelliousness," he wrote in *American Negro Slave Revolts,* "were not only exceedingly common, but, indeed, characteristic of American Negro slaves."

But for a time, at least, the more influential challenge to Phillips came from those who claimed that he had neglected the brutality of the system and the damage it did to those who lived under it. Kenneth Stampp's *The Peculiar Institution* (1956), the first comprehensive study of slavery since Phillips, emphasized the harshness of the system— not only its physical brutality but its psychological impact on men and women kept in a virtual prison, with little room to develop their own social and cultural patterns. An even more devastating portrait of slavery came from Stanley Elkins, whose *Slavery* (1959) argued that many slaves had, indeed, displayed childlike, submissive, "Sambo"

unquenchable spirit of rebelliousness. Here, too, there may at times have been personality disorders at work (as is suggested by newspaper advertisements for runaways who were described as having stutters or other behavioral quirks). It was, after all, a somewhat abnormal act to rise up in rebellion against odds so overwhelming that there existed virtually no chance

of success. Yet to attribute slave rebellions to mental disorder is to accept a largely white point of view. It is also possible to see in the rebellious slave signs of a strength and courage far greater than most white Southerners were disposed to admit black people could possess.

Actual slave revolts were extremely rare, but the

─── WHERE HISTORIANS DISAGREE ───

personalities, as Phillips had suggested. But to Elkins, such personalities were evidence of the terrible damage the institution had inflicted on them. Comparing the slave system to Nazi concentration camps in World War II, he cited the effects on the individual of enforced "adjustment to absolute power" and the tragic distortions of character that resulted.

Stampp and Elkins reflected the general belief of white liberals in the 1950s and early 1960s that their society bore a large measure of guilt for the injustices it had inflicted on blacks, that whites must work to undo the damage they had done in the past. By the early 1970s, however, racial attitudes had changed again, with the emergence of the "black power" ideology and the widespread belief among blacks and some whites that blacks themselves should determine their own future. The new emphasis on black pride and achievement, therefore, helped produce a new view of the black past, emphasizing the cultural and social accomplishments of blacks under slavery. John Blassingame, in *The Slave Community* (1973), echoed the approach of Herskovits thirty years before in arguing that "the most remarkable aspect of the whole process of enslavement is the extent to which the American-born slaves were able to retain their ancestors' culture." Herbert Gutman, in *The Black Family in Slavery and Freedom, 1750–1925* (1976), provided voluminous evidence to support his claim that the black family, far from being weakened and destroyed by the slave system, survived with remarkable strength—although with some differences from the prevailing form of the white family. The slave community, Gutman claimed, was so successful in preserving and developing its own culture that the master class was unable, despite its great legal power, to affect it in any significant way.

This emphasis on the ability of blacks to maintain their own culture and society under slavery, and on their remarkable achievements within the system, formed the basis of two studies in 1974 that claimed to present comprehensive new portraits of the entire system. *Time on the Cross,* by Robert Fogel and Stanley Engerman, used quantitative methods to show not only that slaves were skilled and efficient workers, not only that the black family was strong and healthy, but that the institution of slavery was a prosperous one that benefited masters and slaves alike. Slave workers, Fogel and Engerman claimed, were generally better off than Northern industrial workers. Slaves often rose to managerial positions on plantations. Whippings were few, and families were rarely broken up. The findings of *Time on the Cross* soon came under harsh attack—both from those who were offended by what they considered its apology for slavery and, more important, from historians who claimed to have discovered crucial flaws in Fogel and Engerman's methods. More influential in the long run was Eugene Genovese's *Roll, Jordan, Roll: The World the Slaves Made.* Genovese revived the idea of "paternalism" as the central element of the slave system. But in his view, paternalism was not an expression of white generosity; it was a powerful instrument of control. And it worked in two directions, enabling blacks to make demands of whites as well as the other way around. Moreover, within this paternal system, Genovese claimed, blacks retained a large cultural "space" of their own within which they developed their own family life, traditions, social patterns, and above all religion. Indeed, slaves had by the mid-nineteenth century developed a sense of themselves as part of a separate black "nation"—a nation tied to white society in important ways, but nevertheless powerful and distinct.

knowledge that they were possible struck terror into the hearts of white Southerners everywhere. In 1800, Gabriel Prosser gathered 1,000 rebellious slaves outside Richmond, but two blacks gave the plot away, and the Virginia militia was called out in time to head it off. Prosser and 35 others were executed. In 1822, the Charleston free black Denmark Vesey and his

followers—rumored to total 9,000—made preparations for revolt; but again the word leaked out, and retribution followed. In 1831, Nat Turner, a slave preacher, led a band of blacks who armed themselves with guns and axes and, on a summer night, went from house to house in Southampton County, Virginia. They slaughtered sixty white men, women, and children before being overpowered by state and federal troops. More than a hundred blacks were put to death in the aftermath. Nat Turner's was the only actual slave insurrection in the nineteenth-century South, but slave conspiracies and threats of renewed violence continued throughout the section as long as slavery lasted.

For the most part, however, resistance to slavery took other, less drastic forms. In some cases, slaves worked "within the system" to free themselves from it—earning money with which they managed to buy their own and their families' freedom. Some had the good fortune to be set free by their master's will after his death—for example, the more than 400 slaves belonging to John Randolph of Roanoke, freed in 1833. From the 1830s on, however, state laws made it more and more difficult, and in some cases practically impossible, for an owner to manumit his slaves. The laws, when permitting manumission, often required the removal of the freed slaves from the state. Slaveowners objected to the very presence of free blacks, who by their existence set a disturbing example for the slaves.

By 1860, there nevertheless were about 250,000 free blacks in the slaveholding states, more than half of them in Virginia and Maryland. A few (generally on the northern fringes of the slaveholding regions) attained wealth and prominence. Some owned slaves themselves, usually relatives whom they had bought in order to ensure their ultimate emancipation. Most, however, lived in abject poverty, under conditions worse than those afflicting blacks in the North. Law or custom closed many occupations to them, forbade them to assemble without white supervision, and placed numerous other restraints on them. They were only quasi-free, and yet they had all the burdens of freedom: the necessity to support themselves, to find housing, to pay taxes. Yet great as were the hardships of freedom, blacks usually preferred them to slavery.

Some blacks attempted to resist slavery by escaping from it, by running away. A small number managed to escape to the North or to Canada, especially after sympathetic whites began organizing the so-called underground railroad to assist them in flight. But the odds against a successful escape, particularly from the Deep South, were almost impossibly great. The hazards of distance and the slaves' ignorance of geography were serious obstacles. So were the white "slave patrols," which stopped wandering blacks on sight throughout the South demanding to see travel permits. Without such a permit, slaves were presumed to be runaways and were taken captive. For blacks who attempted to escape through the woods, slave patrols often employed bloodhounds. Despite all the obstacles to success, however, blacks continued to run away from their masters in large numbers. Some did so repeatedly, undeterred by the whippings and other penalties inflicted on them when captured.

But perhaps the most important method of resistance was simply a pattern of everyday behavior by which blacks defied their masters. That whites so often considered blacks to be lazy and shiftless suggests one means of resistance: refusal to work hard. Slaves might also steal from their masters or from neighboring whites. They might perform isolated acts of sabotage: losing or breaking tools (Southern planters gradually began to buy unusually heavy hoes because so many of the lighter ones got broken) or performing tasks improperly. In extreme cases, blacks might make themselves useless by cutting off their fingers or even committing suicide. Or, despite the terrible consequences, they might on occasion turn on their masters and kill them. The extremes, however, were rare. For the most part, blacks resisted by building into their normal patterns of behavior subtle methods of rebellion.

Slave Religion and the Black Family

But resistance was only part of the slave response to slavery. The other was an elaborate process of adaptation—a process that did not imply contentment with bondage but a recognition that there was no realistic alternative. One of the ways blacks adapted was by developing a rich and complex culture, one that enabled them to keep a sense of racial pride and unity. In many areas, they retained a language of their own, sometimes incorporating African speech patterns into English. They developed a distinctive music, establishing in the process what was perhaps the most impressive of all American musical traditions. The most important features of black culture, however, were the development of two powerful institutions: religion and the family.

A separate slave religion was not supposed to exist. Almost all blacks were Christians, and their masters expected them to worship under the supervision of white ministers—often in the same chapels as whites. Indeed, autonomous black churches were banned by law. Nevertheless, blacks throughout the South developed their own version of Christianity, at times incorporating such African practices as voodoo, but more often simply bending religion to the special circumstances of bondage. Natural leaders emerging within the slave community rose to the rank of preacher; and when necessary, blacks would hold services in secret, often at night.

Black religion was far more emotional than its white counterparts, and it reflected the influence of African customs and practices. Slave prayer meetings routinely involved fervent chanting, spontaneous exclamations from the congregation, and ecstatic conversion experiences. Black religion was also more joyful and affirming than that of many white denominations. And above all, black religion emphasized the dream of freedom and deliverance. In their prayers and songs and sermons, black Christians talked and sang of the day when the Lord would "call us home," "deliver us to freedom," "take us to the Promised Land." And while their white masters generally chose to interpret such language merely as the expression of hopes for life after death, blacks themselves were undoubtedly using the images of Christian salvation to express their own dream of freedom in the present world.

The slave family was the other crucial institution of black culture in the South. Like religion, it suffered from certain legal restrictions—most notably the lack of legal marriage. Nevertheless, the nuclear family consistently emerged as the dominant kinship pattern among blacks. Such families did not always operate precisely according to white customs. A black couple would often begin living together before declaring any intent to marry; and a black woman would often bear a child before becoming wed. But family ties were generally no less strong than those of whites, and many slave marriages lasted throughout the course of long lifetimes.

When marriages did not survive, it was often because of circumstances over which blacks had no control. Up to a third of all black families were broken up by the slave trade. And that accounted for some of the other distinctive characteristics of the black family, which adapted itself to the cruel realities of its own uncertain future. Networks of kinship—which grew to include not only spouses and their children, but aunts, uncles, grandparents, even distant cousins—remained strong and important and often served to compensate for the breakup of nuclear families. A slave suddenly moved to a new area, far from his or her family, might create "fictional" kinship ties and become "adopted" by a family in the new community. Even so, the impulse to maintain contact with a spouse and children remained strong long after the breakup of a family. One of the most frequent causes of escape from the plantation was a slave's desire to find a husband, wife, or child who had been sent elsewhere. It was not only by breaking up families through sale that whites intruded on black family life. Black women, usually powerless to resist the sexual advances of their masters, often bore the children of whites—children whom the whites seldom recognized as their own and who were consigned to slavery from birth.

In addition to establishing social and cultural institutions of their own, slaves adapted themselves to slavery by forming complex relationships with their masters. However much blacks resented their lack of freedom, they often found it difficult to maintain an entirely hostile attitude toward their owners. Not only were they dependent on whites for the material means of existence—food, clothing, and shelter; they also often derived from their masters a sense of security and protection. There was, in short, a paternal relationship between slave and master—sometimes harsh, sometimes kindly, but almost invariably important. That paternalism, in fact, became (even if not always consciously) a vital instrument of white control. By creating a sense of mutual dependence, whites helped to reduce resistance to an institution that, in essence, was designed solely for the benefit of the ruling race.

SIGNIFICANT EVENTS

1831 Nat Turner slave rebellion breaks out in Virginia

1834 Cyrus McCormick patents mechanical reaper

1837 Oberlin becomes first men's college to accept woman students

Mount Holyoke Seminary for women founded

1842 Massachusetts supreme court, in *Commonwealth* v. *Hunt,* declares unions and strikes legal

1844 Samuel F. B. Morse sends first telegraphic message

1845 Irish potato famine begins, spurring major emigration to America

1846 Rotary press invented, making possible rapid printing of newspapers

Associated Press organized

1848 Failed revolution in Germany spurs emigration to America

1849 Rise in cotton prices spurs production boom

1852 American party (Know-Nothings) formed

Chapter
5

Your Health

Outline

Objectives

When you finish this chapter, you will be able to do the following:

Language and Study Skills

1. Quickly find information in written material by using skimming and scanning.
2. Use effective test preparation and test-taking skills.
3. Answer an essay-type test question.
4. Analyze essay test questions by focusing on key words.

Content Mastery

1. Explain some of the causes of stress.
2. Describe the General Adaptation Syndrome.
3. List some positive and negative ways of coping with stress.
4. Describe your own habitual behaviors in terms of their impact on your overall ability to cope with stress.
5. Show how particular personality traits can affect our ability to cope with stress.

Everyone experiences stress from time to time. For example, many people find speaking in front of an audience stressful. You may feel stress because of midterm exams. In this chapter, we take a closer look at stress: its causes, how it affects our health, and how to cope with it. The material for this chapter is similar to what is covered in a basic psychology class.

Important Terms and People

As you listen to the lecture and read the passage for this chapter, note the following important terms and their meanings. When you finish the chapter, you should be able to define each one.

alarm phase   assertive
arthritis   asthma

cardiovascular system	lymphocyte
cholesterol	meditation
coping	negative affectivity
emphysema	negative emotions
Cynthia Epstein	pathogenic
eustress	phagocyte
exhaustion phase	psychological stress
fight-or-flight response	psychoneuroimmunology
General Adaptation Syndrome (GAS)	psychosomatic
hardiness	resistance phase
Holmes & Rahe	salutogenic
hypertension	Hans Selye
immune system	stress
internal locus of control	stressor
life-change events	Type A behavior pattern

TEST-TAKING TIPS

Most college courses have midterm and final examinations. Since this is the middle chapter of this book, your teacher may soon be giving you a midterm exam. This section will help you develop study and test-taking skills that will help you in preparing for such an exam.

Reviewing

Scientific studies have shown that unless material is reviewed, most of it will be forgotten in a surprisingly short amount of time. Therefore, you should review your notes periodically throughout the course in order to keep the information fresh in your mind. In addition, review before a test.

About one week before an important examination, begin your review and test preparation. As you do the following steps, mark your papers (you might want to use colored ink) in order to highlight things you feel are particularly important to remember.

1. Review all quizzes (if any). Be sure you know the right answers to any questions you answered incorrectly. Your teacher can help you if you have problems finding answers.
2. Review questions and answers for all reading (and in this text listening) comprehension exercises. Many textbooks have comprehension questions at the end of each chapter.
3. Review lecture notes.
4. Review reading notes. This is when taking notes on your text pays off. If you haven't taken notes, you will need to review the textbook chapters, which is more difficult and time consuming.
5. Get together with a classmate and quiz each other. This will test your knowledge and help you find any areas you need to study further.

Taking the Test

Test strategy is the method you use to take tests. It does not refer to your knowledge of the subject matter. There are two parts to test strategy. The first is to be familiar with the types of test questions you will encounter. The second is to manage your time effectively during the test. We will take a look at each of these aspects in the following pages.

Types of Test Questions

Objective

1. Multiple choice

   Example

   The "peculiar institution" refers to
   a. the unique system of slavery in the American South.
   b. the odd system of slavery in the American South.
   c. an unusual system that existed in the mid-nineteenth century.
   d. none of the above.

   Notes: Watch out for choices such as "all of the above" and "none of the above." Also beware of words such as *no, not, always,* and *never*. Sometimes more than one choice appears to be correct. In this case, you must decide which is the *best* answer (usually the more exact one).

2. Fill in the blank

   Example

   In the American South, slavery was also called the _____ _____ .
   Notes: The grammatical structure of the sentence must be taken into account in order to fill in the blanks correctly.

3. Short answer or definition question

   Example

   What is the General Adaptation Syndrome?
   Notes: Although this kind of question is called "short answer," many teachers expect a thorough explanation, including examples.

4. True/False

   Example

   T   F   Stress is always unhealthy and should be avoided if possible.
   Notes: If any part of the statement is incorrect, the statement is false.

Subjective (essay questions)   A detailed exercise on how to answer essay questions appears in the writing section of this chapter.

Example

1. Describe the body's physiological reaction to stress, illustrating with examples.
   Notes: Essay answers generally consist of at least three paragraphs, including an introduction, body, and conclusion. The first paragraph generally contains a straightforward answer to the question. Also, important terms should be defined. The following paragraph(s) explain and develop the answer with examples and logical arguments. The final paragraph summarizes the essay and points out how the essay has answered the test question.

Managing Time

Many students find it difficult to complete a test in the time allowed. Finishing on time takes practice and requires you to budget the time you have. Before beginning a test, quickly look through the exam to see how many questions there are, the types of questions, and their relative importance or weight. Then mentally make a schedule for completing the test by reserving specific amounts of time for each section or question.

Example

You look through your exam and find that it contains 50 multiple-choice questions worth one point each and two essay questions worth 25 points each. You have 2 hours to finish. How much time should you spend on each part of the test?

If you allow 30 minutes to write each essay, you can use 1 hour to answer the multiple-choice section. Since there are 50 questions, you will have slightly more than 1 minute to answer each one.

LECTURE: "COPING WITH STRESS"

Students tend to feel very stressed at exam times and when major assignments like research papers are due. How can we cope with stress? This lecture will explain some constructive ways. It was given by Joan J. Lewis, a Student Health Center counselor at California State University, Los Angeles. It is a talk she has given as a guest speaker to a variety of classes and organizations on campus in order to increase awareness of stress and constructive ways to cope with it.

Comprehension Questions

Refer to your notes as needed to answer the following questions.

1. In regard to stress, what is the importance of our perception of events?
2. List some causes of stress, and indicate whether they are negative or positive events.
3. What are some common reactions to being overstressed?
4. What are some of the diseases that result from prolonged stress?
5. What are some ways the speaker recommends to control stress?

Questions for Analysis

1. In what ways do you cope with the stress of an upcoming examination, such as a mid-term or final? Have you found any ways of coping with "test anxiety" that you feel are especially effective?
2. Living in a foreign country can be very stressful at times. What do you feel is particularly stressful about living in the United States? What are some ways of coping with these stresses?
3. Discuss some ways that people might react to stress that actually *increase* the harmful effects of stress?
(hints: drinking, smoking)

HOW VULNERABLE ARE YOU TO STRESS?

Our day-to-day habits affect our ability to cope with stress. The following stress vulnerability scale was developed by Lyle H. Miller and Alma Dell Smith of Biobehavioral Associates to help determine how likely you are to be affected by stressors. Beside each item, indicate how much of the time each statement applies to you. Score each item based on the scale shown below. When you finish, calculate your total score.

1	Always	4	Some of the Time
2	Almost Always	5	Never
3	Most of the Time		

_____ **1.** I eat at least one hot, balanced meal a day.

_____ **2.** I get 7 to 8 hours sleep at least four nights a week.

_____ **3.** I give and receive affection regularly.

_____ **4.** I have at least one relative within 50 miles on whom I can rely.

_____ **5.** I exercise to the point of perspiration at least twice a week.

_____ **6.** I smoke less than half a pack of cigarettes a day.

_____ **7.** I take fewer than five alcoholic drinks a week.

_____ **8.** I am the appropriate weight for my height.

_____ **9.** I have an income adequate to meet basic expenses.

_____ **10.** I get strength from my religious beliefs.

_____ **11.** I regularly attend club or social activities.

_____ **12.** I have a network of friends and acquaintances.

_____ **13.** I have one or more friends to confide in about personal matters.

_____ **14.** I am in good health (including eyesight, hearing, teeth).

_____ **15.** I am able to speak openly about my feelings when angry or worried.

_____ **16.** I have regular conversations with the people I live with about domestic problems (e.g., chores, money, and daily living issues.)

_____ **17.** I do something for fun at least once a week.

_____ **18.** I am able to organize my time effectively.

_____ **19.** I drink fewer than three cups of coffee (or tea or cola drinks) a day.

_____ **20.** I take quiet time for myself during the day.

_____ TOTAL POINTS – 20 = _____ (Your stress score)

Interpretation

To get your score, add up the answers and *subtract 20*.

0–30	Good resistance to stress.
30–50	Some vulnerability to stress.
50–75	Seriously vulnerable to stress.
75+	Extremely vulnerable to stress.

Discussion Question   Are there any habits you could change in order to reduce your vulnerability to stress?

TIME MANAGEMENT LOG EXERCISE

In the United States, time is viewed as an important commodity that is highly valued, and which can be bought, spent, or wasted, among other things. You may be familiar with the expression, "Time is money." This describes the typical American view of time.

One important factor in the amount of stress Americans experience is whether their time is used effectively. Americans believe an inefficient use of time results in missed assignments, late or forgotten appointments, and a stressful feeling of not having enough time in the day. Regardless of original cultural time patterns, people living in the United States tend to be pushed and pulled along by American time patterns, often resulting in stress.

What do *you* do with your time? Try the following standard exercise used by American colleges and businesses as an introduction to time management. Follow the directions for using the time management log to keep a careful record of how you use your time during one week.

Using the Time Management Log

1. Fill in the "Time" column with the hours of the day, beginning with the time you usually get up in the morning and ending with the time you usually go to sleep at night.
2. Block in hours that are committed to certain activities. For example, the times when you are in class are not flexible, so they can be blocked in right away. You can also pencil in activities that you normally do at a certain time. For example, you can write in "breakfast" in the space each day at the time when you eat breakfast.
3. For the rest of the log, fill in what you *actually do* for every hour each day for a week.
4. At the end of the week, discuss the questions about your time management log in class.

TIME MANAGEMENT LOG

Date:

Time	Monday	Tuesday	Wednesday	Thursday	Friday

Questions

1. Does anything about your time log surprise you?
2. How much time do you spend studying?
3. Do you take study breaks when studying?
4. Do you have time to relax each day?
5. Is anything about your schedule causing stress?
6. Would you like to change the way you use your time?

Key Factors for Efficient Use of Time

1. Make a list of things to be done each day, but be reasonable in your expectations. Don't try to do too much in one day.
2. Do the most important things first.
3. Make a weekly schedule to follow, using the time management log as a guide.
4. Give yourself some time to relax every day.

Review: Guessing Meaning From Context

In the following paragraphs from the reading passage, guess the meanings of the underlined words from the context. Write your guesses next to each word listed below. When you finish, discuss your guesses with your classmates in small groups or as a class.Remember that your guesses do not need to be exactly accurate. In most cases all you need is a general idea of the meaning, just so that you can continue reading the sentence and understand the main point. For example: In paragraph 1, *toxins* must be something harmful to the body. This guess is good enough.Exactly what kind of harmful things they are isn't important for an understanding of the sentence.

Paragraph 1

In his 1956 book *The Stress of Life*, Canadian physician Hans Selye (1907–1982) popularized the idea of stress and advanced its study. Selye noted that many environmental <u>factors</u> throw the body out of <u>equilibrium</u>—heat, cold, pain, <u>toxins</u>, viruses, and so on—and require the body to respond. These factors, called *stressors*, include anything that requires the body to mobilize its resources. The body responds to a stressor with an <u>orchestrated</u> set of physical and chemical changes, which, as we will see in Chapter 9, prepare an individual to fight or <u>flee</u>. To Selye, "stress" consisted of this package of reactions, which he called the **General Adaptation Syndrome** (with the memorable <u>acronym</u> GAS). Usually, the body will meet the challenge of the environment and <u>adapt</u> to the stress.

factors _____

equilibrium _____

toxins _____

stressors _____

orchestrated _____

flee _____

acronym _____

adapt _____

Paragraph 2

Stress is the <u>bane</u> of modern civilization because our physiological alarm mechanism now chimes too often. When human beings had to contend with <u>woolly mammoths</u>, a dramatic <u>fight-or-flight response</u> was adaptive. Today, when the typical stressor is a <u>mammoth</u> traffic jam and not a mammoth <u>mammal</u>, the fight-or-flight response often gets <u>revved up</u> with nowhere to go. When your teacher announces that you will have an unexpected writing assignment, you don't really need to respond as if you were fighting for your life, but your body may still <u>sweat</u> to dispose of excess body heat. When you see your sweetheart <u>flirting</u> with someone else, you don't really need to breathe hard to get oxygen to your muscles, as you would if you were fleeing to safety.

bane _____

woolly mammoths _____

fight-or-flight response _____

mammoth _____

mammal _____

revved up _____

sweat _____

flirting _____

SKIMMING AND SCANNING FOR INFORMATION

Skimming means quickly reading something in order to find the general idea. *Scanning* means looking through written text to find a particular word, number, or other piece of information. These two skills are used together to quickly find information in written material.

Skimming and scanning are especially useful when doing library research, as for a research paper, and when taking reading tests such as the TOEFL, where the goal is to answer a set of questions correctly. You will practice these skills on the reading passage for this chapter; however, it may not always be advisable to do your reading homework this way. Some assignments require more careful reading than others. By learning a variety of skills, you can choose the best ones to use for a particular assignment.

How to Skim for Information

Skimming will give you a general idea of what the reading material is about and how it is organized.

1. Begin by checking the index or table of contents if you are using a book.
2. Use titles, headings, and subheadings as guides to the likely organization of ideas.
3. Read the introductory paragraph and the first sentence of each following paragraph. If there is a summary at the end of the material, read that as well.

How to Scan for Information

Scanning is used to find information; for example, to find the answers to a list of questions or to find definitions of key terms. Before scanning, it is helpful to have skimmed the reading material so that you know generally how it is organized.

1. When scanning, you must look for specific information. Picture the shape of a *key word or phrase* as you look at the print on a page. Look for this shape, rather than reading words or sentences.

   Also have in mind alternate ways that the information might be given. For example: If you are scanning for the date of the beginning of the Civil War, picture the answer as numbers and look for them in the text, but be ready to spot dates written in words as well.
2. If you are scanning an index, telephone book, or other list, look for the first letter of the word you want. For example, if you want to find the words *General Adaptation Syndrome* in a vocabulary list, look on the list for all words beginning with *G*, and skip any words beginning with another letter.

Practice

1. Find the words *fight-or-flight* on the first page of the reading passage. Remember. . .Don't *read* the material! Just look at the shapes of the words.
2. Locate the sections of the reading passage that discuss how a feeling of control over events affects stress.
3. Practice these skills when you do the reading exercises for this chapter.

READING EXERCISES: "STRESS"

Reading Goal   Skim the reading material to become acquainted with its content and organization. Then scan to find answers to the comprehension questions.

The reading for this chapter (5,562 words) is from a freshman-level psychology textbook, *Psychology*, by Carole Wade and Carol Tavris. The complete chapter is 33 pages long, and there are 18 chapters in the book.

1. Read the comprehension questions first. Then, instead of reading each section completely, skim the entire chapter. Next, scan to find the answers to each question.
2. Write your answers in outline form.

Reading Comprehension Questions

1. What is the General Adaptation Syndrome?
2. What is eustress?
3. Explain what the following diagram shows about the relationship between stress and illness.

4. What is a psychosomatic illness?
5. List and briefly describe some sources of stress.
6. What is Cynthia Epstein's main point about whose stress counts?
7. Describe personality characteristics that some psychologists think tend to result in more stress and stress-related illnesses.
8. What do some researchers think are the characteristics of a stress-resistant personality?

Questions for Analysis

1. Look at Table 15.1 in the reading passage. From your own experience, which measurement of stress do you think is better? Explain the reasons for your choice.
2. It is quite common for a person experiencing culture shock to become ill with a cold, the flu, or sometimes a more serious illness. Explain some possible reasons for this, using what you have learned about stress.

Word Parts

Match the words in the list of examples with the correct word part; then write your guess for its meaning. Check your answers with your teacher or the list in Appendix A. Make a point of learning any of the word parts that are new to you.

Root	Meaning	Example
1. lect, leg, lig	_____	_____
2. log	_____	_____
3. loqu, loc	_____	_____
4. luc	_____	_____
5. manu	_____	_____
6. mar	_____	_____
7. mater	_____	_____
8. med	_____	_____

Prefix

9. il-, in-, im-, ir-	_____	_____ _____
10. inter-	_____	_____
11. intra-	_____	_____
12. mal-	_____	_____
13. mega-	_____	_____

Suffix

14. -ion, -tion, -ity	_____	_____ _____
15. -ism	_____	_____

Examples

eloquent	lucid	megabyte
humility	malformed	monologue
improper	manufacture	precision
interpersonal	marine	select
intramural	maternity	socialism
irrational	mediate	

WRITING: TACKLING ESSAY QUESTIONS

The writing exercise for this chapter consists of a practice "essay test." Use the following guidelines to answer the practice "test question" that follows.

Understanding Essay Questions

You need to understand exactly what an essay question means in order to answer it correctly, so a knowledge of the vocabulary used in essay questions is essential. The following is a list of words commonly used in essay questions.

1. *Analyze*	to divide into component parts, examine these parts and explain them
2. *Comment*	to use the freedom to express an opinion about a subject
3. *Compare*	to point out both similarities and differences between two things

4. *Contrast*	to point out just the differences between two things
5. *Criticize/Critique*	to point out both strengths and weaknesses, advantages and disadvantages, good points and bad points, etc., of something.
6. *Define*	means either to give the meaning of something or to point out the essential qualities or characteristics of something
7. *Describe*	to tell the details of something
8. *Diagram*	to make a drawing of something and label or tell about its parts
9. *Differentiate*	to tell about the differences between two things that are similar (also *Distinguish*)
10. *Discuss*	to tell about something in detail, looking at all sides
11. *Enumerate*	to name, one by one (also *List*)
12. *Evaluate*	to make a judgment about something based upon its good and bad points
13. *Explain*	to tell how to do something, to give reasons for something or to make something clear and easy to understand
14. *Illustrate*	to make something clear by giving examples or drawing a diagram or picture
15. *Interpret*	to tell about the importance of something or the meaning of the results or effects of something
16. *Justify*	to give facts to support something
17. *Outline*	to organize the main points and subordinate points of something to show the relationship of the points to each other
18. *Prove*	to show something is true by giving facts or logical reasons
19. *Relate*	to tell how things are alike or connected
20. *Summarize/Review*	to briefly give the main points
21. *Trace*	to tell about something in the order or sequence that it occurs or occurred

Practice   Review Chapters 1 through 5. Find comprehension questions or questions for analysis that use words from the preceding list. In groups or as a class, discuss how you would organize an answer for each question.

Guidelines for Taking an Essay Test

    I. Use a time schedule.
        A. Use less time per question than the actual time allowed. Example: A 90-minute test has 3 essay questions. The time/question ratio is 30 minutes per question. You should spend *less than* 30 minutes on each question.
        B. Stick to your time schedule (three abbreviated answers are better than only two detailed ones).
        C. Use the extra time to check your essay.
    II. Read the entire test once before beginning.
        A. Underline direction words.
        B. Note and number any individual parts of questions.
        C. Jot down your immediate reactions and key words needed for your answer.
    III. Plan before you write.
        A. Start with the easiest question first.
        B. Mentally restate each question in your own words to make sure you understand it. Don't hesitate to ask the teacher for clarification if you don't understand the question.
        C. Write a brief outline.
           1. Write a thesis sentence that answers the test question directly.
           2. Note down details supporting your thesis, and be sure not to get off the subject.

    IV. Write your answers.
        A. Start with an introduction that includes your thesis sentence.
        B. Follow your outline.
        C. Summarize and show how you answered the question in the conclusion.
        D. Check time; use only allotted time for each question.
     V. Check your essay.
        A. Modify questionable statements (if you're not sure of the facts, better not to mention specific dates or numbers. Use "approximately" and similar expressions.
        B. Add points you may have omitted—writing late additions on the back of your paper is permissible, as long as you indicate on the front so that the teacher knows to read the back.
        C. Check numbers, dates, and statistics for accuracy.
        D. Correct misspellings.

Test Question

Analyze your own personality and behavior based on what we have studied about stress. Would you say that you tend to have stress-prone behaviors or personality traits, or do you have stress-resistant behaviors and attitudes?

Gathering Information

Before you decide what information you will use, consider carefully what this question is really asking. It is asking you to *apply* the information from this unit to your own life. You must show that you understand the concepts well enough to relate them to your situation. First of all, it is necessary to include relevant information from the lectures and text. Next, you will need to consider including any applicable information from class activities and discussions. Finally, you can mention your own experiences and ideas.

Narrowing the Topic

On essay tests, you will have to narrow the topic just as you would for any essay. When deciding on how to narrow the topic, choose points to discuss that allow you to demonstrate your understanding of the subject. Remember that the purpose of an essay question is to test whether you have understood the course material, so you must show this in your answer.

Planning the Essay

Make a brief outline to follow so that you don't forget important points. Also jot down key words you'll need to define.

Follow-up Exercise

Work in groups. Your teacher will collect and redistribute the essays. Imagine that you are college professors grading essay exams. Base your grades on the content and organization of the answers only, not on grammar.

1. Decide whether to award letter grades or to grade on a percentage system.
2. Read each essay your group receives, and on a separate piece of paper, list each author's name and what grade you would give the essay. Also write down a brief comment about the reason for your grade decision.
3. When each member of the group has read all the group's essays, compare and discuss grade decisions.

4. On a separate sheet of paper for each essay, write the group's final grade decision and reasons, and return the essays and grade sheets to the authors.

SAMPLE ESSAY QUESTIONS

The following are actual questions that were given on college examinations and were collected by the author. You may notice that they are considerably more difficult than the essay topics given in this book. For each essay question, discuss the following points:

1. What key words in the question can help you understand what the teacher wants?
2. What information will you need in order to answer the question?
3. Propose a way of organizing the answer.

From an anthropology course:

1. How would you explain the relevance of the concept of evolution for an understanding not only of our human past, but also the cultural present?
2. "The life of the primitive hunter is a precarious one, a continual search for food. Leisure time is almost totally lacking, and life is nasty, brutish and short." Criticize or support this statement in every way you can, drawing on your readings on the !Kung, Arunta, or other societies covered in the textbook.

From a history course:

1. The fifteenth- and sixteenth-century voyages of exploration produced lasting changes in the political and social structure of Western Europe. Would you say that these voyages tended to hasten or delay the growth of national states? Explain.
2. If you had to take the position that due to the psychological, environmental and ideological necessities of the American experience, the period 1607-1865 had a basic intellectual continuity, what would be your argument, your analysis and your evidence?

From an English course:

1. Based on your reading of *A Connecticut Yankee in King Arthur's Court*, in your judgment, what is the essential difference between the procedures Hank uses to blow up (a) Merlin's antique tower in Chapter VII and (b) the obstruction to the holy fountain in Chapter XXIII? What does this say about him?
2. What is your estimate of the psychological accuracy of Emily Dickinson's "After Great Pain"?

Stress

What's Ahead

- *Bad stress and good stress*
- *What is stress, anyway?*
- *The immune connection between stress and illness*
- *Crises, hassles, and negativity: Some sources of stress*

Throughout history, "stress" has been one of those things that everyone has experienced but few can define. In a thorough review of 35 years of stress research, members of an Institute of Medicine panel wrote that "no one has formulated a definition of stress that satisfies even a majority of stress researchers" (Elliott & Eisdorfer, 1982). Why has it been so difficult to agree on something all of us have felt?

Alarms and adaptation: The physiology of stress

In his 1956 book *The Stress of Life*, Canadian physician Hans Selye (1907–1982) popularized the idea of stress and advanced its study. Selye noted that many environmental factors throw the body out of equilibrium—heat, cold, pain, toxins, viruses, and so on—and require the body to respond. These factors, called *stressors*, include anything that requires the body to mobilize its resources. The body responds to a stressor with an orchestrated set of physical and chemical changes, which, as we saw in Chapter 9, prepare an individual to fight or flee. To Selye, "stress" consisted of this package of reactions, which he called the **General Adaptation Syndrome** (with the memorable acronym GAS). Usually, the body will meet the challenge of the environment and *adapt* to the stress.

According to Selye, the general adaptation syndrome consists of three phases. The first is the *alarm* phase, in which the organism mobilizes to meet the threat. The second is the phase of *resistance*, in which the organism attempts to resist or cope with the threat. If the stressor persists, however, it may overwhelm the body's resources. Depleted of energy, the body enters the phase of *exhaustion*, becoming vulnerable to fatigue, symptoms, and, eventually, illness. The very reactions that allow the body to resist short-term stressors—boosting energy, shutting out signs of pain, closing off digestion, raising blood pressure—are unhealthy as long-range responses. Increased blood pressure can become chronic hypertension. Closing off digestion for too long can lead to digestive disorders.

Stress is a bane of modern civilization because our physiological alarm mechanism now chimes too often. When human beings had to contend with woolly mammoths, a dramatic fight-or-flight response was adaptive. Today, when the typical stressor is a mammoth traffic jam and not a mammoth mammal, the fight-or-flight response often gets revved up with nowhere to go. When your teacher announces that you will have an unexpected writing assignment, you don't really need to respond as if you were fighting for your life, but your body may still sweat to dispose of excess body heat. When you see your sweetheart flirting with someone else, you don't really need to breathe hard to get oxygen to your muscles, as you would if you were fleeing to safety.

Not all stress is bad, however. Some stress, which Selye called **eustress,** is positive and feels good, even if it also requires the body to produce some short-term energy: competing in an athletic event, falling in love, working hard on a project you enjoy. Selye did not believe that all stress could be avoided or that people should aim for a stress-free life. "Just as any inani-

General Adaptation Syndrome (GAS) *According to Hans Selye, the bodily reactions to environmental stressors.*
eustress [YOU-stress] *Positive or beneficial stress.*

mate machine gradually wears out," he said, "so does the human machine sooner or later become the victim of constant wear and tear." The goal is to minimize the wear and tear, not get rid of it.

Selye recognized that psychological stressors (such as emotional conflict or grief) can be as important as physical stressors (such as heat, toxic chemicals, or noise). He also observed that some factors *mediate* between the stressor and the stress. A warm climate or a nutritious diet, for example, can soften the impact of an environmental stressor such as pollution. Conversely, a harsh climate or a poor diet can make such stressors worse. But by and large, Selye concentrated on the biological responses that result from a person's attempt to adapt to environmental demands. He defined a stressor as any event that produces the stress (that is, the General Adaptation Syndrome). A diagram of his view is:

Stressor — — –> Stress (GAS) — — –> Healthy adaptation or illness

Later studies, however, have found that stress is not a purely biological condition that leads directly to illness. First, between the stressor and the stress is *the individual's evaluation of the event.* For this reason, an event that is stressful for one person may be challenging for another and routinely boring for a third. Becoming pregnant, losing a job, traveling to China, or having "too much" work to do are stressful to some people and not to others. Second, between the stress and its consequences is *how the individual copes with the stress.* Not all individuals who are under stress behave the same way. Not all get ill. Thus a revised diagram might look like this:

Stressor – – –> Stress (GAS) – – –> Healthy adaptation or illness

↑   ↑

interpretation   coping
of stressor

Psychologists have had a hard time defining stress precisely because people differ in how they interpret events and in how they respond to them. Many now prefer a definition of stress that takes into account aspects of the environment, aspects of the individual, and how the two intersect. **Psychological stress** is the result of a relationship between the person and the environment, in which the person believes that the situation strains or overwhelms his or her resources and is endangering his or her well-being (Lazarus & Folkman, 1984).

psychological stress *The result of a relationship between the person and the environment, in which the person believes the situation is overwhelming and threatens his or her ability to cope.*

psychosomatic *A term that describes the interaction between a physical illness or condition and psychological states; literally, mind (psyche) and body (soma).*

Illness and immunology: The psychology of stress

A different approach to the origins of illness came from the field of *psychosomatic medicine*, which developed within psychiatry at the turn of the century. **Psychosomatic** describes the interaction of mind (*psyche*) and body (*soma*). Freud was one of the main contributors to this field, arguing that physical symptoms were often the result of unconscious conflicts. Other psychodynamic theorists maintained that certain disorders—notably rheumatoid arthritis, asthma, ulcers, migraine headaches, hypertension— are caused by neurotic personality patterns or needs (Taylor, 1986).

Many of these early theories have not been supported by modern research, but they unfortunately left the public with two wrong ideas. One is that "psychosomatic" means an illness that is "just in your head." Today's field of psychosomatic medicine has expanded to include all aspects of the mind-body relationship—not only how mind affects body, but also how body affects mind. The other misconception is that if you get sick, it is somehow the fault of your personality. The current view is that psychological factors are only one link in a long chain that connects stress and illness.

Some researchers, borrowing ideas from Selye and from psychosomatic medicine, are studying the effects of physical stress and psychological factors on the immune system. The immune system is designed to do two things: recognize foreign substances (antigens), such as flu viruses, bacteria, and tumor cells, and destroy or deactivate them. There are basically two types of white blood cells in the immune system: the *lymphocytes* [LIM-foe-sites], whose job is primarily to recognize and destroy foreign cells, and the *phagocytes* [FAG-oh-sites], whose job is to ingest and eliminate them (*phago* means "eating").

To defend the body against foreign invaders, the immune system deploys different weapons (cells), sometimes together and sometimes alone, depending on the nature of the enemy. For example, *natural killer cells*, a type of lymphocyte, are important in tumor detection and rejection; *killer T cells* help destroy antigens that they have been exposed to previously. Prolonged or severe stress can suppress these cells and others that normally fight disease and infection.

The marriage of immunology and psychology has produced an offspring with the cumbersome name **psychoneuroimmunology.** This new field explores the connections between psychological processes (such as emotions, attitudes, and perceptions), the nervous system, and immune function. A basic assumption in this work, according to one of the field's founders, is that *all* disease is the result of relationships among the endocrine, nervous and immune systems, behavior, and emotions (Solomon, 1985). These relationships explain, for example, why of two people who are exposed to a flu virus, one is sick all winter and the other doesn't even get the sniffles (Schwartz, 1984; Strickland, 1985).

Some sources of stress

What are the stressors that might affect the immune system and thus lead to illness? Some psychologists study events, such as the death of a spouse or child, that take an emotional toll. Others count nuisances, the small straws that break the camel's back. Still others study people who seem to create their own stress for no apparent reason. Table 15.1 shows three methods of measuring the causes of stress.

Major events.   Two decades ago, Thomas Holmes and Richard Rahe (1967) identified 43 events that seemed to be especially stressful. By testing thousands of people, they were able to rank a series of "life-change events" in order of their disruptive impact. Holmes and Rahe then assigned each event a corresponding number of "life-change units" (LCUs). At the top was death of a spouse (100 LCUs), followed by divorce (73), imprisonment (63), and death of a close family member (63). Not all of the events were unpleasant. Marriage (50) was on the list, as were pregnancy (40), buying a house (31), and Christmas (12). Among people who had become ill, the large majority had had 300 LCUs or more in a single year.

psychoneuroimmunology
(psycho/neuro/immu/nology) The field that studies the relationships among psychology, the nervous system, and the immune system.

——— *TABLE 15.1* ———

Events, hassles, and perceptions: Three ways to measure stress

Measure #1: *Counting major life events and their "life-change units," such as:**	Measure #2: *Counting frequency of "daily hassles," such as:†*	Measure #3: *Assessing perceptions of stress:‡*
100 Death of spouse 73 Divorce 63 Jail term 63 Death of close family member 53 Major personal injury or illness 50 Marriage 47 Being fired at work 45 Marital reconciliation 40 Pregnancy 38 Major change in financial state 29 Trouble with in-laws 28 Outstanding personal achievement 26 Beginning or ending school 24 Change in personal habits 16 Change in sleeping habits 15 Change in number of family get-togethers 13 Vacation 12 Christmas	Household chores Health of self or family member Time pressures: too many things to do, not enough time in day (related to symptoms for women but not for men) Inner conflicts Environmental worries: neighborhood deterioration, noise, crime Financial worries Work problems Future financial security worries	Answer each question using the following scale: 0 = never; 1 = almost never; 2 = sometimes; 3 = fairly often; 4 = very often. *In the last month, how often have you:* 1. been upset because of something that happened unexpectedly? 2. felt nervous and "stressed"? 3. found that you could not cope with all the things that you had to do? 4. been angered because of things that were outside your control? 5. found yourself thinking about things that you had to accomplish? 6. felt difficulties were piling up so high that you could not overcome them?

*Selected items from the Social Readjustment Rating Scale (Holmes & Rahe, 1967).
†Eight major hassles factors (Lazarus et al., 1985).
‡Selected items from the Perceived Stress Scale (Cohen, Kamarck, & Mermelstein, 1983).

Research has confirmed that the events at the top of the list, death of a spouse and divorce, are indeed powerful stressors that are linked to a subsequent decline in health. Grieving widows and widowers are more susceptible to illness and physical ailments—including pneumonia, diabetes, ulcers, and rheumatoid arthritis—and their mortality rate is higher than expected (Klerman & Izen, 1977). Divorce also often takes a long-term health toll. Divorced adults have higher rates of emotional disturbance, heart disease, pneumonia, and other diseases than comparable adults who are not divorced (Jacobson, 1983; Weiss, 1975). Bereaved and divorced people may be vulnerable to illness because of other changes in their lives, such as insomnia, poor diets, increased smoking, drinking, and drug consumption. But animal and human studies suggest that separation itself creates changes in the cardiovascular system, a lowered white blood cell count, and other abnormal responses of the immune system (Laudenslager & Reite, 1984).

Other studies, though, have found numerous flaws in the idea that all major life events are stressful and lead to illness:

■ As many as 29 of the 43 items of the Holmes-Rahe Scale may be the *result* of psychological problems or illness, not their *cause* (such as "problems at work" and "major changes in sleeping habits") (Hudgens, 1974).

- Some events become more stressful once a person already is depressed or ill (Dohrenwend, 1979).

- The Holmes-Rahe scale assumes that every event has the same stress impact on everyone. But, as we saw in Chapter 14, many changes, such as retirement or having children leave home, are not especially stressful for most people.

- Happy, positive events are not related (thank goodness) to illness or poor health (Taylor, 1986).

Newer measures of stress attempt to correct these problems. For example, they assess your *perception* of how stressful an event or accumulation of events is. Having 80 things to do in one week in not necessarily stressful unless you feel overwhelmed by them (Cohen, Kamarck, & Mermelstein, 1983; Sarason, Johnson, & Siegel, 1978).

Daily hassles.   Some psychologists argue that we handle most of the big problems of life quite well; it's the daily grind that can get us down. "Hassles" are the irritations and frustrations of everyday routines, such as traffic jams, bad weather, annoying arguments, broken plumbing, lost keys, and sick cats. Some research suggests that hassles are better predictors of psychological and physical symptoms than are major life events (DeLongis et al., 1982; Kanner et al., 1981).

Of course, a major event, such as divorce, can have a strong influence by increasing the number of hassles a person must contend with (new financial pressures, custody questions, moving). Also, a major event, such as having fought in a war, might make a person more intolerant of small hassles. By and large, though, people's reports of being hassled are independent of life events. In a study of 210 police officers, the most stressful things they reported were not the dramatic dangers and arrests you see on TV, but daily paperwork, annoyance with "distorted" accounts of the police in the press, and the snail-like slowness of the judicial system (Grier, 1982).

Notice, though, that when people report that something is a hassle, they are really reporting their *feelings* about the activity. The activity itself might be neutral. A young mother who says that making meals every day is a "hassle" is revealing her attitudes and emotions about this "chore." Perhaps because she has so many other things to do every day, preparing dinner feels to her like the last straw. Her husband might look forward to cooking as an enjoyable way to reduce tension. Similarly, one commuter finds taking the train a "hassle" because he is in a hurry to get to work, whereas another welcomes the commuting time to read novels. So the measure of "hassles," like that of "stressful events," may be confounded with existing symptoms of emotional distress (Dohrenwend & Shrout, 1985).

Continuing problems.   Stressors differ in their duration as well as in their intensity. Some are brief, one-shot events, such as awaiting surgery or news about admission to graduate school. Others are continuous or recur frequently: living with an abusive or tyrannical parent; working in a situation in which you are at a disadvantage because of your color, religion, gender, or age; feeling trapped in a relationship that you can't live with and can't live without.

Many stress researchers believe that people have a good ability to withstand acute (short-term) stress, even a massive blow. The real problem, they say, occurs when stress becomes interminable. Prolonged or repeated stress (from occupations such as air traffic control or from circumstances such as unemployment) is associated with heart disease, hypertension, arthritis, and immune-related deficiencies (Taylor, 1986). Black men in America who live in stressful neighborhoods (characterized by poverty, high divorce and unemployment rates, crime, and drug use) are particularly vulnerable to hypertension and related diseases (Gentry, 1985; Harburg et al., 1973). Female clerical workers who feel they have no support from their bosses, who are stuck in low-paying jobs without hope of promotion, and who have financial problems at home, are the women most at risk of heart disease (Haynes & Feinleib, 1980). (The "Think About It" box raises the question of whose stress and what kind of stress generally gets public attention.)

What seems to be most debilitating about these circumstances is the feeling of powerlessness, of having no control over what happens to you. People can tolerate years of difficulty if they feel they can *control* events or at least *predict* them (Laudenslager & Reite, 1984). These are not necessarily the same thing. You may not be able to control the stressful experience of an exam, but you can usually predict and prepare for exams. When people know that they will be going through a stressful time or living in a stressful environment, they can take steps to reduce stress (see "Taking Psychology with You"). We will return to this important topic later.

Negative emotions.   The events we have described—major changes, little hassles, and continuing problems—often generate anger, grief, anxiety, and other uncomfortable emotions. Recent studies find that prolonged negative emotions, whether they are associated with life events or not, are themselves far more stressful than happy ones.

For example, men who are chronically angry and resentful, and who have a hostile attitude toward others, have a much higher risk than nonhostile men of getting coronary heart disease and other ailments (Williams, Barefoot, & Shekelle, 1985). In a longitudinal study of 255 male physicians, the hostile physicians were five times as likely as the nonhostile men to get coronary heart disease or to have died from it. Another study followed 1877 middle-aged men who were free of heart disease at the time of the interviews. Twenty years later, the researchers found that hostility was again a strong predictor of death from a variety of causes.

Other unhappy emotions, notably depression, helplessness, loneliness, panic, and anxiety, have also been linked to illness. In a study of medical students who had herpes virus, researchers found that herpes outbreaks were more likely to occur when the students were feeling loneliest or were under the pressure of exams. Loneliness and stress suppressed the cells' immune capability, permitting the existing herpes virus to erupt (Kiecolt-Glaser et al., 1985a, 1985b).

"Stress-prone personalities."   Some people always seem to be in a state of stress for no apparent reason. Put them on a tranquil beach far from civilization, and they worry about what's happening at home. Show up at their offices with two tickets to the World Series, and they snap at you for

Think About It

WHOSE STRESS COUNTS?

Stress has become as popular an issue as money, power, and sex. Stories in the media warn about it, worry about who has it, and advise us on how to control it. These messages, and the money that goes to fund stress research, are not dispensed equally. Cynthia Fuchs Epstein (1985) argues that some people's stress is considered worse than other people's and gets more public attention. The usual recommendations about what a person should do to be "unstressed," she adds, are different for different groups.

Who is worst off? Epstein observes that the problems that get government funding—alcoholism, executive stress, Type A behavior and heart disease—are the problems that many Congressmen have. Although these concerns are worthy of study, she maintains, the fact is that in terms of stress, successful white males do not have the most to worry about. They are a lot less "stressed" or at risk of illness than black men in poor neighborhoods, or than single mothers, now the largest group who live below the poverty line. Men at the high end of the job hierarchy are much better off than the men and women at the low end of the totem pole, who are poorly paid, who are first to be fired during a recession, who make no decisions in the work they do, and who have the least chance to develop those desirable components of "hardiness"—commitment, challenge, and control (Kohn & Schooler, 1983).

Whose stress matters? Attention has been focused on career stress, and on how it costs billions of dollars a year in lost time and employee productivity. But some employees and occupations get more attention than others do. The stress of motherhood gets less concern than the stress of the "career woman." The stress of an underpaid high-school teacher with crowded classes gets less concern than the stress of a banker or business executive.

What are the solutions to stress? Men in powerful jobs are often advised to reduce their drinking, take more vacations, or try meditation. Women in powerful jobs, says Epstein, are often advised to quit. They are warned that it might be "too stressful" for them to be "superwomen," combining families and careers. Women are advised that entering the world of work is harmful to their health because they will pick up all that male stress. They aren't always informed that they will also pick up more satisfaction and income. Women are expected to solve by themselves the real conflicts of managing children, employment, and husbands. In Scandinavian countries, this juggling act is considered a social problem, with social solutions such as quality day care for children and paid maternity (and paternity) leave (Tavris & Wade, 1984).

We note in this chapter that there are many solutions to stress. You can try to change the stressful problem. You can run away from the problem. You can try to live with the problem. Obviously, the consequences of attacking the problem are different from those of accepting the problem. If you decide that the reason for your stress is "all in your mind," you will probably look for solutions within yourself. If you decide that you can take action to improve things, you may look for solutions in your circumstances.

How might your ways of coping be affected by the kinds of problems you have? How would the approach you take affect your level of stress and sense of control? Are occupational stress and the stresses of parenthood individual problems or social ones? What do you think?

---

interrupting them.

A notable difference between easygoing people and tense worriers seems to be in the frequency with which the latter feel stressful negative emotions. Indeed, two psychologists have identified a dimension of personality they call *negative affectivity* (NA)—a person's tendency to feel negative emotions such as anger, scorn, revulsion, guilt, rejection, and sadness (Watson & Clark, 1984). High NA people frequently feel worried and tense, even in the absence of objective stress. Their low self-esteem and negative moods are linked to their tendency to brood about (and magnify) their mistakes and disappointments. They are particularly sensitive to hassles and frustrations, and report greater distress for a longer time than low NAs do.

A cluster of stressful characteristics that has been the most thoroughly analyzed is called the **Type A behavior pattern** (Friedman & Rosenman,

1974; Glass, 1977). Although Type A has been measured in different, often inconsistent ways, it basically refers to a constant struggle to achieve, a sense of time urgency, impatience at anyone or anything that gets in the way, irritability, and an intense effort to control the environment. Type B people are calmer, less impatient, less intense. The hard-driving aspects of Type A, especially anger and hostility, have been linked to an increased likelihood of coronary artery disease (Spielberger et al., 1985). However, it is not known if Type A is really a stable pattern or a behavioral response to certain conditions. So some scientists prefer to use the term "coronary-prone behavior" instead of "Type A" personality (Review Panel, 1981).

Psychologists disagree about the links between Type A behavior, stress, and heart disease. One theory argues that people with Type A personalities are "hot reactors" (Eliot, Buell, & Dembroski, 1982). When faced with a challenge, they physically react very fast. Their heart rates and endocrine responses shoot up and stay high, which ultimately damages the cardiovascular system. However, it turns out that different tasks and situations produce different physiological responses in the same people—you might be a "hot reactor" while playing a video game and a "cold reactor" during exams—and overreactivity itself is not a risk factor in heart disease (Krantz & Manuck, 1984). Type A people do set themselves a fast work pace and a heavy work load, but many cope with it better than Type B people who have a lighter work load, and without a high physiological price (Frankenhaeuser, 1980). Further, people who are highly involved in their jobs, even if they work hard, have a relatively low incidence of heart disease. What is going on?

In accord with our earlier discussion, it seems likely that Type A behavior becomes stressful (and leads to illness) when an individual (1) feels out of control of the environment, (2) feels external pressure to work, rather than intrinsic pleasure, (3) feels frequent anger, resentment, or hostility, and (4) lacks close friends and intimate attachments.

Type A behavior pattern *A set of characteristics consisting of time urgency, irritability, impatience, a need to control the environment, and a struggle to achieve; it is believed to be a risk factor in coronary heart disease.*

Quick Quiz

A. Match the stressors on the left with their examples:

1. life-change event	**a.** feeling enraged at being mugged
2. hassle	**b.** having to work for a hostile boss
3. continuing situation	**c.** death of a parent
4. negative emotion	**d.** losing your books before a big exam

B. Selye called the body's response to stressors the_____.
C. A person who has a sense of time urgency, is irritable and impatient at interruptions, and intensely needs to control the environment is said to have a_____pattern or_____-prone behavior.

ANSWERS:

A. 1. c **2.** d **3.** b **4.** a **B.** General Adaptation Syndrome **C.** Type A; coronary

What's Ahead

- *The hardy personality*
- *When to go with the flow*
- *The selfish benefits of unself-ishness*

---

pathogenic [path-o-GEN-ik]
Causing disease or suffering.
salutogenic [sa-loot-o-GEN-ik]
Causing health.

THE INDIVIDUAL SIDE OF HEALTH AND WELL-BEING

Scientific psychology and medicine typically focus on the causes of a problem or an illness. Their method, tracking down the sources of pathology, is called **pathogenic** (from *patho*, disease or suffering, and *genic*, producing). According to Aaron Antonovsky (1979, 1984), we also need to know what generates health, by taking the **salutogenic** approach (from *salut*, health).

The pathogenic approach, Antonovsky argues, divides the world into the healthy and the sick, although many healthy people have occasions of "dis-ease" and many sick people are able to get along with life. It seeks a single cause to a problem: Type A causes heart attacks, bereavement causes illness. The salutogenic approach, in contrast, regards health and disease as a continuum. "Everyone, by virtue of being human, is in a high-risk group," says Antonovsky (1984). "The question is no longer 'How can we eradicate this or that stressor?' but rather 'How can we learn to live, and live well, with stressors, and possibly even turn [them] to our advantage?' " To find out, Antonovsky and other researchers are studying the exceptions—the people who theoretically should have trouble coping but don't, and the people who face difficult problems in life but who do not give in, physically or emotionally.

The stress-resistant personality

From studies of people who have successfully overcome the experience of concentration camps, poverty, or discrimination, Antonovsky concludes that the healthy personality is based on what he calls the "sense of coherence." People who share this psychological orientation believe that their lives are *comprehensible* (the world is meaningful, orderly, and consistent instead of chaotic, random, and unpredictable). They feel that events are *manageable*, that they are able to cope. They believe that life is *meaningful* and that life's demands are worthy of commitment.

Hardiness. In another version of the salutogenic approach, a team of psychologists studied 259 business managers, ages 32 to 65, over a five-year period (Kobasa, 1979; Kobasa, Maddi, & Kahn, 1982). At the end of five years, many of the men had undergone numerous stressful events, such as job transfers, illness of a family member, and uncertain job evaluations. The researchers then compared those who developed illness (whether mild, such as the flu, or more serious, such as hepatitis) with those who did not. The latter group turned out to have what the researchers called "hardy" personalities. "Hardiness" consisted of three psychological components, which are very similar to those in the sense of coherence:

- *Commitment*, like Antonovsky's "meaningfulness," is the feeling of attachment to one's activities and relationships, and the belief that they are important. What matters is the sense of commitment, not the object of the commitment, which could be personal goals, friends, family, work, or religion.
- *Challenge* is the willingness to accept and to enjoy new and unpredictable experiences, to see opportunities in change rather than only losses, to feel curiosity and interest.
- *Control*, like "manageability," reflects the belief that one is not helpless, but can influence many events and other people.

The hardy managers were not younger, wealthier, or higher on the career ladder than those who succumbed to stress. Hardiness was not related to demographic factors, such as age, education, religion, job level, or years at that job level. Nor did the hardy managers simply have stronger constitutions, as measured by their parents' medical history. "Hardiness" and genetic vulnerability were unrelated (Kobasa, Maddi, & Courington, 1981). These findings about hardiness have held up in subsequent studies of lawyers (Kobasa, 1982), telephone company executives, U.S. Army officers, college students, and working women.

Moreover, hardiness was more important than exercise in reducing stress. Consider two men who leave work after an argument with the boss. The one who is low in hardiness goes to his gym for a good workout, feels refreshed, and goes home for a relaxed evening. The next day, though, as he walks into his office, his unresolved tensions return. He anticipates another battle with the boss, which he feels unable to avoid, and before long his neck muscles tighten and his palms are sweating. The hardy manager, however, sees this conflict as a challenge that he can turn to his advantage. He looks forward to resolving the disagreement with his boss and getting on with his work.

Locus of control.   One of the most important personality factors that offset stress, it seems, is feeling in control of one's life. In Chapter 11 we discussed internal and external locus of control, a personality dimension that is related to stress. People who feel that they are in charge of their lives often deal more effectively with problems and decisions than people who lack this sense of mastery. "Internals" modify their coping efforts depending on what the problem is, selecting the appropriate tactic from a range of possibilities (Parkes, 1984). In contrast, people who feel powerless tend to respond to stress with anger, depression, drug use, or physical symptoms (Langer, 1983). They are inclined to see the worst in every situation, and are not as flexible in choosing the best method of coping.

Psychologists have developed a version of the locus of control scale that measures people's beliefs in control over their own health. Is it all a matter of faith and luck, or can you take action to stay well? An internal locus of control is related to the ability to stop smoking, lose weight, get inoculations and dental checkups, follow medical regimens, wear seat belts, and otherwise take care of yourself (Lau, 1982; Walston & Walston, 1982).

Yet, is a sense of control always a good thing? Believing that an event is controllable does not always lead to a reduction in stress, and believing that an event is uncontrollable does not always lead to an increase in stress (Folkman, 1984; Thompson, 1981). The question must always be asked: control over *what?* As we saw in the study of cancer patients, it isn't beneficial to "take control" for becoming sick, but for staying well.

It also doesn't help people to believe they have control over an event if they then feel unable to cope with it. Victims of abuse or other crimes, for example, often suffer because they blame themselves for having "provoked" their attackers, as if they could have controlled the criminal's behavior.

Finally, if an unrealistically confident person tries to control the uncontrollable ("I'm going to be a movie star in 60 days!"), the resulting failure may lead to unrealistic helplessness (Fleming, Baum, & Singer, 1984). In one study of 45 adults, those who had the strongest internal health locus of control were the *most* vulnerable to stressful events that were out of their control, as measured by their cellular immune functioning (Kubitz, Peavey, & Moore, 1985).

So a critical step in promoting health and well-being is to learn the difference between what can be controlled and what cannot.

Five things you can do for 72¢ or less...

1

Enjoy a cup
of coffee…

2

Pick up a
newspaper…

3

Buy a few
stamps…

4

Have a soft
drink…

5 Or make a lasting difference in the
life of a child and family overseas
through Foster Parents Plan.

Here at home, 72¢ is the kind of pocket change
you spend every day without thinking much
about it. But for a child overseas, born into
a world of desperate poverty, it can lead to
a future full of promise and achievement.

**Your spare change can change the
life of a child. Forever.**

As a Foster Parent, you'll be helping a
needy child in the most critical areas of
development. Like education. Better
nutrition. Improved health. At the
same time, your help will give your
Foster Child the gift of hope.

It's hope that springs from Foster
Parents Plan's comprehensive programs,
built on your support combined with the
hard work and determination of your

Foster Child's family to help themselves.
Programs that produce ways to make
a better living. That build confidence
and self-sufficiency, and that result
in long-lasting improvements for
all their lives.

What's more, you'll be able to share in
these accomplishments through photographs, progress reports and letters about
your Foster Child and family.

Don't wait—a child needs your help now.

Think about all the good you can do for just
72¢ a day, the cost of a morning coffee break.
Then send your love and support to a child and
family overseas, who need a chance for a better life.
Please, do it now.

Chapter
6

English Communication

Outline

Lecture: "Propaganda"
Debate: Anti-Smoking Legislation
Quotation and Paraphrase
Reading Exercises: "Persuasion"
Advanced Questions for Analysis: Logical Fallacies
Word Parts
Writing: Analyzing a Persuasive Message
"Persuasion"

Objectives

When you finish this chapter, you will be able to do the following:

Language and Study Skills

1. Take an active role in a class debate.
2. Write an essay analyzing a persuasive message.
3. Use quotation and paraphrase correctly.
4. Participate in a seminar-style class activity.

Content Mastery

1. Use appropriate methods of persuasion to put forth your own arguments.
2. Recognize and label logical fallacies.
3. Identify persuasive devices used in advertisements.

Persuasion is a communication skill used extensively in college, both in writing and in speaking. It also is very useful in daily life, for example, if you want to persuade your parents to buy you a new car. This chapter takes a look at the elements of persuasion as they are formally taught in freshman-level public speaking (speech) classes and freshman composition (writing) classes.

Important Terms

As you listen to the lecture and read the passage for this chapter, note the following important terms and their meanings. When you finish the chapter, you should be able to define each one.

appeal to authority	conviction
appeal to tradition	cost-benefit analysis
argument from analogy	cross-ranking
attack on the person	deception
Card Stacking Device	deductive reasoning
consistency	determination

distraction
dramatic example
emotional appeals
equivocation
fallacies
fear appeals
flattery
generalization
Glittering Generalities
　Device
hasty generalization
idealism
inductive reasoning
justified fear

logical conclusion
Maslow's hierarchy of needs
Name Calling Device
one-sided approach
pity
Plain Folks Device
post hoc, ergo, propter hoc
prejudice
propaganda
provocation
Testimonial Device
transcendence
Transfer Device
two-sided approach

LECTURE: "PROPAGANDA"

You are surrounded by persuasive messages, many of them propaganda. Advertisements are one example. This lecture will introduce ways of recognizing common propaganda methods. It was a lecture given by the author in an advanced reading and writing class for international students at California State University, Los Angeles.

Comprehension Questions

Refer to your notes as needed to answer the following questions.

1. What is propaganda?
2. List three logical fallacies and give an example for each.
3. In one or two sentences, explain each propaganda device.
   a. Name Calling Device
   b. Glittering Generalities Device
   c. Transfer Device
   d. Testimonial Device
   e. Plain Folks Device
   f. Card Stacking Device

Questions for Analysis

1. Look at a magazine or newspaper. Read the advertisements and find one that uses a propaganda device discussed in the lecture. Quote or paraphrase the advertisement to show exactly how the propaganda device is being used.
2. Aside from advertisements, can you give examples of other propaganda that you have encountered?

DEBATE: ANTI-SMOKING LEGISLATION

As an introduction to persuasion, you will participate in a debate where you will need to use your persuasive skills to support your position.

Debate Topic　Should new laws be passed to restrict smoking?
　The class should form two teams. One team will be for anti-smoking legislation (the "pro" team), and the other team will be against it (the "con" team).

Debate Procedures

1. Members of each team meet for ten to fifteen minutes. Choose a team captain and plan your arguments. Every team member should take notes, listing all the arguments. The "pro" team should decide exactly what legislation to propose (see following list of examples).
2. Arrange the classroom so that each team sits together facing the opposing team. The debate begins with a statement by the team captain of the "pro" team, followed by a rebuttal by the team captain of the "con" team.
3. a. In turn, a member from one team and then the other speaks. A person speaking should rebut the point of the opposing team before putting forth a new point. Questions can be asked to clarify the opposing point before answering.
    b. No student may speak a second time until every member of his or her team has had a chance to speak.
    c. Team members can help each other, consulting before a member answers.
    d. It is a good idea to limit each debate statement to just one rebuttal and one additional point.

The following are some ideas to get you started.

Laws Restricting Smoking

1. Expand the use of smoking/no smoking divisions in public areas (bus stops, banks, offices, restaurants, public buildings).
2. Ban smoking in public entirely. Smokers can light up in their own homes and private offices only.
3. Increase tax on cigarettes so smokers pay a penalty for their habit. Use the revenue for medical research into cancer, heart disease, and other smoking-related illnesses.
4. Declare cigarettes an illegal drug and make it a crime to buy, sell, grow, or smoke tobacco. (The U.S. Surgeon General has determined that nicotine is an addictive drug.)
5. Require a doctor's prescription in order to buy cigarettes, just as with other drugs.

Arguments Against Restrictions

1. Social pressure will control smoking. The government should not get involved in this type of personal issue.
2. Each individual has a right to make the decision whether to smoke or not. We are guaranteed the right to ". . . liberty and the pursuit of happiness" by the Constitution.
3. Increasing cigarette tax or making smoking illegal could trigger a black market for cigarettes. This is what happened with liquor during Prohibition.
4. Nonsmoking areas are not enforced anyway, so why expand them?
5. The government should not discriminate against any group, and that includes smokers.

QUOTATION AND PARAPHRASE

In your writing, you may want to use information from a source other than your own experience. One way to do this is by summarizing, as explained in Chapter 4. There are two other ways to use material from a source in your writing. These are quotation and paraphrase. Both give a more detailed and exact rendering of information than a summary.

If quotation and paraphrase are not done correctly, a student may be accused of plagiarism, a kind of cheating in which someone else's work is presented as a student's own.

Plagiarism is considered a serious offense, so students should be especially careful to list sources of information when quoting and paraphrasing. The directions in this section follow the guidelines in the *MLA Handbook for Writers of Research Papers* (3rd ed., Joseph Gibaldi and Walter S. Achtert, New York: The Modern Language Association of America, 1988). For science courses the guidelines may be different. There are style manuals for specific disciplines such as chemistry, mathematics, psychology, and so on. These are available in most university libraries.

Quotation

You are quoting when you copy a source exactly. Generally the reason for doing this is to give more force or credibility to a statement by keeping the original wording. Quotation should be used sparingly. It is most often used for stating someone's opinion, especially the opinion of an expert.

Rules for Quoting a Source

1. Any time you use original wording, you must put quotation marks (" ") at the beginning and end of the passage you copy.
2. You should cite your source, either in your sentence or with a note, or both.
3. If you choose to omit part of a sentence when quoting, use an ellipsis (three dots: . . .) in place of the words you left out. Be sure that you don't change the author's meaning when you omit words.
4. Introduce the quotation in a way that shows how the quoted material is related to the point you are making.

Example

An indication of when the United States will balance the budget can be found in an article in the *Wall Street Journal* (21 December 1987: A1), in which Kenneth Bacon points out: "The October 19 stock-market crash created an opportunity for significant budget action, but President Reagan and Congress failed to seize it. As a result, there's little hope for any bold attempt to lower the deficit until after a new president takes office in 1989."[1]

In essays, notes can be placed at the bottom of the page on which the note number appears, but in reports they are most often grouped together at the end of the report, on a separate page titled "Notes."

Sample Note

[1] Kenneth H. Bacon, "The Struggle for Economic Equilibrium," *The Wall Street Journal* 21 Dec. 1987: A1.

Practice   Use quotations from the reading passage for this chapter to define the following terms: inductive reasoning, provocation, deception, one-sided approach. Include notes.

Paraphrase

Paraphrase is more commonly used than quotation. When you paraphrase, you restate ideas in your own words. Use paraphrase when you want to give detailed information from a source, and exact accuracy of wording is not necessary. Paraphrase is most appropriate for factual information.

Rules for Paraphrasing

1. Change the vocabulary of the passage.
2. Change the grammatical structure.
3. Change the order or organization of ideas.

4. Do not add any information that is not in the passage.

5. Be careful not to change the meaning of the passage.

6. State the source, either in the sentence or in a note or both.

Examples

(Original) Good management is the art of making problems so interesting, and their solutions so constructive, that everyone wants to get to work and deal with them.

   Paul Hawken, "The Mind of a Manager," *Inc.* Sept. 1987: 24.

(Paraphrase) According to Paul Hawken's article in the Sept. 1987 issue of *Inc.* (24), a good manager motivates people to work on problems by getting people interested in them and showing how the results will be helpful.

(Original) Caffeine is one of the most commonly consumed substances, found naturally in coffee and tea, added to soft drinks, and compounded into more than 1,000 over-the-counter drugs.

   "Is Coffee Safe?" *Consumer Reports* Sept. 1987: 529.

(Paraphrase) Coffee, tea, carbonated beverages, and over 1,000 commonly used medicines all contain caffeine, a chemical that is very often taken into the body.[2]

[2]"Is Coffee Safe?" *Consumer Reports* Sept. 1987: 529.

Paraphrase Exercise

On a separate sheet of paper, paraphrase the following passages. Remember to mention the source in your sentence or write a footnote.

1. The development of the Humboldt County timber industry was a direct result of the gold rush.

  California Business Sept. 1987: 40.

2. Today, because of the increasing demand for urban housing, center-city property values have skyrocketed.

  Barbaralee Diamonstein, "The Old Versus the New," *Los Angeles Times Magazine* 6 Dec. 1987: 52E.

3. Humans have many unusual characteristics, not least of which is our intense curiosity about our relationships with the world around us.

  Richard E. Leakey, *The Making of Mankind* (New York: E.P. Dutton, 1981) 9.

4. There are also the vast cultural differences between the United States, a relatively young nation, and Europe and Japan. The latter two have long traditions of appreciating the arts, which have permeated the executive ranks of the business world.

  Pamela S. Leven, "Design or Die," *California Business* Sept. 1987: 21.

5. Our society gives more leeway to the individual to pursue her own ends, but since the culture defines what is worthy and desirable, everyone tends, independently but monotonously, to pursue the same things in the same way.

  Phillip Slater, *The Pursuit of Loneliness* (Boston: Beacon Press, 1976) 14–15.

6. The greater the mobility of the individual, the greater the number of brief, face-to-face encounters, human contacts, each one a relationship of sorts, fragmentary and, above all, compressed in time.

  Alvin Toffler, *Future Shock* (New York: Bantam Books, 1970) 102.

7. It may sound like a futurist's fantasy, but American Voice & Robotics in Fort Lauderdale, Fla., is installing custom home-automation systems that hear and speak and do almost everything except fold the laundry.

  Phillip Godwin, "Houses with High IQs," *Changing Times* Sept. 1987: 103.

8. When mistakes are not tied to personal worth, they are less overwhelming.

  Dorothy Corkille Briggs, *Your Child's Self-Esteem* (Garden City, NY: Doubleday & Company, 1975) 95.

READING EXERCISES: "PERSUASION"

Reading Goal Read to prepare an oral answer for one comprehension question. Use skimming and scanning to locate the answer.

The reading material for this chapter (6,129 words) is from a freshman speech textbook, *Confidence in Public Speaking*, by Paul Edward Nelson and Judy Cornelia Pearson. The complete chapter has 42 pages, and there are 14 chapters in the book.

The Seminar Approach

1. To simulate a seminar class, work on the comprehension questions in small groups. Each group is responsible for one of the comprehension questions.
2. One member of the group will report its answer to the class.
3. Members of the class should take notes for each answer, based on group reports.
4. For homework, your teacher may ask you to write answers to all the comprehension questions.

Reading Comprehension

When answering, be sure to use quotation and paraphrase appropriately.

1. List five important principles of persuasion and briefly explain each one.
2. Define the following terms. Be sure to include the three parts of a good definition, as discussed in Chapter 3. Use quotation and paraphrase when appropriate.
   a. inductive reasoning
   b. deductive reasoning
3. What are some important things to consider in evaluating evidence to support your argument?
4. Give examples (your own or from the reading passage) for each of the following logical fallacies.
   a. hasty generalization
   b. post hoc, ergo, propter hoc
   c. cross-ranking
   d. equivocation
   e. argument from analogy
5. a. According to the reading passage, what are some unacceptable emotional appeals? Why are they unacceptable?
   b. What are some acceptable emotional appeals?
6. According to the passage, in what different situations should the one-sided approach and the two-sided approach be used?

Questions for Analysis

1. Persuasive methods differ from culture to culture. Would the methods discussed in the reading passage be appropriate in your culture? Which persuasive methods are preferred in your culture? Discuss.
2. Imagine that you are trying to convince your parents to buy you a new car. What persuasive methods would you use?
3. In the following exercise from *Confidence in Public Speaking*, identify each of the following arguments with an "I" for inductive or a "D" for deductive reasoning. When you finish, discuss any flaws in the logic of the statements.

_____ **a.** Sam, Fred, and Joan are all rich; therefore, most people in this community must be rich.

_____ **b.** College students always cause mischief; so Andy must be a college student.

_____ **c.** Other states have raised the drinking age to reduce accidents; therefore, this state should raise the drinking age also.

_____ **d.** Americans practice freedom of speech, so those students in the public speaking class must be Americans.

_____ **e.** Every time I drink milk I break out with hives; so I must have an allergy.

ADVANCED QUESTIONS FOR ANALYSIS: LOGICAL FALLACIES

How sharp is your ability to recognize false arguments? Each of the following sentences contains a fallacy. Identify the fallacy by the letter from the following list and place that letter in the left-hand column opposite the sentence.

a. *Appeal to tradition.* Inappropriately using tradition or the customary way of doing things as support for an argument.

b. *Appeal to authority.* Using the statement of a well-known person (living or dead) or organization that is not an expert in the subject.

c. *Attack on the person.* Attacking a person's character instead of the issue (an attack on the person is valid if the person's character is the issue).

d. *Hasty generalization.* Coming to a conclusion based on inadequate evidence.

e. *Post hoc, ergo, propter hoc.* Arguing that one thing is the cause of another because the two things happened one after the other.

f. *Cross-ranking.* Basing a comparison on more than one characteristic, risking comparing something to itself.

g. *Equivocation.* Using words inappropriately, allowing more than one interpretation of the meaning of a statement.

h. *Argument from analogy.* Comparing two unlike things and incorrectly saying that the characteristics of one automatically fit the other.

_____ **1.** Cori studied for her English test, but she didn't pass it; therefore, studying results in bad grades.

_____ **2.** Mom, insisting that I clean my own room is child abuse!

_____ **3.** The human body is like a car. They both require fuel to operate. You wouldn't put sugar in your car's gas tank, would you? Therefore, you should not put sugar in your body, either.

_____ **4.** In shopping in Los Angeles, I never encountered a clerk who couldn't speak Spanish. It is not necessary to speak English to shop in Los Angeles.

_____ **5.** It is obvious that this proposed gun control law is no good, because for many years Senator Brown—the author of the bill—has had a love affair with his secretary.

_____ **6.** It's a good idea to spend more money than you earn; after all, that's what the U. S. government does.

_____ **7.** You should buy brand X toothpaste because Michael Jackson recommends it.

_____ **8.** Interracial marriages are bound to fail, because marriage within races has been the norm for hundreds of years.

_____ **9.** That chemist says the city water is unsafe to drink, but he is a socialist; therefore what he says must be false.

_____ **10.** My research shows that students with glasses get better grades than Chinese students.

WORD PARTS

Match the words in the list of examples with the correct word part, then write your guess for its meaning. Check your answers with your teacher or the list in Appendix A. Make a point of learning any of the word parts that are new to you.

Root	Meaning	Example
1. min	_____	_____
2. mit, miss	_____	_____
3. mort	_____	_____
4. naut	_____	_____
5. neo	_____	_____
6. neuro	_____	_____
7. nomin, nomen	_____	_____

Prefix

8. micro-	_____	_____
9. mis-	_____	_____
10. mono-	_____	_____
11. non-	_____	_____
12. peri-	_____	_____
13. poly-	_____	_____

Suffix

14. -logy, -ology	_____	_____
15. -ment	_____	_____

Examples

commitment	misunderstand	nominate
cosmonaut	monogram	nonmaterial
manumission	mortal	peripheral
microscopic	neoclassic	polygamy
minimum	neurosis	sociology

WRITING: ANALYZING A PERSUASIVE MESSAGE

Writing Topic

Choose an advertisement from a magazine or newspaper. Write an essay analyzing what persuasive devices the advertisement uses to influence the reader. Attach the advertisement to your finished essay.

Practice   Look at the advertisement at the beginning of the chapter. Discuss which persuasive methods are being used. These can be principles of persuasion, propaganda devices, or logical fallacies.

Some Unspoken Rules about Academic Essays

Generally, teachers give assignments in the form you see in the preceding writing topic; however, there are many unspoken conventions involved that you may or may not be aware of. The following are some things the teacher will expect you to include in your writing.

First, the teacher expects a *summary* of the material before your explanation and discussion. This is not always clearly stated in the assignment instructions, but the teacher assumes that you know it is required.

Second, you need to *mention specific parts of the material* when you discuss it. For example, you need to quote or paraphrase parts of the advertisement and also appropriate parts of the lecture or textbook.

Third, you have to do a lot of independent thinking to complete the assignment. In a sense, you are giving your opinion. You shouldn't worry about whether your answer is "right" or "wrong," but rather whether you have given convincing reasons for your conclusions. Generally, in an assignment like this, teachers are more concerned with whether you *give adequate support* for your answer than which persuasive methods you choose. The assignment is designed so that the teacher can see which students really understand and can apply the information they have studied.

Gathering Information

Choose an advertisement for your essay and bring it to class. Work in groups of three or four. Group members share their advertisements and discuss the methods being used to persuade the reader.

Narrowing the Topic

Although the advertisement may employ several persuasive methods, you should not choose more than three key methods to write about.

Planning the Essay

In an essay of analysis, the following organization would be typical. According to the following example, write an outline for your essay.

    I. Introduction
       Describe the material to be analyzed by giving a brief summary. Tell what aspects your analysis will focus upon.

    II. Body
       Devote a paragraph for each key element of your analysis. For example, if you will discuss more than one persuasive method, devote one paragraph to each one.

           Define the terms of your analysis. For example, if you use a term such as "testimonial device," explain what the testimonial device is before going on to your analysis.

       Use quotation and paraphrase (and descriptions of pictures, drawings, etc.) of the material to illustrate your points. In other words, don't just say that the advertisement uses emotional appeals to persuade. Use a quotation or paraphrase to pinpoint specific statements to prove your point.

    III. Conclusion
       Summarize your main points. In addition, for this assignment you may want to make a general statement about the effectiveness of the advertisement, based on the persuasive methods it uses.

Follow-up Exercise

Teachers often have a list of items that they expect students to include in their essays. Often grading is done by checking the essay for the items on the list. The more items included, the higher the essay grade. You can try this yourself. Using the following checklist, find and mark each item in your essay.

1. Underline with pencil your thesis and focus.
2. Put a star (*) at the beginning of your summary of the advertisement.
3. Underline with pen the names and definitions of any persuasive methods (principles of persuasion, logical fallacies, propaganda devices) you used.
4. Circle any quotations or paraphrases of the advertisement.
5. Put brackets ([ ]) around your opinion of the effectiveness of the advertisement.
6. Put a star (*) at the beginning of your essay summary.

Do you have all the listed items in your essay? If not, add them and rewrite.

Persuasion

Principles of Persuasion

> **Principles of Persuasion**
>
> 1. Consistency persuades
> 2. Small changes persuade
> 3. Benefits persuade
> 4. Fulfilling needs persuades
> 5. Gradual approaches persuade

Consistency Persuades

The first principle of persuasion is that audiences are more likely to change their behavior if the suggested change is consistent with their present belief, attitudes, and values.

People who have given money for a cause (a behavior) are the likely contributors to that and other related causes in the future. People who value competition (a value) are the most likely candidates to enter into another competition. People who want to segregate old people in communities of their own (a belief) are the most likely to promote bond issues that provide separate housing for the aged. Finally, people who dislike immigrants (an attitude) are likely to discourage immigrants from moving into their neighborhood.

Fortunately for public speakers, people tend to be relatively consistent. They will do in the future what they did in the past. The public speaker uses this notion of **consistency** by linking persuasive proposals to those old consistencies. Some examples of appeals based on consistency are:

> The members of this audience were among the first in their neighborhoods to buy home computers, VCRs, and centralized home security systems. Now you can be among the first to own a laser disk sound system. I know that you are basically conservative folks who do not spend money without deep thought and careful scrutiny. That is why you will find this new sound system so appealing: it is expensive, but will outlast every appliance in your house; it is small, but more powerful than any previous system; and it is new, but designed to bring to your ears with great clarity all the songs that you like to hear.

The public speaker shapes, reinforces, and changes by showing how the promoted activity is consistent with the audience's past behavior.

Small Changes Persuade

The second principle of persuasion is that audiences are more likely to alter their behavior if the suggested change will require small rather than large changes in their behavior. A common error of beginning speakers is that they ask for too much change too soon for too little reason. Audiences are reluctant to change, and any changes they do make are likely to be small ones. Nonetheless, the successful persuasive speaker determines what small changes an audience would be willing to accept consistent with the persuasive purpose.

What if you, as a persuader, are faced with an audience of overweight Americans who are loath to exercise and resistant to reduced eating? Your temptation might be to ask for too much too soon: quit eating so much and start losing weight. The message would likely fall on unreceptive ears, because it is both inconsistent with present behavior and asking for too much change too soon. You could limit your persuasive message by encouraging the audience to give up specific foods, or a specific food that is part of their problem. However, an even better example of a small change consistent with the audience's present behavior would be to have them switch from regular to dietetic ice cream. An audience that would reject a weight-loss program might be more willing simply to switch from one form of food to another, because that change would be minimally upsetting to their present life patterns.

Are there any qualifications or limitations on this second principle of persuasion? One factor that needs to be considered in deciding how much to ask of an audience is commitment level. Studies in social judgment show that highly committed persons, people who believe most intensely or strongly about an issue, are highly resistant to any positions on the issue except their own or ones very close to it. To such an audience, reinforcement would be welcome, shaping would be a challenge, and change would be very difficult indeed. On the other hand, audience members who do not feel strongly about an issue are susceptible to larger changes than are those who already have established positions to which they are committed.

To state the principle more concretely: a speaker addressing a religious rally of persons who abhor drinking, dancing, and smoking can get warm acceptance for a persuasive message that reinforces or rewards those ideas; he would be greeted with cautious skepticism with a speech attempting to shape any responses different from those already established; and he would be met with outright rejection if he requested changes in behavior that run counter to those already embraced. On the other hand, a heterogeneous audience of persons uncommitted on the issue of regular exercise would be susceptible to considerable response shaping, and an audience of the already committed would receive reinforcement and would at least consider adopting some small changes in behavior. The successful persuader is skilled at discerning which small changes, consistent with the persuasive purpose, can be asked of an audience.

Benefits Persuade   The third principle of persuasion is that audiences are more likely to change their behavior if the suggested change will benefit them more than it will cost them. **Cost-benefit analysis,** for example, is considered every time we buy something: "Do I want this new jacket even though it means I must spend $50.00 plus tax? The benefits are that I will be warm and will look nice. The cost is that I will not be able to get my shoes resoled or buy a new watch." The persuader frequently demonstrates to the audience that the benefits are worth the cost.

A student who sold vacuum cleaners told of a fellow sales representative who donned white gloves and a surgical mask when he looked at the customer's old vacuum cleaner. By the time he had inspected the brush and changed the bag, he was filthy. He would then demonstrate that the old vacuum threw dust all over the house as it dragged across the carpet. By the end of his sales pitch, the sales representative was going to try to convince the customer that the old vacuum was not only ineffective, but also increased the amount of dirt flying around the house. The cost of the new vacuum would, according to this salesman, be worth the benefit of owning a cleaning machine that picked up dirt instead of spreading it around. Remember that you need to reveal to your audience the benefits that make your proposal worth the cost.

How can you use cost-benefit analysis in your classroom speech? Consider the costs to the audience of doing as you ask. What are the costs in money, time, commitment, energy, skill, or talent? Consider one of the most common requests in student speeches: write to your representative or senator. Many student speakers make that request without considering the probability that nobody in class has ever written to a senator or representative. Even if the speaker includes an address, the letter writing will take commitment, time, and even a little money. Few students are willing to pay those costs. On the other hand, if the speaker comes to class with an already written letter and simply asks for signatures from the class, then the cost is a few seconds of time, and the speaker is more likely to gain audience cooperation. Whenever you deliver a persuasive speech, consider the costs and how you can reduce them so the audience will feel they are worth your proposed benefits.

The fourth principle of persuasion is that audiences are more likely to change their behavior if the change meets their needs. Abraham Maslow has an often-quoted **hierarchy of needs**[7] that can be depicted like this:

Fulfilling Needs
Persuades

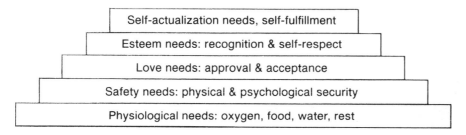

Maslow's pyramid makes sense. As a human being you do need all of the items in the hierarchy, though many people never get very far above the second level and few think they have achieved complete self-fulfillment.

You can use Maslow's hierarchy in your public speeches. Are you in a place where the air and water are so bad that it threatens public health? If so, speeches on those issues are about the basic physiological needs. Do the people in your audience have decent places to live? If not, then speeches about space and psychological health are appropriate. Is everyone in your audience happy with his or her relationships? If not, then speeches about approval and acceptance are in order.

You can analyze your audience for specific needs. Do they need money? Jobs? Day care? Do they need help in dealing with government bureaucracies? Do they need better living conditions? Do they need to learn how to study, how to handle children, or how to live with spouses? Check out your own audience and determine what they need because a speech that meets the audience's needs is likely to be successful.

Gradual approaches work best when the audience is likely to be unreceptive to your message. With a friendly audience you can ask them to do what you already know they are likely to accept and then simply give them reinforcement and a good rationale for doing so. But many persuasive speeches ask for audience changes that they may not wholeheartedly endorse just because you say they should.

Gradual
Approaches
Persuade

Do not ask a hostile audience for too much too soon. Persuading a reluctant audience is a kind of seduction in which the audience is more likely to cooperate after courtship than after an abrupt proposition. Start with common ground to show the audience that you share their basic humanity. Move from arguments and evidence that they will find quite acceptable to that which they find harder to accept.

One of the authors watched a Democratic governor face a highly Republican audience of radio and television owners and managers. The governor disarmed his potentially hostile audience by beginning with a story about how he sent his young son to school that morning. The story was amusing, but more importantly it showed that the governor—like most of the people in the audience—had the same kinds of things going on in his life that they had in their own. This common ground set the stage for the rest of the speech, in which he gently pushed the audience toward his position on the issues.

Similarly, in a persuasive speech do not start by saying, "I want you to donate your eyes to the eye bank." Instead, start gently with "safe" information about how many people have been saved from blindness by cornea transplants. Mention that the program is sponsored by the local Lion's Club. Reveal how many other people in the community, students in particular, have signed papers to allow their eyes to be used to help another person. Only after this careful courtship do you reveal that you have pledge cards for them to sign if they have compassion for their fellow human beings. The behavioral change—the signing of a commitment card—is the end result of a gradual approach.

Remember, as you prepare your persuasive speech, that audiences are more likely to change their behavior if the suggested change is consistent with their present beliefs, attitudes, and values; if it requires small rather than large changes in their lives; if it benefits them more than it costs them; if it meets their needs; and if it is a culmination of acceptable ideas. With these principles to apply in your persuasive speeches, you can move to the matter of content in the persuasive speech.

Reasoning in Persuasive Speaking

How can you convince an audience that your idea meets their needs? How can you demonstrate the benefits of your plan? How can you show that your idea is consistent with the audience's present beliefs, attitudes, and values? One of the two primary methods of persuading an audience is through reasoning—through the use of arguments with reasons, evidence, and inferences. To begin to understand reasoning, you will need to know the difference between inductive and deductive reasoning, two of the categories into which reasoning can be divided.[8]

As an overview of reasoning, you can start with the idea that inductive reasoning starts with a generalization and demonstrates its validity with various types of evidence. In deductive reasoning, you proceed to a conclusion from a major and minor premise. Let us look at these two kinds of reasoning in more detail.

Inductive Reasoning

Inductive reasoning consists of reasons, usually in the form of evidence, that lead to a generalization. The following example illustrates the form of inductive reasoning:

> Professor X gave me a D in history.
> Professor X gave Fs to two of my friends in the same course.
> Professor X posted a grade distribution with many Ds and Fs.
> Professor X boasts about his rigorous grading standards. Therefore,
> Professor X is a hard grader [generalization].

Inductive reasoning, then, provides evidence that gives you an "inferential leap" to the generalization. Inductive reasoning requires an inference because a generalization is drawn that is probably, but not unquestionably, true—based on the evidence.

In the argument above, the **generalization** that Professor X is a hard grader remains only a probability, even with the evidence presented. What if both you and your friends are poor history students, and the posted distribution was for a "bonehead" history course open only to students with poor academic records? You need to remember that in inductive reasoning, the persuader gathers evidence that leads to a *probable* generalization, but that generalization can always be questioned by reinterpretation of old evidence or the introduction of contrary evidence.

Deductive reasoning is a second way to apply logic to your argument. In inductive reasoning you have a generalization supported by or induced from the evidence; in deductive reasoning you have a **conclusion** deduced from a major and a minor premise. Instead of resulting in a probability, as inductive reasoning does, the deductive argument results in a conclusion that necessarily follows from the two premises. A deductive argument looks like this:

Deductive Reasoning

> Major premise: All insects have six legs;
> Minor premise: ants are insects;
> Conclusion: therefore, ants have six legs.

Notice that if the premises are true, then the conclusion must necessarily be true also, because in a sense the two premises are the same thing as the conclusion.

In conversation and even in most speeches, a deductive argument usually does not sound or look quite as formal as it appears above. In fact, the argument cited above would more likely appear in a speech like this: "Since all insects have six legs, ants must too." The reasoning is still deductive, except that the minor premise is implied rather than openly stated. This can make deductive arguments difficult to analyze—or even detect—in actual speeches. For this reason, it is necessary to listen closely to the reasoning in speeches, in order to determine what has been implied—or *seemed* to be implied, but actually wasn't—in addition to what has been stated openly.

On the other hand, if you feel you have particularly strong deductive arguments in your own speech, you should take the time to state them clearly and completely. Well-reasoned deductive arguments can have great persuasive power because once the audience has accepted the validity of the premises, *the conclusion is inescapable*. Mathematical proofs commonly take the form of deductive arguments, and the reasoning in your own speech should have all the clarity and impact of such proofs: if A equals B, and if B equals C, then A equals C.

You can apply several "tests" to correctly identify inductive and deductive reasoning. One test is to observe if the argument moves from the general to the particular ("All adolescents have skin problems; therefore, since Amanda is an adolescent, she must have skin problems"). If so, the argument is probably deductive. A second test is to see if the argument moves from a big category to a small or individual one ("All people have fears; so our enemies must have fears also"). If so, the argument is probably deductive. A third test is to observe if the argument moves from a small group or collection of individuals to a large one ("Randy drinks beer, Cindy drinks beer, and Rod drinks beer; so they must be alcoholics"). If so, then the argument is probably inductive. [9]

Try application exercise 3 to test your own skill at identifying inductive and deductive reasoning.

Evaluating
Reasoning

There are at least four ways to evaluate your own reasoning and that of other speakers. One way is to ask critical questions about the use of evidence. A second way is to invite inspection of your own sources of evidence. A third way is to learn how to recognize common fallacies. And a fourth way is to systematically analyze your detailed outline.

Chapter 7 on support material included questions to ask about testimony, statistics, examples, comparisons, and analogies. You might want to review those questions that refer to specific kinds of support material and consider some of these more general questions:

1. Is your evidence consistent with other known evidence? An example is the current controversy over insurance rates. Cities, counties, and even transit authorities are facing rates that they cannot afford to pay. The federal government claims that those high rates are partly because of all the law suits, a claim that they back with evidence. The lawyers counter with their evidence that the actual number of lawsuits involving insurance have increased only with the increase in population. The point is that the amount of evidence you have that consistently supports your position can help you persuade an audience. At this point in the lawyer-government-insurance controversy none of the combatants have really won the public's endorsement with their evidence.

2. Is there any evidence to the contrary? When you try to reason with evidence, you must always be aware of any evidence that does not support your cause. An opponent can do much damage to your arguments and your credibility if he or she can find contrary evidence that you did not mention. Usually, you are better off mentioning any conflicting evidence, especially if you can argue against it in your presentation.

3. Does your generalization go beyond your evidence? Speakers always face the danger of overstating what their evidence shows. A small study that shows grade inflation is treated like a university-wide problem. Evidence of a local problem becomes a national problem in the speech. Always be careful that you do not go beyond what your evidence demonstrates.

4. Is your evidence believable to the audience? In persuasive speaking you need to provide only enough evidence to have the audience believe and act as you wish. More than that is too much, less than that is too little. A large amount of evidence that the audience finds unacceptable will not persuade them; a small amount that the audience finds acceptable will be sufficient to persuade.

Asking critical questions is just one way that the speaker as persuader can evaluate evidence and reasoning. Another method is to invite your listeners to check on your evidence themselves. The speaker does this through oral footnotes to indicate where he or she found the information, evidence, or idea.

One research study indicated that an authority-based claim, in which you state who said what, may slightly improve your own credibility. Also, using a claim made by an authority slightly improved the speaker's chance of changing the audience's attitude.[10] Standard classroom practice, the rules of scholarship, and the ethics of persuasive speaking all support the idea that the persuasive speaker should reveal the sources of information to the audience.

A third means of evaluating your own reasoning and that of others is to learn how to recognize **fallacies,** violations of the rules of inference.[11] There is not room or time enough to enumerate all of the common fallacies here, so you may wish to consult a book on argumentation or debate where more fallacies are discussed. For now, we will look at five fallacies that will serve as examples of the many fallacies described in the literature.

Common Fallacies

1. Hasty generalization
2. Post hoc, ergo, propter hoc
3. Cross-ranking
4. Equivocation
5. Argument from analogy

The hasty generalization violates the rules of inference by drawing a generalization based on too little evidence. Example: I have in the past employed two white, male workers. Both proved to be poor employees. Therefore, I have vowed never again to hire a white, male employee. Problem: the sample—two persons—was too small and not random; also, the generalization does not account for the many other reasons why the employees may have been inadequate.

The post hoc, ergo, propter hoc ("after this; therefore, because of this") fallacy confuses correlation with causation. Just because one thing happens *after* another does not necessarily mean that it was *caused* by it. Example: I found that I was pregnant right after our trip; therefore, going on a trip must cause pregnancy. Problem: the trip may have correlated (occurred at the same time) with the onset of pregnancy, but the trip is not necessarily the cause.

The cross-ranking fallacy violates the rules of inference by using more than one basis of comparison at the same time. Example: I want to classify the basketball players in the NBA into (a) tall players, (b) black players, and (c) high-scoring players and then compare their performances. Problem: height, color, and skill are three different bases of comparison; so a tall, black, high-scoring player fits in all three categories and in a sense is merely being compared with himself.

The equivocation fallacy means that a word is used in several different ways to make it appear more relevant than it is. Example: Johnny is a juvenile delinquent for talking to his mother that way. Problem: the term *juvenile delinquent* is a legal term for under-aged children who commit serious crimes; verbal abuse to one's mother is not such a crime.

The argument from analogy fallacy means that an analogy compares two unlike things, asserts that they have something in common, but then goes too far by suggesting that still another characteristic is common to both. Example: Both **England and the United States have democratic governments, both have laws** that spring from "common law," and both have problems with crime. England has fewer deaths from police bullets because their police, the bobbies, do not carry guns. Therefore, we should disarm our police to reduce the problem of police killing citizens. An argument from analogy necessarily omits important differences (fewer English criminals are armed), making the argument from analogy a weak form of argument.

A fourth way to evaluate your own reasoning in a persuasive speech is a systematic analysis of your detailed outline. Major arguments should appear as main points in the outline, and each argument should be followed by the supporting materials. Analysis of your outline should allow you to determine both the quantity and the quality of the evidence and the probable acceptance by the audience.

Critically questioning, verifying sources, identifying fallacies, and analyzing the detailed outline are all methods of assessing your own evidence, arguments, and reasoning.

Appeals to the Emotions

So far in this chapter, you have considered reasoning and logical appeals. However, you need to recognize that reasoning is not the only means of securing change in an audience's mind or actions. As one writer put it:

> The creature man is best persuaded
> When heart, not mind, is inundated;
> Affect is what drives the will;
> Rationality keeps it still.[12]

Among the multitude of ways that a persuader can persuade, the use of reason has the highest regard. Appeals to the audience's emotions, on the other hand, are often regarded as a less reputable means of persuading. **Emotional appeals** are in this book not because we encourage their unqualified use, but because we hear them and occasionally use them.

Monroe Beardsley, in his book *Thinking Straight*,[13] provides over 300 pages on how reasoning and logic apply in everyday discourse. Some of the appeals he discusses are seen as unacceptable or downright unethical in public speaking or debate over issues. Learn to recognize these appeals to be an enlightened critic of public speeches. After examining a sampling of some of these illegitimate emotional appeals, we will look at some that you should know, because they do have a place in public speaking.

Unacceptable Emotional Appeals

1. Pity
2. Flattery
3. Provocation
4. Deception
5. Distraction
6. Prejudice

We will dwell but briefly on the unacceptable emotional appeals because they need only to be recognized, not practiced. These appeals are "unacceptable" in public speaking because they short-circuit the reasoning process. They try to persuade an audience to do something for the wrong reasons.

Pity is an unacceptable emotional appeal because it attempts to persuade an audience to do something because of misplaced anguish. An example is the candidate who tries to secure votes for himself because he is poor and needs the money. You should vote for a candidate whose qualities will advance your community, your state, or your nation, but you should not vote for someone simply because he is pitiable.

Flattery is an equally unacceptable reason for submitting to someone's persuasive purpose. Although flattery of an individual or an audience can be enticing, its problem as an appeal is that seductive attempts to stroke an audience's collective ego do not play to real qualifications but to an exaggerated bit of puffery. "You are such a wonderful audience," "People as terrific as you must find this product very tempting," or "This audience is the best we have had in our entire tour" are all examples of appeals that invite further scrutiny.

Provocation is an attempt to incite an audience to action, usually by making the audience angry over some issue. Provocation is the stuff of which lynch mobs, gang fights, and wars are made. When people are riled about an issue anyway, then provoking them to anger is something almost any fool can do. The difficult task is turning an angry crowd to any constructive activity.

Deception is an attempt to convince an audience to do something for the wrong reasons. They are "deceived" because they do not know the real reasons for the speaker's persuasive attempt. The speaker gives an apparently objective speech about the merits of personal property insurance and recommends one broker over all others—without revealing that the recommended broker is his brother-in-law.

Distraction is an attempt to circumvent reasoning by throwing audience attention toward some unrelated aspect of the issue. In a hot public debate about the issue of rezoning a residential area for commercial use, one speaker points out that the developer who is asking for the variance was once arrested for alleged possession of marijuana. The speaker hopes to distract attention away from the zoning issue and throw it instead on the credibility of the developer.

Prejudice is another unacceptable emotional appeal that raises an audience's hackles over the age, race, creed, color, or sexual preference. People can be prejudiced about almost anything. But the speaker who uses prejudice as an appeal tries to use it to divert attention from the issue itself and motivate the audience to dislike people who might be involved. The tough part about solving problems and settling issues is doing so without resorting to base appeals.

Let us look next at emotional appeals justifiable in public speaking.

Acceptable Emotional Appeals

1. Idealism
2. Transcendence
3. Justified fear
4. Determination
5. Conviction
6. Dramatic example

Among the acceptable emotional appeals is idealism, the communication of humanity's lofty possibilities, however rare their reality in practice. Martin Luther King, Jr., was an idealist who believed that human rights could be achieved for all people through peaceful resistance to laws, policies, and practices that treated some people as second-class citizens. Appeals to idealism are loaded with emotional content, but they are seen as appealing to our best qualities.

Transcendence is an emotional appeal that says differences can be overcome (transcended) by looking at greater and more basic commonalities among people. We do not look at what blacks, Hispanics, or poor people need; we look instead to what human beings need to exist in the richest country in the world. Gandhi is an example of a person who believed that India could overcome its ethnic and religious rivalries to forge a nation. Here again the speaker who seeks to transcend is appealing to humanity's finer qualities.

Some people would classify **fear appeals** as unacceptable because they short-circuit reasoning and encourage alarm. But justified fear refers to fear appeals in situations where we should truly be afraid, where a real threat exists to life and property. Although some researchers have found that milder fear appeals work better than stronger ones,[14] others have found that stronger appeals work better than mild ones.[15] The most solid conclusion from the research is that reassurance is an important part of any fear appeals. That is, if you are going to scare someone, you had better also tell them how to avoid or overcome the fear.[16] Otherwise, you might succeed in scaring them so much that they repress the message to avoid it.

Speakers who are working on long-term causes have to rely on an emotional appeal called sheer determination, a drive to bring about change or reform regardless of obstacles. Determination is not rational; it is a hard-headed, single-minded will to carry a cause to its completion. Caesar Chavez exhibited such determination in his attempts to organize laborers. Speakers who urge audiences to complete a task no matter how much sacrifice or time it takes are using determination as their appeal.

Conviction is your depth of belief, your certainty in the truth, righteousness, and virtue of your cause. Union leaders have strong convictions about unions, corporate executive officers have strong convictions about free enterprise, and students often have convictions about education. Convictions have an emotional component that is unmistakable in the words and actions of the true believers. A person with convictions usually communicates those convictions to an audience.

The last of the legitimate emotional appeals is the dramatic example, the narrative or story that illustrates a message. In the Bible, dramatic examples are called parables; in children's stories they are called fables; and in speeches they are called dramatic examples or stories. Sometimes one actual example can give life to your statistics about drunken driving. The dramatic example plays more to the audience's emotions than to their rationality, but ordinarily it is not seen as disreputable to use dramatic examples in a sermon, a broadcast, or a public speech.

Presenting Sides and Citing Sources

After you have developed an argument that meets the tests of evidence and the requirement of believability—and now that you are at least familiar with the basic emotional appeals—what are you supposed to do? This section answers these questions: When should you present only arguments in favor of your case? When should you present both sides of an issue? What does the educational level of your audience have to do with presenting a one-sided or two-sided treatment of the issue? Why should you be careful not to omit important arguments in your presentation? And what other factors should you keep in mind as you put together your persuasive speech?

First, when should you present a **one-sided approach**—that is, only arguments and evidence in favor of your position on an issue? Research seems to indicate that pro-arguments and evidence are more effective when the audience already agrees with your position; in fact, a two-sided approach appears to work less well for such an audience. A **two-sided approach** tends to work better when the audience is basically opposed to your point of view. An educated audience, like your classmates, are also usually more favorably disposed to a two-sided approach, while less-educated persons tend to favor only a one-sided presentation with supporting arguments. Why should you be careful to include relevant arguments that the audience knows? The absence of a relevant argument is more noticeable to an audience in a two-sided approach than in a one-sided approach with supporting arguments only. [17] Finally, if your audience is likely to hear arguments against your position from others, you can reduce the impact of those counter-arguments by mentioning them openly in your own persuasive speech.

Chapter 7

Sociology

Outline

Objectives

When you finish this chapter, you will be able to do the following:

Language and Study Skills

1. Summarize a section of a reading passage.
2. Analyze research data from a survey.
3. Recognize facts and opinions.
4. Write an essay applying a theory.

Content Mastery

1. List and explain different theories of deviance.
2. Describe different types of deviant behavior.
3. Use a survey as a sociological research method.

In this chapter, you are introduced to the field of sociology, which is the study of human societies. Sociologists are concerned with what makes up a society and what forces operate within societies to either maintain or change them. This chapter focuses on one area of sociology: deviance, or the study of what happens when people break social rules. The lecture and reading material deal mainly with criminal behaviors, but it is important to keep in mind that the information is generally based on U.S. society. Other societies might define normal and abnormal, legal and criminal behaviors quite differently. Remember to approach the material with an inquiring mind.

Important Terms and People

As you listen to the lecture and read the passage for this chapter, note the following important terms and their meanings. When you finish the chapter, you should be able to define each one.

corporate crime
cultural relativity
Cultural Transmission Theory
deviance
deviant behavior

goal disjunction
index offenses
Labeling Theory
Robert Merton
National Crime Survey

neurosis
peer group
psychosis
public consensus
social causation
social forces

Strain Theory
social selection/drift
socialization
Edwin Sutherland
Uniform Crime Reports

LECTURE: "THEORIES OF DEVIANCE"

Have you ever wondered why there is so much crime in the United States? This lecture will introduce some theories about why deviance, especially crime, occurs. This is an excerpt from a freshman-level sociology class lecture given by Dr. Bernard B. Berk, Associate Professor, California State University, Los Angeles. As you take notes, pay particular attention to definitions of important terms and the explanations of theories.

Comprehension Questions

Refer to your notes as needed to answer the following questions.

1. What are some social forces that influence us?
2. a. What is deviance?
   b. According to sociologists, what is the basic cause of deviance?

For each theory below, state the general idea in one or two sentences. Then list some key aspects of the theory.

3. Cultural Transmission Theory
4. Strain Theory
5. Labeling Theory

Questions for Analysis

1. Does the speaker seem to favor one theory over the others? Be prepared to explain why you decided on your answer.
2. Describe an incident that happened in your own country that you feel illustrates one of the theories. Name the theory and briefly explain how the incident illustrates the theory.
3. Do you feel any one of the theories is more accurate? Support your answer with concrete examples.

CLASS SURVEY: PREFERRED SOCIETAL SANCTIONS

One common tool used by sociologists is the survey. In this exercise, you will conduct a class survey, discuss and tabulate the results, and compare it to the results of an actual sociological survey.

Survey Directions   Place a check in the column that represents the social reaction you believe is appropriate for each action.

Treatment = probation, mental hospital, or other treatment
Punishment = prison, fines, corporal or capital punishment, other
Nothing   = warning only, or no action taken

Act	Treatment	Punishment	Nothing
Robbery			
Incest			
Homosexuality			
Abortion			
Taking drugs			
Factory pollution			
Public protest			
Not helping			

Exercise

1. Form groups of students from different countries. Compare answers with group members. On which points do you agree? On which do you disagree? Explain the reasons for your choice of sanctions.
2. Form groups according to nationality (the groups may be of different sizes). Students who are the only representatives from their countries can form a group together. Compare answers. Do students from the same country tend to give similar answers? What norm or value might underlie some of the answers members of the group agree on?
3. Compile all the class survey results by making a table on the board. On which points is there general agreement? On which points is the class divided? Discuss possible reasons for disagreement for these points. You will use the table of class survey results again in the following exercise.

Survey Comparison

The following table shows the results of a survey of people in four different countries done in 1976. It is similar to the one you filled out in the previous exercise. Refer to the table to answer the following questions.

1. If your country appears in the table, compare your own answers to the survey results for your country. If your country does not appear in the table, compare your survey answers to the results for the United States. On which points do your answers agree with the majority view in the survey? On which do you disagree?
2. How does the table of class survey results that you wrote on the board in the previous exercise compare to the following table? (You may wish to convert the class results to percentages for easier comparison.)
3. According to the table, about which acts do people in all the countries surveyed generally agree?

THE PREFERRED SOCIETAL SANCTIONS (PERCENTAGES)

Act and Sanction	India (N = 497)	Indonesia (N = 500)	Iran (N = 475)	USA (N = 169)
Robbery				
Treatment[a]	6.2	0.8	5.4	16.8
Punishment[b]	85.6	89.6	87.0	79.6
Nothing[c]	8.0	5.2	7.6	0.0

Act and Sanction	India (N = 497)	Indonesia (N = 500)	Iran (N = 475)	USA (N = 169)
Incest				
Treatment	29.3	12.4	17.2	62.7
Punishment	45.7	55.0	82.3	12.4
Nothing	24.9	25.4	2.8	16.0
Homosexuality				
Treatment	26.9	14.4	26.8	33.7
Punishment	20.2	21.6	60.9	5.9
Nothing	52.9	57.6	12.3	60.4
Abortion				
Treatment	5.6	6.4	13.5	14.9
Punishment	9.2	43.8	48.4	4.0
Nothing	85.1	45.2	38.1	77.5
Taking Drugs				
Treatment	23.0	19.8	68.9	78.1
Punishment	21.4	25.4	15.8	15.4
Nothing	55.8	48.0	15.1	1.2
Factory Pollution				
Treatment	3.0	2.6	1.1	1.2
Punishment	82.3	46.8	78.2	87.0
Nothing	14.7	42.2	20.8	6.5
Public Protest				
Treatment	1.6	3.6	5.3	3.0
Punishment	19.2	10.6	22.6	5.3
Nothing	79.4	73.2	71.9	91.7
Not Helping				
Treatment	5.4	2.4	7.1	11.6
Punishment	15.2	8.4	22.6	14.7
Nothing	77.3	84.0	70.1	56.2

Source: Graeme Newman, Comparative Deviance: Perception and Law in Six Cultures, New York: Elsevier, 1976, 142–143. Reprinted by permission.
[a] "Treatment" = Choice of probation, mental hospital, other treatment.
[b] "Punishment" = Choice of prison, fines, corporal or capital punishment, other punishment.
[c] "Nothing" = Choice of "nothing" or "warning only."

RECOGNIZING FACTS AND OPINIONS

Recognizing facts and opinions is an important academic skill that will help you when participating in class discussions, writing essays, and doing research for reports.

What is a Fact?   A fact is something that has been verified or proven to be true.
    Example: James Brown is married to Adrienne.

What is an Opinion?   An opinion is something that hasn't been proven true. Some opinions become facts because somebody does prove them to be true.
    Example: James Brown allegedly shot at his wife's mink coat.

Some opinions cannot be proven true or false.
    Example: James Brown is the greatest musician who ever lived.

Practice   Read the article "Soul Brother No. 155413." Underline all the factual statements with a pen. Underline the opinions with a pencil. Then compare with one or two classmates. Discuss any statements that you marked differently.

Soul Brother No. 155413

A legendary singer winds up in the slammer

By Alessandra Stanley

I Feel Good pounds in the background of a TV commercial for spark plugs. *Papa's Got a Brand New Bag* sells a brand of rice. It's been a long time since the raw, driving soul music of James Brown sounded dangerous to mainstream white America. The rhythm-and-blues man, who says he is 55, belonged to a presidential task force and is in the Rock and Roll Hall of Fame. He has won two Grammy Awards and has had an audience with the Pope. When the phone rings in his office in Augusta, Ga., a receptionist crisply answers, "Godfather of Soul." But the boss can't come to the phone right now. James Brown, the self-styled Hardest-Working Man in Show Business, is 70 miles away in South Carolina's State Park Correctional Center, serving a six-year sentence.

There he is listed as James J. Brown, No. 155413. "I'm just sitting quiet, not saying a thing, serving my time," says Brown from a pay phone inside the minimum-security facility. Every day he rises at 5:15 to dish out breakfast in the cafeteria, wearing a cook's white uniform and cap, embellished by purple wraparound sunglasses and a matching purple foulard scarf. He directs the chapel choir, and attendance has doubled since he got there. On Saturdays, his wife Adrienne, a former hair stylist with the television show *Solid Gold*, brings a dryer and a bag of salon products to primp his curly coiffure.

Brown's fall from the top of the charts to a four-man prison cell has been going on for several years. In 1985 the IRS slapped a lien on his 62-acre spread on rural Beech Island, about ten miles outside Augusta, and he was forced to auction it off. His eight-year marriage to Adrienne, his third wife, has been tempestuous. Last April she filed suit against him for assault, then dropped the charge. (Among other things, he allegedly ventilated her $35,000 black mink coat with bullets.)

About a year ago, rumors that Brown had a drug problem began to surface. He was arrested last summer for possession of PCP (he claimed his wife had planted the drug on him), illegally carrying a firearm and resisting arrest. He was given a $1,200 fine and ordered to stage a benefit concert for abused children. In September, Brown stormed into an insurance company next door to his office, waving a gun and complaining that strangers were using his bathroom. When the police arrived, Brown sped away in his pickup truck, touching off a high-speed chase through Georgia and South Carolina that ended only after the cops shot out his tires. The city of Augusta, which had honored him three years ago with a James Brown Appreciation Day, turned on him. Enough was enough, says Mayor Charles DeVaney.

It is not Brown's first stint in the slammer. Born in a shack in rural South Carolina, Brown grew up dirt poor, shining shoes and dancing for pennies. At 15 he was sentenced to eight years for breaking into cars. He sang in the prison choir (his nickname was "Music Box") and, on his release after three years, started a band. Brown's pioneering rhythm and blues soon had black audiences up on their feet dancing to funky drums, taut horn riffs and sweat-drenched lyrics that sometimes rose to the level of pungent urban poetry. A 1968 hit gave a slogan to an era: "Say it loud, I'm black and I'm proud."

Before he started to slide, Brown racked up 15 No. 1 R.-and-B. hits; amassed a personal empire that included radio stations in Augusta, Knoxville and Baltimore; and inspired later generations of rock 'n' rollers, including Mick Jagger and Michael Jackson. So great was his influence with young blacks that he was summoned to Boston and Washington to cool off race riots during 1968. He eagerly ticks off the Presidents he has met and supported, including George Bush. "I've been the American Dream," Brown plaintively notes. "When you say Old Glory, I'm a part of it. It's just very bad that sometimes the country forgets."

These days, Brown feels abandoned by the black and white musicians who became famous by copying his style and gyrating dance techniques. He says, "The only two people who have shown love and respect for James Brown are Little Richard and Al Sharpton," the New York City preacher who stirred up a storm over the purported rape of Tawana Brawley and is now organizing a campaign to gain Brown's early release. Complains Sharpton, who sports a Brown-style hairdo: "The country would never have done this to Elvis."

Brown is not eligible for parole until 1992. His lawyers, who are working on an appeal, may seek a form of work release. Brown says what he missed most are his fans, touring overseas and fooling around until 3 or 4 in the morning with friends. "I'm well rested now," says the Hardest-Working Man in Show Business, "but I miss being tired."

Questions for Analysis

1. What are some deviant acts Brown is accused of that haven't been proven?
2. What facts caused Brown to be imprisoned?
3. Based on the theories of deviance discussed in the lecture, how could you explain Brown's deviance? Use facts and opinions from the article to support your point.

READING SPEED CHECK

You will have 1 minute to read the following passage. Mark the word that you are reading at the end of that time.

18   A man, recently fired, returns to the office where he has worked, rifle in hand, and begins firing.
32   Executives from several companies conspire to keep prices for their products artificially high. In
54   a dark alley, a mugger waits for a victim to pass by. In a nice home, a woman goes through the daily
71   routine of drinking to the point of intoxication. In the pursuit of thinness, a young woman starves
90   herself until she looks like a scarecrow. When two police officers try to arrest a man, he spits on
108 them thinking that he can transmit his AIDS virus to them in this way. These actions may appear
125 to have little in common, but they are all examples of deviant behavior. Deviant behavior is gener-
142 ally defined as any act that violates a social norm. But the phenomenon is more complex than
158 that. How do we know whether an act violates a social norm? Is homosexuality deviant—a viola-
176 tion of social norm? Some people think so, but others do not. This suggests that deviance is not
197 absolute, not real in and of itself. It is relative, a matter of definition. A deviant act must be defined
208 as such by someone before it can be said to be deviant.
222   Since many people have different views, they are bound to define deviant behavior differently.
238 It is no wonder that practically all human acts have the potential for being considered deviant.
254 When sociologist J. L. Simmons (1969) asked people what they defined as deviant, he ended up
267 with a list of 252 acts and persons, including homosexuals, prostitutes, alcoholics, murderers,
277 communists, atheists, Democrats, Republicans, movie stars, smart-aleck students, and know-it-all
292 professors. If you are surprised that some of these people are considered deviant, your surprise
305 simply confirms that there are countless *different* definitions of deviance, including your own.
319 Even among sociologists, there is disagreement on what deviance is. Most sociologists define devi-
332 ance as something negative. To them, deviance is what the public considers negative, objectiona-
348 ble behavior. But a few sociologists argue that deviance can also be positive. To them, then, heroes,
362 saints, geniuses, reformers, and revolutionaries are just as deviant as criminals because they all
369 deviate from being average persons (Thio, 1988).
384   All definitions of deviance, however, do not carry the same weight. Rock stars may be
402 regarded by some people as deviant, but they are not put in prison. Murderers, on the other hand,
419 are widely considered to be seriously deviant, so that many are put on death row. What determines
434 that murder is more deviant than being a rock star? What determines which definitions of devi-
448 ance have more serious consequences for the deviants? There are at least three determining fac-
456 tors: time, place, and public consensus or power. . . .
471   In view of those three determinants of deviant behavior, we may more precisely define *devi-
487 ant behavior* as any act considered deviant by public consensus or the powerful at a given time
489 and place.

GO ON TO COMPREHENSION QUESTIONS

Comprehension Questions

Answer the questions without referring to the passage. Focus on the questions for the lines that you read. You may guess the answers of questions for lines that you didn't have time to read.

1. (18–125) Which of the following is an example of deviant behavior?
    a. listening to rock music
    b. waiting in a dark alley to mug a victim
    c. being infected with AIDS
    d. breaking up with a boyfriend or girlfriend
2. (142–208)   T   F   People tend to disagree about exactly which behaviors are deviant.
3. (222–369) Most sociologists define deviance as something negative, but some sociol-
    ogists
    a. don't think deviance can be defined.
    b. believe more research is needed to find a definition.
    c. think all deviance should be punished.
    d. think it can be positive also.

4. (384–489) T F Three key factors in any definition of deviance must be the punishment, the criminal, and the police.

Your Reading Speed

Find the mark you made when the teacher announced that one minute had passed. Count the number of words on the line that you didn't have time to read. Subtract this from the number at the beginning of the line. The result is reading speed in words per minute. Check your reading comprehension answers. If you missed any questions for the lines that you read, you may need to slow down your reading speed a little.

READING EXERCISES: "DEVIANCE"

Reading Goal Read one part of the passage in order to prepare a summary. Quickly skim through the rest of the passage to find the main ideas.

The reading passage for this chapter (6,580 words) is excerpted from a freshman-level sociology textbook, *Sociology: An Introduction*, by Alex Thio. The complete chapter is 24 pages long. The book has 23 chapters.

Review: Summarizing

In this exercise you will review and practice your skills by summarizing a section of the reading passage. Review these steps in preparing a summary:

1. Read the material, marking key words and ideas.
2. Combine the key points of each paragraph into a summary. Be sure to connect the points in some logical way. When summarizing a longer piece, as you will do in this exercise, you may not need to include a point from every paragraph.

Exercises

Individual Work Practice these steps on the first three paragraphs of the reading passage (the introduction). Compare your summary with a classmate's and discuss any differences. Your teacher will ask students to help write a sample summary on the board.

Pair Work Work with a classmate to summarize one section of the reading passage. Your teacher will assign each pair of students a different section from the list below. When you are finished, you will share your summary with the class. Take notes as you listen to other students' summaries, as they may be helpful when you read the complete passage and answer the comprehension questions.

Section subheadings

What Is Deviance?

Crime Indicators

Murder

Corporate Crime—Three Distinct Characteristics

Corporate Crime—Costs of Corporate Crime

Mental Illness

Is Deviance Always Harmful?

Reading for Main Ideas

1. Read the rest of the passage and mark main ideas.
2. Set a time limit on your reading, based on what you know about your study-reading speed. Try to make the time a little shorter than what is comfortable, in order to increase your speed and efficiency in reading.
3. You may want to read the comprehension questions before you start, and keep them in mind as you read.

Reading Comprehension

1. How is deviant behavior defined in the reading passage?
2. Why do FBI *Uniform Crime Reports* statistics tend to be inaccurate?
3. In order to adjust for inaccuracies in the *Uniform Crime Reports*, the National Crime Survey was started. What have been some of the findings of this survey?
4. Based on the information in the section on murder, give a typical scenario for a murder. (This means describe a typical, although fictional, murder, including the weapon, who did it, who was the victim, their socioeconomic levels, relationship to each other, etc.)
5. **a.** What are three distinct characteristics of corporate crime?
   b. What are some ways in which corporate crime hurts individuals and society?
6. **a.** What are two types of mental illness?
   b. About what proportion of Americans suffer mental illness, and which socioeconomic level are they more often from?
7. Although deviance may seem to be a negative characteristic of society, it serves several positive functions. List and briefly describe each one.

Questions for Analysis

1. Compare the deviance you see in the United States, through the media and your own experience, to the deviance you were exposed to in your own country. How might you explain any differences?
2. Is there any behavior that is considered normal in the United States but criminal in your country, or vice versa? Give examples.
3. Have you ever been the victim of a crime? If so, briefly describe the incident.
4. In many discussions of crime, the subject of weapons, especially guns, seems to come up. How common is it for people in your country to own a weapon? What kinds of weapons, if any, are most common? What are some of the reasons that people might own a weapon? In the United States, do you think that owning a weapon is a good idea? Why or why not?

WORD PARTS

Match the words in the list of examples with the correct word part; then write your guess for its meaning. Check your answers with your teacher or the list in Appendix A. Make a point of learning any of the word parts that are new to you.

Root	Meaning	Example
1. nom	_____	_____
2. pater	_____	_____
3. path	_____	_____
4. ped, pod, pus	_____	_____

5. pend   _____   _____

6. phil   _____   _____

7. phob   _____   _____

8. phon   _____   _____

9. phot, phos   _____   _____

Prefix

10. post-   _____   _____

11. pre-   _____   _____

12. pro-   _____   _____

13. re-   _____   _____

Suffix

14. -ship   _____   _____

15. -able, -ible   _____   _____

Examples

astronomy	paternal	prerequisite
claustrophobia	pathological	promote
divisible	philanthropist	quadruped
kinship	photon	return
microphone	postgraduate	suspend

WRITING: APPLYING A THEORY

Writing Topic

Find an article (newspaper or magazine) that is about a deviant act. Write about the deviant act based on the material covered in this chapter. In your essay, discuss the following points.

1. What is the deviant behavior described in the article?
2. Choose one of the theories of deviance that were presented and discuss how this particular news item can be explained by the theory. (If no theory seems to apply, choose one and discuss why it does not explain the behavior in the news article.)

Practice Reread the article about James Brown. Notice descriptions of any deviant behavior. In groups or as a class, discuss which theories might explain this deviant behavior. As you discuss, keep in mind that there is no "right" or "wrong" answer. Any theory can be applied, as long as you can support the theory with evidence from the article.

Gathering Information

Bring the news article you have chosen (or a photocopy) to class. Work in groups of three or four. In turn, each group member will summarize his or her article for the group, and propose a theory of deviance to explain the information. Discuss each article briefly, asking questions and giving suggestions, before going on to the next group member.

Narrowing the Topic

The essay topic is already narrowed. Notice that it asks you to write about only *one* theory of deviance, although more than one theory may apply.

Planning the Essay

Using the following general outline, write an outline for your essay. Include your thesis and focus in the introduction.

I. Introduction

Introduce the material (in this case the deviant behavior) by giving a brief summary. Tell what theory you will use.

II. Body

Generally an essay applying a theory will first give the data or observations, and then explain these with a theory. Therefore, a typical organization pattern would be:

A. Data or observations. (Describe the deviant behavior in detail.)

B. Explanation based on a theory. (Show how the theory explains the deviant behavior.)

Remember to define any special terms, including a brief description of the theory of deviance you are using. Use quotation, paraphrase, and summary of the article to illustrate your points.

III. Conclusion

Summarize your main points. Be sure that your summary shows how you have addressed the topic. (In other words, review how the evidence supports the theory.)

Follow-up Exercise

Check your essay for the following items.

1. Put brackets around your summary of the article.
2. Underline with two lines your statement about which theory explains the article.
3. Circle your definition of the theory.
4. Put a bullet (•) next to each piece of evidence you give in support of the theory.
5. Underline any quotations or paraphrases of the article.
6. Put a star next to key terms you used.
7. Put two stars next to definitions of key terms.
8. Put brackets around your essay summary.

Do you have all the preceding items in your essay? If not, add them and rewrite.

Deviance

Most of us are probably accustomed to thinking of deviants as creatures foreign to us, as "nuts, sluts, and perverts." But deviance is widespread. Even in a society of saints, as Durkheim long ago suggested, its rules would be broken. In a classic study (Wallerstein and Wyle, 1947) a random sample of Americans were given a list of 49 acts that were actually criminal offenses punishable by at least one year in prison. A whopping 99 percent of them admitted to at least one offense. It is quite possible that the remaining 1 percent had either lied or could not recall, because crime is not something they could be proud of having committed.

Despite the prevalence of deviance, many people's ideas about it are simplistic and erroneous. Virtually everyone thinks that armed robbery is more dangerous in every respect than unarmed robbery. In reality, it is unarmed robbery that is far more likely to result in sending the victim to the hospital. One study, for example, shows that 66 percent of unarmed robbery victims, compared with 17 percent of armed robbery victims, were seriously injured (Feeney and Weir, 1975). Many people also believe that mental illness runs in a family. This may be true for a few patients, but most have acquired the illness through socialization rather than genes. Many people assume, too, that traditional crimes such as murder, assault, and robbery are more harmful to society than corporate crimes such as selling defective cars, industrial pollution, and tax fraud. Actually the reverse is closer to the truth (Thio, 1988).

There are many more popular misconceptions about these deviant acts. We take a closer look at three of them (murder, corporate crime, and mental illness) in this chapter. But let us first discuss what deviance is and what the current indicators of crime are. Then we examine those three examples of deviance, various explanations for its occurrence, and society's attempts to control it.

DEVIANCE IN AMERICA

A man, recently fired, returns to the office where he has worked, rifle in hand, and begins firing. Executives from several companies conspire to keep prices for their products artificially high. In a dark alley, a mugger waits for a victim to pass by. In a nice home, a woman goes through the daily routine of drinking to the point of intoxication. In the pursuit of thinness, a young woman starves herself until she looks like a scarecrow. When two police officers try to arrest a man, he spits on them thinking that he can transmit his AIDS virus to them in this way. These actions may appear to have little in common, but they are all examples of deviant behavior.

What Is Deviance?

Deviant behavior is generally defined as any act that violates a social norm. But the phenomenon is more complex than that. How do we know whether an act violates a social norm? Is homosexuality deviant—a violation of social norm? Some people think so, but others do not. This suggests that deviance is not absolute, not real in and of itself. It is relative, a matter of definition. A deviant act must be defined as such by someone before it can be said to be deviant.

Since many people have different views, they are bound to define deviant behavior differently. It is no wonder that practically all human acts have the potential for being considered deviant. When sociologist J. L. Simmons (1969) asked people what they defined as deviant, he ended up with a list of 252 acts and persons, including homosexuals, prostitutes, alcoholics, murderers, communists, atheists, Democrats, Republicans, movie stars, smart-aleck students, and know-it-all professors. If you are surprised that some of these people are considered deviant, your surprise simply confirms that there are countless *different* definitions of deviance, including your own. Even among sociologists, there is disagreement on what deviance is. Most sociologists define deviance as something negative. To them, deviance is what the public considers negative, objectionable behavior. But a few sociologists argue that deviance can also be positive. To them, then, heroes, saints, geniuses, reformers, and revolutionaries are just as deviant as criminals because they all deviate from being average persons (Thio, 1988).

All definitions of deviance, however, do not carry the same weight. Rock stars may be regarded by some people as deviant, but they are not put in prison. Murderers, on the other hand, are widely considered to be seriously deviant, so that many are put on death row. What determines that murder is more deviant than being a rock star? What determines which definitions of deviance have more serious consequences for the deviants? There are at least three determining factors: time, place, and public consensus or power.

First, what constitutes deviance varies from one historical period to another. Jesus was nailed to the cross as a criminal in his time, but he is widely worshipped as God today. About 30 years after Jesus' birth, the Roman Empress Messalina won a bet with a friend by publicly having a prolonged session of sexual intercourse with 25 different men. At the time, Romans were not particularly scandalized, though they were quite impressed by her stamina. Today, if a person with similar social standing engaged in such behavior, we would consider it extremely scandalous (King, 1985). In the last two centuries, opium was a legal and easily available common drug; today its use is a criminal offense. Nowadays cigarette smoking is legal in all countries, but in the seventeenth century it was illegal in most countries. In fact, in some countries at that time, smokers were punished harshly: their noses were cut off in Russia and their lips sliced off in Hindustan (Goode, 1984a). Second, the definition of deviance varies from one place to another. A polygamist is a criminal in the United States but not in Saudi Arabia and other Moslem countries. Prostitution is illegal in the United States (except in some counties in Nevada), but it is legal in Denmark, West Germany, France, and most other countries. In 1987 the Iran-Contra affair, like the Watergate scandal in the mid-1970s, was considered major news in the United States, especially by the American media and Congress, but people in Europe wondered what the fuss was all about. Third, whether a given act is deviant depends on public consensus. Murder is unquestionably deviant because nearly all people agree that it is. In contrast, long hair on men is not deviant because hardly anybody considers it so. Public consensus, however, usually reflects the vested interests of the rich and powerful. As Marx would have said, the ideas of the ruling class tend to become the ruling ideas of society. Like the powerful, the general public tends to consider, for example, bank robbery to be a crime but not fraudulent advertising, which serves the interests of the powerful.

In view of those three determinants of deviant behavior, we may more precisely define **deviant behavior** as any act considered deviant by public consensus or the powerful at a given time and place.

Crime Indicators

Deviance may be either criminal or noncriminal. Noncriminal deviance is less likely to harm someone else. Examples include mental disorders, alcoholism, and suicide. Criminal deviance—such as murder, rape, and price fixing—is generally more serious. More accurately, criminal deviance is behavior that is prohibited by law.

Sinced 1930, when it was first published, the FBI's annual *Uniform Crime Reports* has been a major source of information for studying crime in the United States. Every year it presents a large amount of data on numbers of crimes and arrests, which the police all over the country have sent to the FBI. It has remained the most comprehensive source of official data on crime in the United States, as more than 95 percent of all Americans live in police jurisdictions reporting to the FBI. Even so, it is still far from being an accurate indicator of crime.

First, it reports only what the FBI calls **index offenses,** which it regards as major, serious crimes. There are eight of them: murder, rape, robbery, aggravated assault, burglary, larceny (theft of $50 or more), auto theft and arson. The official statistics do not include victimless crimes such as prostitution and gambling. Neither do they present most of the white-collar crimes, such as income tax evasion, committed by seemingly respectable citizens; fraud against consumers and price fixing committed by corporations; and bribe taking and illegal wiretapping perpetrated by government officials.

Second, the FBI statistics even underreport index offenses. To know how much crime has been committed, the police rely heavily on citizens to come forward with the information. In fact, 85 to 90 percent of the offenses appearing in official statistics are based on citizen reports. However, about two-thirds of crime victims fail to report offenses to the police. Most of these victims feel that the offense is not important enough, that it is a private matter, or that nothing can be done about it (U.S. Dept. of Justice, 1983). Moreover, in nearly one-fourth of the cases where a citizen's complaint is received, the police do not consider the incident a crime. In his classic study of police-citizen encounters in three large American cities, Donald Black (1970) discovered a certain bias in the way police handled citizens' complaints. The officers were less likely to define an incident as a crime if it was less serious, if the suspect was not a stranger to the complainant, and if the complainant was not respectful to the police, did not want to have the suspect prosecuted, and was a working-class rather than a white-collar person. Even in serious cases of assault, the police are less likely to make arrests if the victims are black or female (Smith, 1987). Due to victim nonreporting and police discretion, then, the FBI data miss a lot of crimes (see Table 7.1).

Third, police politics is a major source of bias in the FBI statistics. Law enforcers know that local politicians, businesses, the mass media, and the public at large often find out the crime situation in their areas from official reports. More importantly, they all interpret the reports in a certain way: low crime rates mean police effectiveness; high crime rates mean the problem is out of control. Therefore, when a police department is seeking additional funds or personnel, it is likely to make more arrests and report more crimes. Thus increases in crime rates shown in official statistics may sometimes be misleading (Thomas and Hepburn, 1983).

Given the limitations of official figures, researchers working with the President's Commission on Law Enforcement and Administration of Justice began in 1967 to ask national samples of Americans whether they had been victims of crime. Since 1973 this victimization survey, known as the National Crime Survey, has been providing yearly data on such things as the characteristics of victims and the "dark figure" of crime, which is not reported to the police. The most dramatic finding is the tremendous amount of criminal activity and victimization in the United States. The surveys show, for example, that in 1981 almost 25 million households—a third of all households—fell victim to at least one crime of violence or theft. Since many of these households were victimized more than once, the total number of victimizations—or criminal offenses—was far higher than 25 million; it came up to 41 million, three times the number known to the police. The prevalence of crime also comes across in the finding that the average American runs a higher risk of being victimized by a violent crime than he does of being hurt in a traffic accident.

The crime surveys further reveal who are more likely to be the victims: men more than women; the divorced or never married more than the married or widowed; young people more than elderly; lower-income more than higher-income people; the unemployed and students more than the employed, retirees, and housewives; and city dwellers more than rural residents (U.S. Dept. of Justice, 1983). Most of these differences seem to result from at least three risk factors: exposure (frequent contact with potential offenders), proximity (being in high-crime areas), and lack of guardianship (not having neighbors, police, burglar alarms, barred

Table 7.1 How FBI Statistics Miss the Mark

Most victims of crime do not call the police, who in turn fail to regard some victim-reported incidents as crimes. Thus official data, such as the FBI crime statistics, underreport even major crimes.

	Number of crimes in 1981	
	FBI statistics[a]	Actually occurred[b]
Forcible rape	81,540	178,000
Robbery	574,130	1,381,000
Aggravated assault	643,720	1,796,000
Burglary	3,739,800	7,394,000
Larceny/theft	7,154,500	26,039,000
Motor vehicle theft	1,074,000	1,439,000
TOTAL	13,267,690	38,227,000

[a] As reported by citizens to police.
[b] As told by victims to interviewers, in national surveys.
Source: U.S. Department of Justice, Bureau of Justice Statistics, *Report to the Nation on Crime and Justice: The Data, 1983*, p. 7.

windows, and so on). Given these factors, people who engage in activities outside of the household, such as going to the movies or attending sports events, are more likely to be victimized than those who stay home to watch television or read a book. Thus young people, for example, suffer a greater chance of being victimized than do older citizens because the former go out more, thereby increasing their exposure and proximity to potential offenders and leaving behind the guardianship against them (Cohen, Kluegel, and Land, 1981; Messner and Blau, 1987).

While they get closer than the FBI statistics to the "true" level of crime, victimization surveys are not perfect, either. When asked whether they have been victimized during the past year, people may give inaccurate reports. An object that has simply been lost may be remembered as stolen. "Memory decay"—poor recall—can creep into victimization survey data. Interviewees may get involved in "backward telescoping," remembering that a crime took place earlier than it did, or they may be given to "forward telescoping," thinking that it occurred more recently than it did. Either way it can reduce the validity of victimization surveys because such studies define crimes as those that have occurred during a specified period of time only (Gottfredson and Hindelang, 1981; Thomas and Hepburn, 1983). Sometimes people simply cannot remember whether they have been victimized within a certain time frame. In one study where the respondents were known from police files to have been victims of crime, about 20 percent failed to report the offenses to survey interviewers (Gottfredson and Hindelang, 1981). These recall problems, however, do not invalidate victimization surveys seriously because they may cancel each other—with some overreporting and others underreporting victimizations.

Another method for measuring crime is the self-report study. While victimization surveys focus on victims, self-report studies concentrate on offenders, asking people whether they have committed a crime. The results have by and large shown that there are no class and race differences in *overall* criminality, which refute the popularly held theory and the FBI finding that lower-class people have higher crime rates than do those of higher classes (see Johnson, 1980; Krohn et al., 1980; Tittle, 1983; but also Thornberry and Farnworth, 1982, for contrasting findings). Other self-report studies, however, have shown status differences in *specific* forms of offenses. Delbert Elliott and Suzanne Ageton (1980), for example, found that lower-class youths are more likely than their middle-class peers to commit serious criminal offenses. In his review of numerous studies, John Braithwaite (1981) concluded that the lower classes are more likely to be involved in "directly interpersonal crimes" such as murder, rape, robbery, and as-

sault, but that the middle and upper classes tend more to commit "less directly interpersonal crimes" such as tax evasion, employee theft, and fraudulent advertising. Let us, then, take a closer look at these two types of crime by analyzing murder and corporate crime.

Murder

Murder is a relatively rare crime. It occurs less often than any of the other major offenses such as rape, robbery, and aggravated assault. We are even less likely to be murdered by others than to get ourselves killed in a car accident. But murder does not appear reassuringly rare if we see it from another angle. According to the FBI (1988), one American is murdered every 26 minutes. The chance of becoming a murder victim for all Americans is 1 out of 157. The odds are especially high for nonwhite males, who have a 1 out of 29 probability of being murdered. Regardless of our race or gender, our chance of murder victimization peaks when we reach the age of 25 (Farley, 1980; Akiyama, 1981).

Homicide occurs most frequently during weekend evenings, particularly on Saturday night. This holds true largely for lower-class murderers but not for middle- and upper-class offenders, who kill on any day of the week. One apparent reason is that higher-class murders are more likely than lower-class homicides to be premeditated—hence less likely to result from alcohol-induced eruptions during weekend sprees (Green and Wakefield, 1979). Research has also frequently shown that most of the murderers in this country are poor. Marvin Wolfgang (1958) estimated that 90 to 95 percent of the offenders came from the lower end of the occupational scale. A more recent study showed that 92 percent of the murderers were semiskilled workers, unskilled laborers, or welfare recipients (Swigert and Farrell, 1976). The latest analysis by Kirk Williams (1984) confirmed these and other similar findings. We should note, however, that the rich and powerful actually cause far more deaths than the poor. Every year, while fewer than 24,000 Americans are murdered mostly by the poor, over 100,000 U.S. workers die from occupational diseases alone, attributable to corporate disregard for safe working conditions (Simon and Eitzen, 1986).

Whatever their class, murderers most often use handguns to kill (FBI, 1988). Perhaps seeing a gun while embroiled in a heated argument may incite a person into murderous action. As Shakespeare said, "How oft the sight of means to do ill deeds, makes ill deeds done." This may be similar to feeling more inclined to kill after watching a prizefight on TV (see box, above). Of course, firearms by themselves cannot cause homicide, nor can their absence reduce the motivation to kill. It is true that "Guns don't kill, people do." Still, were guns less available, many heated arguments would have resulted in aggravated assaults rather than murders, thereby reducing the number of fatalities. One study suggests that attacks with knives are five times *less* likely to result in death than are attacks with guns (Wright et al., 1983). In fact, the use of less dangerous weapons such as knives in attempted murders has been estimated to cause 80 percent fewer deaths (Newton and Zimring, 1969). Given the enormous number of guns in private hands (about 120 million), it is not surprising that far more deaths result from gun attacks in this country than in Canada, England, and Japan (Rodino, 1986).

Ironically, murder is the most personal crime, largely committed against relatives, friends, or acquaintances. According to the U.S. Department of Justice (1983), at least 55 percent of all murder victims were related to or knew their murderer. An earlier study showed the figure to be 80 percent (Swigert and Farrell, 1976). Many of us may find it incredible that the people we know or even love are more likely to kill us than are total strangers. "This should really not be very surprising," Donald Mulvihill and Melvin Tumin (1969) have explained. "Everyone is within easy striking distance from intimates for a large part of the time. Although friends, lovers, spouses, and the like are a main source of pleasure in one's life, they are equally a main source of frustration and hurt. Few others can anger one so much." The act of murder requires a great deal of emotion. It is a crime of passion carried out under the overwhelming pressure of a volcanic emotion. It may be more difficult for us to kill a stranger for whom we don't have any sympathetic or antagonistic feelings. Only psychotic or professional killers can do away with people in a cold-blooded, unemotional manner (Levi, 1981). But such impersonal killings are rare.

Corporate Crime

Unlike murder, corporate crimes are committed by company executives without the overt use of force, and their effect on the victims is not readily traceable to the culprit. If a miner dies from a lung disease, it is difficult to prove beyond reasonable doubt that he had died *because* his employer violated mine safety regulations (Braithwaite and Geis, 1982). Corporate crimes may be perpetrated not only against employees, but also against customers and the general public. Examples are disregard for safety in the workplace, consumer fraud, price fixing, production of unsafe products, and violations of environmental regulations. Compared to traditional "street crime," corporate crime is more rationally executed, more profitable, and less detectable by law enforcers. In addition, crime in the suite is distinguished from crime in the street by three characteristics.

Three Distinct Characteristics First is the victim's unwitting cooperation with the corporate criminal, which results mostly from carelessness or ignorance. In a home-improvement scheme, the victims do not bother to check the work history of the fraudulent company that solicits them, and they sign a contract without examining its contents for such matters as the true price and the credit terms. Some victims purchase goods through the mail without checking the reputation of the firm. Doctors prescribe untested dangerous drugs after having relied on only the pharmaceutical company's salespeople and advertising. It may be difficult for the victims to know they are victimized, even if they want to find out the true nature of their victimization. Grocery shoppers, for example, are hard put to detect such unlawful substances as residues of hormones, antibiotics, pesticides, and nitrites in the meat they buy.

A second characteristic is the society's indifference to corporate crimes. Generally, little effort is made to catch corporate criminals, and on the rare occasions when they are caught, they seldom go to jail. Even if they do go to prison, they are likely to stay there for less than three days (Clinard, 1979). If their terms are longer, they need not worry too much, either, because their companies will take care of their families and give them their old jobs back when they get out. In recent years there has been less societal indifference toward corporate crime. In price-fixing cases, fines of up to $1 million for the company and $100,000 for individuals can be imposed, and corporate executives can be sent to prison for three years (Clinard and Yeager, 1978). It is doubtful, however, that the government can wage an all-out war against corporate criminals because they are too powerful economically and politically. Moreover, while most people consider corporate crime more serious today than they did in the early 1970s, they still regard it as less serious than traditional crimes such as burglary and robbery (Cullen, Link, and Polanzi, 1982). Therefore, corporate criminals continue to receive lighter punishment than street criminals. In 1985, the giant investment firm of E. F. Hutton was found guilty of 2000 counts of mail and wire fraud, for which it must pay a $2 million fine. This may look like a lot of money, but actually it is peanuts to E. F. Hutton, which has annual revenues of $2.8 billion and profits of $52 million. Besides, not a single Hutton official was indicted. In the same year, the Bank of Boston pleaded guilty to violating a federal law by secretly funneling $1.22 billion in suspected organized crime money to and from European banks. The Bank was fined only $500,000 and not a single one of its officials was indicted (Thio, 1988).

These facts probably account for a third characteristic of corporate crime: the perpetrators often see themselves as respectable people rather than common criminals. Often they maintain their noncriminal self-image through rationalization. Violators of price-fixing laws, for example, may insist that they are helping the nation's economy be "stabilizing prices" and serving their companies by "recovering costs." There is no such crime as price fixing in their book.

Costs of Corporate Crime   The economic cost of corporate crime is high—about 27 to 42 times greater each year than the losses from traditional property crimes such as robbery and burglary. Estimates of the total cost of corporate crime range from $50 to $200 billion a year. Price fixing alone costs this nation about $45 billion annually. All this makes the annual estimated loss of $3 or $4 billion from traditional crimes look like small potatoes (Conklin, 1977; Pauly, 1979).

Corporate crime also exacts a high physical cost. Bodily injury and even death may result from violations of health and safety laws, housing codes, and environmental regulations. The violence inflicted on the public by corporate criminals in their pursuit of profit far exceeds the violence by lower-class street criminals. According to the National Commission on Product Safety, 20 million Americans have suffered injuries from using consumer products, and among these victims 110,000 are permanently disabled and 30,000 are dead (Simon and Eitzen, 1986). It has been estimated that each year some 500,000 workers are needlessly exposed to toxic substances such as radioactive materials and poisonous chemicals because of corporate failures to obey safety laws (Anderson, 1981). Of the 4 million workers who have been exposed to asbestos in the United States, about 1.6 million are expected to die from lung cancer, a figure much higher than the total U.S. loss of 372,000 lives during World War II and subsequent wars (Balkan, Berger, and Schmidt, 1980).

There is also a high social cost imposed by corporate crime. Though unmeasurable, the social cost may be more far-reaching than the economic and physical toll. As a former U.S. attorney general wrote: "White-collar crime is the most corrosive of all crimes. The trusted prove untrustworthy; the advantaged, dishonest. . . . As no other crime, it questions our moral fiber" (Clark, 1971). Corporations sometimes weaken the democratic process by making illegal campaign contributions. In foreign countries American corporations operating there often make political payoffs. Such bribes interfere with

the political process of those nations by strengthening the existing power structure and reinforce their image of America as an imperialist nation (Jacoby et al., 1977; Simon and Eitzen, 1986).

Mental Illness

While corporate crime and murder are criminal acts, other forms of deviance are not. A clear example is mental illness. Contrary to popular belief, mental illness is extremely common. Surveys have consistently shown that about 20 percent of American adults suffer from mental disorders serious enough to need professional help or hospitalization. It also has been estimated that over 80 percent experience some degree of impaired mental health—in the form of psychosomatic disorder; feelings of nervousness, tension, and restlessness; and difficulties in interpersonal relations (Srole et al., 1962; Weissman et al., 1978; Myers et al., 1984). In fact, all of us have been or shall be mentally ill in one way or another. Of course, most of our mental disorders are not serious at all. We occasionally come down with only a brief anxiety or depression, "the common cold of mental ailments." But the types of mental illness that sociologists—and psychiatrists—study are rather serious. They include **psychosis,** typified by loss of touch with reality, and **neurosis,** characterized by a persistent fear, anxiety, or worry about trivial matters. A psychotic can be likened to a person who thinks incorrectly that 2 plus 2 is equal to 10 but strongly believes it to be correct. On the other hand, a neurotic can be compared to a person who thinks correctly that 2 plus 2 is equal to 4 but constantly worries that it may not be so (Thio, 1988).

Sociologists have long suspected that certain social forces are involved in the development of mental disorder. The one that has been most consistently demonstrated by many different studies to be a key factor in mental illness is social class: the lower the social classes, the higher the rates of mental disorder (Faris and Dunham, 1939; Hollingshead and Redlich, 1958; Srole et al., 1962; Myers et al., 1984).

This finding, however, has prompted two conflicting explanations. One, known as *social causation,* suggests that lower-class people are more prone to mental disorder because they are more likely to have the following experiences: being subjected to social stress such as unemployment, family problems, or threat of criminal victimization; suffering from psychic frailty, infectious diseases, and neurological impairments; and lacking quality medical treatment, coping ability, and social support. The other explanation, called *social selection* or *drift,* suggests that the heavy concentration of mental disorder in the lower-class neighborhood results from the downward drift of mentally ill people into the neighborhood coupled with the upward movement of mentally healthy people out of it. This means that being a member of the lower class is a consequence rather than a cause of mental illness. Both explanations have been found to have some basis in fact, although a majority of the more recent studies favor the social causation interpretation (Eron and Peterson, 1982; Wheaton, 1978, 1980; Mirowsky and Ross, 1983; Kessler, 1979; Rushing and Ortega, 1979; Liem and Liem 1978; Turner and Gartrell, 1978). In general, the evidence for the drift theory comes from studies of extremely serious mental illness such as schizophrenia. The early onset of such illness usually causes individuals to lose their jobs or suffer downward mobility. But the evidence for social causation comes from studies of less severe disorders such as depression and phobia. These problems are more likely to result from the social stresses of lower-class lives (Kessler, Price, and Wortman, 1985).

Is Deviance Always Harmful?

We are accustomed to thinking of deviance as bad. But deviance is not always or completely harmful to society. It can bring benefits if it occurs within limits. Sociologists have noted at least five positive functions of deviance.

First, deviance may enhance conformity in the society as a whole by defining and clarifying norms. Norms are basically abstract and ambiguous, subject to conflicting interrelations. Even criminal laws, which are far more clear-cut than other norms, can be confusing. Through the crime a criminal commits and is punished for, other citizens obtain a concrete example of what constitutes a crime. During the Watergate scandal of the 1970s, for example, both politicians and the public clarified their opinions about which practices, though shady, were just "politics as usual," and which ones were unacceptable. From deviants we can learn the difference between conformity and deviance—we can see the boundary between right and wrong more clearly. Once aware of this boundary, we are more likely to stay on the side of righteousness (Erikson, 1966).

Second, deviance strengthens solidarity among law-abiding members of society. Differing values and interests may divide them, but collective outrage against deviants as their common enemy can unite them. Because it promotes social cohesion, Durkheim called deviance "a factor in public health, an integral part of all healthy societies" (Durkheim, 1966).

The third function of deviance is the provision of a safety valve for discontented people. Through relatively minor forms of deviance, they can strike out against the social order without doing serious harm to themselves or others. Prostitution, for example, may serve as a safety valve for marriage in a male-dominated society, because the customer is unlikely to form an emotional attachment to the prostitute. In contrast, a sexual relationship with a friend is more likely to develop into a love affair, which would destroy a marriage (Cohen, 1966).

Fourth, deviance also provides jobs for many law-abiding people. The police, judges, lawyers, prison wardens, prison guards, criminologists, and others would be out of work if there were no criminals. Criminals also stimulate some useful developments. As Marx (1964) said, "Would locks ever have reached their present degree of excellence had there been no thieves? Would the making of bank notes have reached its present perfection had there been no forgers?"

Finally, deviant behavior sometimes induces social change. Martin Luther King, Jr., and other civil rights leaders were jeered and imprisoned for their opposition to segregation, but they moved the United States toward greater racial equality.

Despite these positive functions, widespread deviance obviously threatens the social order. First, it can destroy interpersonal relations. Alcoholism has torn many families apart. If a friend flies into a rage and tries to kill us, it will be difficult to maintain a harmonious relationship. Deviance can also undermine trust. If there were many killers, robbers, and rapists living in our neighborhood, we would find it impossible to welcome neighbors to our home as guests or babysitters. Finally, if deviance goes unpunished, it can weaken the will to conform throughout society. If we know that most people cheat on their taxes, for example, we may be tempted to do the same.

QUESTIONS FOR DISCUSSION AND REVIEW

1. Why do persons disagree about whether an act is deviant or not?
2. How do we obtain data on criminal forms of deviance, and why is each of these sources somewhat biased?
3. When do murders occur, and who usually commits them?
4. What are the three distinct characteristics of corporate crime?
5. Why is mental illness seen as a form of deviance, and what are some of its causes?
6. What are some of the positive and negative consequences of deviance?

Chapter

8

Computers and Society

Outline

Objectives

When you finish this chapter, you will be able to do the following:

Language and Study Skills

1. Estimate the size of your vocabulary.
2. Use skimming and scanning to answer reading comprehension questions.
3. Define key terms from the chapter.
4. Use conversation skills to conduct a survey.
5. Write a cause-and-effect essay.

Content Mastery

1. Describe computer viruses, how they work, and how to avoid them.
2. Label the important parts of a computer.
3. Give examples of computer crimes and some steps that can be taken to prevent them.
4. Use a word processor as a writing tool.

Computers have become an essential part of modern societies, serving a variety of functions in science, business, the media, education, and the home. For this reason, many colleges have added a computer literacy class as part of their graduation requirements. The positive side of computers, their usefulness in storing and processing large amounts of information, is well known. But computers and society interact in many ways. In this chapter, we look at some other aspects of computers, in particular computer crime and computer viruses. These are two aspects of computers that you should be aware of, both as a person who may use a computer and as a member of society who depends on the correct use of computers.

Important Terms

As you listen to the lecture and read the passage for this chapter, note the following important terms and their meanings. When you finish the chapter, you should be able to define each one.

access code	keyboard
access controls	key disk
backup copy	modem
benign virus	monitor
bit copier	operating system (DOS)
callback system	password
computer virus	positive identification
copy protection	printer
data	program
data encryption	read access
disk drive	replicate
download	scan program
electronic bulletin board	site license
electronic mail	software
embezzlement	software piracy
executable files	Trojan horse programs
execute access	unauthorized access
floppy disk	word processor
hacker	write access
hard disk	write-protect tab
hardware	

LECTURE: "COMPUTER VIRUSES"

Did you know that computers can be infected with "viruses"? This is a growing problem related to computer use. In this lecture you will hear about computer viruses, what they are and what they do. Pay special attention to new words, as the subject of computers has its own special vocabulary. This lecture was given at California State University, Los Angeles, by Professor Paul C. Blakely, who teaches Computers and Society, a basic computer literacy course.

Comprehension Questions

Refer to your notes as needed to answer the following questions.

1. Describe hardware and software, and pinpoint the category into which computer viruses fall.
2. What is an operating system?
3. What is a computer virus and what are its basic functions?
4. What are some primary and secondary effects of computer viruses?
5. Give an example of a computer virus.
6. What steps can you take to (a) detect and (b) avoid computer viruses?

Questions for Analysis

1. Why would anyone want to write a computer virus? Discuss this with your classmates, speculating about possible motives and any possible benefits to the virus writer.
2. Imagine that you are using the school computer when you find that all your data has been scrambled. You suspect a computer virus. What can you do?

COMPUTER HARDWARE

Work with your classmates to identify and label the items in the following picture. The name for each item is included in the Important Terms for this chapter.

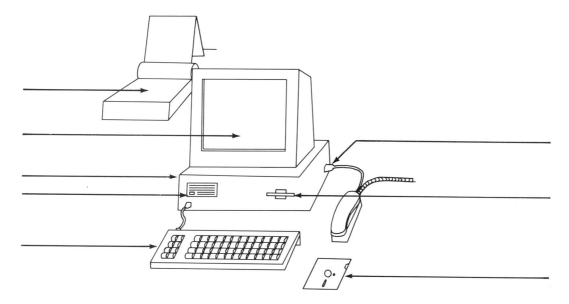

Figure 8.1. Computer Hardware

SURVEY OF COMPUTER USE

In this exercise, you will practice your conversation skills by asking people questions about their use of computers.

Survey Assignment

Interview two or three people and ask them the following questions. There is space for you to add an additional survey question of your own. Take notes on people's answers. You will report your results to the class.

1. Have you ever used a computer?
   a. If yes, how often?
   b. If not, do you plan to use one in the future?
2. If you use a computer, what do you usually use it for?
3. For yourself, what do you feel is (or might be) an important advantage of using a computer?
4. What do you think is (or might be) a disadvantage for you?

5. _____

Practice   Be sure to introduce your survey and yourself before beginning the interview. A good introduction will result in a helpful and conversational interviewee. Discuss the good and bad points of the following examples.

Good Example   Excuse me. I'm doing a survey about computers for my English class. Do you have time to answer a few questions?

Bad Example   Do you mind if I ask you some questions?

Practice the survey by interviewing a classmate first. Be sure to include an introduction.

Survey Results

When you finish the survey, present the answers to each question in class. One person should be the survey recorder. On the board, the survey recorder should make a column for each survey question, and use tally marks and brief notes to indicate results as students report them.

Questions for Analysis

1. What does the survey show about computer use in the local area?
2. Do you think this survey accurately shows how people use computers? Why or why not?
3. Do you agree with the advantages and disadvantages people gave? Explain your answer.

ESTIMATING THE SIZE OF YOUR VOCABULARY

Have you ever wondered how many words were in the English language, or how many words you needed to know? According to the *World Book Encyclopedia*, there are over 600,000 words in the largest dictionaries; however, the average American adult knows only about 30,000 to 40,000 of them. It is interesting to note that although the average American knows the meaning of quite a few words, he or she uses a basic vocabulary of only about 10,000 words in everyday speaking and writing. A college student would use slightly more. The balance of the words are what is called a person's passive vocabulary, meaning words that are understood when reading or listening but that are not actively used in speaking or writing. This means that you can expect to come into contact with somewhere between 10,000 to 40,000 words in everyday use, and perhaps more than that in college. What about the other words in the largest dictionaries? They may be old, slang, technical words, or other kinds of language not used by most people in everyday situations.

How many English words are in your active and passive vocabulary? Get a good English dictionary, set aside about an hour of your time, and follow the directions below to find out.

1. Number from 1 to 20 down the left margin of a sheet of notebook paper. Each number represents a page from the dictionary.
2. Choose a page *at random* from the dictionary.
3. Read the words (not the definitions) on the page. How many do you know? Count words that you understand when you read, even if you may not know all the different meanings for them, and even if you do not use them in your writing or conversation.
4. Write the number of words you knew on the dictionary page next to the number "1" on your sheet of paper.
5. Continue selecting pages at random and counting words you know. On your notebook paper, record the number of words you know on each page until you have looked at twenty dictionary pages.
6. Add up the total number of words you recognized. _____

7. Divide the total by 20 to get the average number of known words per page.

_____

8. Find the number of pages in the main alphabet of your dictionary. _____
Multiply this by the average number of known words per page (the number from

step 7). _____

The final number is approximately the number of words in your dictionary that are part of your vocabulary. Since the dictionary has fewer words than the total words in the language, your number from this exercise might be slightly lower than the number of words you actually know. To compare your vocabulary to other students like you, in field tests of advanced college-bound ESL students using a standard paperback dictionary of about 800 pages, results ranged between 7,000 and 18,000 words.

Follow-up Exercise

Your teacher will ask each student for his or her vocabulary size as calculated from the exercise. Then the numbers will be listed on the board from high to low, so that you can see your knowledge of vocabulary in relation to your classmates! If you are disappointed with the results, you may want to increase the amount of time you spend reading and listening to TV and radio, because one of the best ways to increase your vocabulary is to expose yourself to more words.

REVIEW: GUESSING MEANING FROM CONTEXT

In the following paragraphs from the reading passage, guess the meanings of the underlined words from the context. Write your guesses next to each word listed below. When you finish, discuss your guesses with your classmates in small groups or as a class. Remember that your guesses do not need to be exactly accurate. In most cases all you need is a general idea of the meaning, just so that you can continue reading and understand the main point.

Paragraph 1

We have seen that most money is <u>represented</u> not by paper or metal <u>currency</u> but by numbers stored in the computers of <u>financial institutions</u>. Every day these computers exchange messages representing billions of dollars. By changing the data stored in computers or by transmitting false messages, thieves can transfer funds from the rightful owners to themselves and their <u>accomplices</u>.

represented _____

currency _____

financial institutions _____

accomplices _____

Paragraph 2

The handling of <u>tangible</u> property, such as merchandise, is also often controlled by computers. <u>Unauthorized entries</u> into a computer can cause merchandise to be shipped to people who haven't paid for it. <u>Inventory</u> records can be changed to conceal thefts from a <u>stockroom</u> or <u>showroom</u>.

tangible _____

unauthorized entries _____

inventory _____

stockroom _____

showroom _____

Paragraph 3

Unauthorized access is often the work of <u>hackers</u>. A *hacker* is an enthusiastic and <u>compulsive</u> computer user and programmer, someone who spends most of his or her spare time working with computers. . . . A small minority of hackers. . . specialize in unauthorized access to computer systems. Although a few of these use their skills to commit crimes (such as charging purchases with other people's credit card numbers), most are interested only in the challenge of exploring a computer system and <u>circumventing</u> its security provisions. But even the most well-intentioned intruder can accidentally destroy important data and perhaps even <u>crash</u> (interrupt the operation of) the system. And the ability of hackers to access files containing sensitive information <u>makes a mockery of</u> privacy legislation.

hackers _____

compulsive _____

circumventing _____

crash _____

makes a mockery of _____

REVIEW: DEFINING TERMS

Do you remember the three important parts of a definition? Discuss them as a class briefly before going on with this exercise.

Group Practice

In groups of three or four, work with the important terms listed at the beginning of this chapter.

1. Choose one of the terms from the list.
2. Tell your group the definition of the term.
3. Group members should guess which term is being defined.

Pair Work: Definition Competition

How quickly can you give a definition and have your partner guess the term correctly? In this competition, the fastest teams will be the winners.

1. Make a secret list of three terms that you will define from this chapter, or your teacher may want to assign terms by passing out lists on cards. Don't let your partner see your list. He or she will also have a secret list of three terms.
2. Decide who will give definitions first.
3. When the teacher says to begin, all pairs start simultaneously. Tell your partner the definitions of your terms, one by one. Your partner's job is to guess which term you are defining. If your partner guesses incorrectly, continue to explain your definition. If your partner cannot guess the term, you may pass to the next definition, but any

terms not guessed will receive a one point penalty. As soon as one member of the team finishes, the next member starts to give definitions.

4. Raise your hand when both you and your partner have finished. If you have any penalties from unguessed terms, let your teacher know.

The Championship Round

The fastest three teams can compete in a "championship round." In the championship round, with the class as audience, each team plays in turn as the teacher records its time.

USING A WORD PROCESSOR

In this exercise, you will work with a computer and try out a word processor. It has become a popular way for college students to complete their written work, because they can more easily do their assignments.

What Is a Word Processor?

A word processor is a special computer program designed to allow the computer user to write documents such as research papers, essays, comprehension question answers, and so on. With a word processor, the computer works like a sophisticated typewriter, doing everything a typewriter can do and more. For example, many word processors include spelling checkers, which check what you have written for spelling errors.

When it comes to schoolwork, one of the biggest advantages of a word processor is that it eliminates the need to rewrite material. If you compose at the keyboard—if you type your ideas directly into the computer without writing them down first—all you have to do in order to revise your writing is to change the words that appear on the computer screen. Then the computer sends the complete document to the printer, and the printer types it out. There is no need for you to retype.

Note: To use a computer, one very helpful skill is knowing how to type. If you don't already know how to type, you should make a point of learning, because college assignments almost always must be typed.

The Keyboard

When using a computer, you need to be familiar with important keys on the keyboard. Use the following list of words to identify the keys on the drawings of IBM and Apple keyboards. Then discuss what each key does.

Alternate	Control	Escape
Backspace	Cursor Keys	Indent
Caps Lock	Delete	Shift
Command/Function	Enter/Return	Space Bar
Keys		

How to Get Access to a Computer

In order to use a word processor, you need a computer. There are several ways to get access to a computer.

1. Your school may have a computer lab. If so, work with your teacher to set a time when you can use the lab. It may be possible for the whole class to go to the lab together. Usually there is a computer lab supervisor who can help you get started.

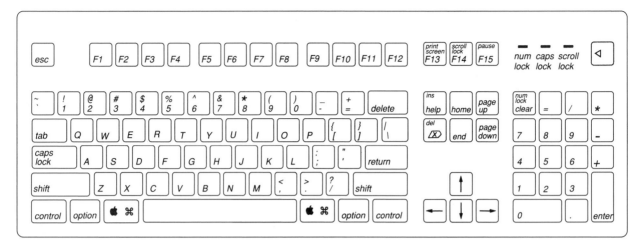

Figure 8.2. Apple II Extended Keyboard

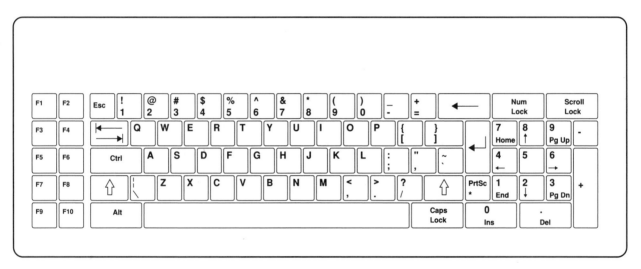

Figure 8.3. IBM Keyboard

2. You can visit a computer store. There a salesperson will be happy to show you what a word processor can do. In this case, it may be better to go with just a small group, since computer stores generally don't have much space for large numbers of people.

3. You may have a friend or relative who has a computer and can introduce you to the system.

Practice Exercise

There are many different brands of computers, and also many word processing programs made by different companies. Each one is slightly different. You will need to get help from someone who is knowledgeable about the particular computer and software you are working with.

Although the following steps look simple, if this is the first time you are working with a computer, you will probably need some time to learn by trial and error. Making mistakes may be frustrating, but don't give up; you will learn if you are persistent.

1. Use the following paragraph for practice. Enter it into the computer just as it appears, even though there are several errors. (There is about one error per sentence.)
2. Then go back and revise it, making the appropriate changes.
3. When you are satisfied with your revisions, print the document (your computer must be connected to a printer in order to do this step).

Should calculators allowed in the classroom? Nowadays, nowadays, calculators are so cheap that almost anyone can buy one. If students are allowed to use them in class, they can concennnn-trate on solving problems, instead of spending a lot of time simply doing arithmetic calculations. are They especially useful in classes such as physics and engineering. By allwoing calculators in classrooms, students can concentrate on the important concepts of the course instead of spending a lot of time doing calculations.

Follow-up Exercise

With your classmates, discuss your experiences using the word processor.

1. Did you have any problems? Find out if anyone else had the same problems and discuss how they can be solved.
2. What are some things that you learned, perhaps shortcuts or special features of the word processor? Describe them to the class.

READING EXERCISES: "COMPUTER CRIME"

Reading Goal   Skim and scan to find answers to the comprehension questions.

The reading passage for this chapter (5,186 words) is from a basic computer literacy textbook, *The Mind Tool*, by Neil Graham. The complete chapter (11 pages) is included. There are 20 chapters in the textbook.

Since this is the first time in this textbook that you are given an entire chapter to read, survey the material carefully.

1. Notice that there is an introduction and also a summary. You may want to read these first when you begin reading the chapter.
2. In addition, the college text includes review questions. In order to get a feel for the kind of comprehension and discussion questions you might find in a college text, they have been included as the comprehension questions and questions for analysis. It is a good idea to read the questions as part of your survey of the chapter.
3. Also note that five of the first seven headings are actually titles for stories of classic computer crime cases.

Review: Skimming, Scanning, Summary, and Paraphrase

1. Begin with the comprehension questions.
2. Read the first question; then skim and scan to find the answer. You may want to highlight the sections of the passage that provide answers.
3. Write your answer, using summary and paraphrase (avoid copying your answer directly from the passage).
4. Continue with the rest of the review questions. Concentrate on going directly to the information you need for each answer, working as quickly as you can.
5. When you are finished, compare answers with your classmates.

Comprehension Questions

1. Describe the following embezzlement cases:
   a. Pacific Telephone
   b. Security Pacific
   c. Wells Fargo
   d. Equity Funding
   e. The Gambling Teller
2. Why may computerized financial institutions be more susceptible to embezzlement than traditional ones?
3. How can unauthorized people get access to computer systems? What problems might they cause?
4. What are hackers?
5. What is software piracy?
6. Describe several approaches to copy protection. What are the advantages and disadvantages of each method?
7. Give the advantages and disadvantages of simple, easy-to-remember passwords for identifying users.
8. Describe read, write, and execute access rights.
9. What are some of the difficulties in enforcing security with software?
10. What security options are generally available to microcomputer owners?
11. What is encryption?
12. Discuss some measures that can be taken to protect data from loss due to theft, fire, natural disaster, and failure of storage media such as disks and tapes.

Questions for Analysis

1. For each of the computer crimes described in this chapter, discuss security measures that might have prevented the crime or permitted its early detection.
2. Discuss the conflict between the need for software users to make backup copies and the need for software vendors to prevent unauthorized copying of their products.
3. Fingerprints seem to be one promising method of identifying users, although some of the technical problems of automatically taking and analyzing fingerprints still remain to be solved. A possible human problem is that many people associate fingerprinting with being arrested and might resist having their fingerprints taken to authorize computer access. Discuss.

WORD PARTS

Match the words in the list of examples with the correct word part; then write your guess for its meaning. Check your answers with your teacher or the list in Appendix A. Make a point of learning any of the word parts that are new to you.

Root	Meaning	Example
1. plic, plex	_____	_____
2. poli	_____	_____
3. poly	_____	_____
4. port	_____	_____
5. pos, pon	_____	_____
6. psych	_____	_____

Root	Meaning	Example
7. reg, rect	_____	_____
8. rupt	_____	_____
9. scop	_____	_____

Prefix

10. retro-	_____	_____
11. se-	_____	_____
12. semi-	_____	_____
13. sub-, suc-,	_____	_____
suf-, sug-,		_____

Suffix

14. -ac, -al, -an,	_____	_____
-ar, -ative,		_____
-en, -ent, -ic,		_____
-ish, -ive,		_____
-ose, -ous,		_____
-ious		_____
15. -ful	_____	_____

Examples

ambitious	maniac	regulation
application	metropolis	retroactive
comatose	microscope	secede
directive	plentiful	semiautomatic
export	monopoly	stellar
idiotic	postpone	submarine
interrupt	psychology	suggest

WRITING: CAUSE AND EFFECT

Writing Topic

Choose one computer application and discuss how it has changed our lives.

Examples of Computer Applications

automatic teller machines

electronic funds transfer (computerized banking)

pocket calculators

home computers

   word processing

   spreadsheets

   computer games

video games (such as in video arcades)

computerized mailing lists/junk mail

computerized telemarketing

government computer databases

    traffic records

    criminal records

    tax records

    social security/welfare records

computerized library databases/library computer searches

computerized code readers at cash registers in stores

Gathering Information

For this essay, you will need to use information mainly from your own sources, since the lecture and reading material don't deal with this subject directly. You will need to get information by thinking about your own experiences, discussing the topic with other people, listening to the news, and reading newspapers and magazines.

What if you don't have any ideas? This typical type of writing assignment tends to be difficult for students because many students don't read or listen to news very much, so a common problem is lack of ideas and information. If you don't read newspapers and magazines or listen to news shows, you are at quite a disadvantage in college, so it is a good idea to develop these habits. For now, if you want to get some ideas, use some research techniques such as interviewing someone, using the library (the periodicals section is best—see the Research Guide in the appendix for how to use the library), and spending some time listening to TV and radio.

Discussion   Form groups of three or four. Each group should choose one item from the list of computer applications and discuss the following questions about it.

1. How does the average person come into contact with this computer application? Have you had any contact with it?
2. What is the usefulness of the application? How does it make life easier or better? Are there any drawbacks of the application?
3. What was life like before this computer application came into use? How were the jobs done before they were handled by computer? Who, if anyone, was affected by the installation of the computer application?
4. Can you find any changes in society that are a result of this computer application? This could include a change in norms, values, or general behavior of members of society.

Narrowing the Topic

The computer application you have chosen may have changed our lives in many ways. It is best to focus your discussion on just a few of these, and to give detailed descriptions and explanations for each effect that you discuss.

Planning the Essay

Use the following general outline to write an outline for your essay.

I. Introduction

Introduce the computer application that you will be discussing. Make a general statement about what effect it has had on our lives.

II. Body

Describe the computer application in detail. Give the reader an idea of how commonly it is used.

Then, discuss what life was like before and after this computer application started to be used. Point out specific effects and why you think they resulted from this computer application. You can use comparison of before-and-after effects of the computer application, or you may want to use a historical approach, documenting in a step-by-step way how life has changed because of this computer application. Be careful to avoid "post hoc, ergo, propter hoc" fallacies.

III. Conclusion

As always, the conclusion must include a summary that shows how your essay has addressed the topic.

Follow-up Exercise

Exchange rough drafts with a classmate. Have a blank sheet of paper ready. Read your classmate's essay and briefly list the following on your paper:

1. the computer application
2. each effect that the essay mentions

Discuss your list with your partner. Also discuss any questions you may have about your partner's essay. Listen to what your partner says about your essay, then revise and rewrite it.

Computer Crime

Introduction

In Chapter 18 we saw some of the (often controversial) ways in which law enforcement agencies are enlisting computers in the fight against crime. Unfortunately, computers can also help people commit crimes such as embezzlement. And they make possible entirely new kinds of offenses, such as software piracy and unauthorized access to computer systems. This chapter focuses on antisocial activities involving computers and on some of the means by which such activities can be combatted.

Theft and Embezzlement

We have seen that most money is represented not by paper or metal currency but by numbers stored in the computers of financial institutions. Every day these computers exchange messages representing billions of dollars. By changing the data stored in computers or by transmitting false messages, thieves can transfer funds from the rightful owners to themselves and their accomplices.

The handling of tangible property, such as merchandise, is also often controlled by computers. Unauthorized entries into a computer can cause merchandise to be shipped to people who haven't paid for it. Inventory records can be changed to conceal thefts from a stockroom or showroom.

Although exact figures are difficult to come by, estimates of the amounts lost to computer crime each year range from $300 million to $5 billion. The thieves are usually not computer experts but ordinary people—clerks, managers, tellers—whose work throws them into contact with computers. In many cases, the thieves stumble on some loopholes in the computer's security system, perhaps by accidentally entering an improper transaction and noticing that the computer accepts it.

Following are some classic cases from the annals of computer crime. People debate whether some of these cases should be called computer crimes, because in some the computer played a fairly minor role in a crime that could have been committed by conventional means. In every case, however, committing the crime would have been more difficult without the computer.

Pacific Telephone

In the Pacific Telephone case, an 18-year-old college student learned how to enter requests into Pacific Telephone's computers for equipment to be delivered to specific locations. He then picked up the equipment and sold it through his own company, Creative Telephone. Frequently he sold the equipment back to the telephone company from which he had stolen it. He was apprehended only when one of his employees caught on to the thefts, demanded to be cut in, was refused, and for revenge reported the scheme to the authorities.

Not a telephone company employee himself, the culprit used a variety of schemes to obtain the information and access codes needed to order the equipment through Pacific Telephone's computer. He obtained operation manuals for the computer system from company trash cans. By posing as a magazine reporter writing an article about the computerized ordering system, he was able to ask questions about the system and get demonstrations of its operation. Posing as a company employee, he telephoned to request current access codes, which were always provided.

Security Pacific

In 1979, Security Pacific National Bank was robbed of $10.2 million by a computer consultant and former college professor. While visiting the bank's wire room, the consultant learned the codes used to authorize transfers of funds by computer. Telephoning the bank later, he posed as a branch manager and used the codes to order that funds be transferred to a New York bank. After ordering the New York bank to transfer the funds to Switzerland, he withdrew the funds and bought diamonds. He was caught only after he bragged about his crime. While awaiting trial, he used similar techniques in an attempt to steal $50 million from another bank.

Wells Fargo

In what has been called the largest bank embezzlement in U.S. history, a boxing promoter and a bank employee stole $21.3 million from the Wells Fargo National Bank. The money was taken in a complicated scheme that made use of the branch settlement system, a procedure for transferring funds from one branch bank to another.

Such transfers were done with a branch settlement form, which had both a debit part and a credit part. The branch to receive the funds filled out the debit part of the form and sent it to the computer for processing. It sent the credit part to the branch that was to supply the funds. That branch filled out the credit part and sent it in within ten days of the date the debit part was sent in.

The Wells Fargo fraud, called a "roll-over," worked like this. The bank employee made an unauthorized payment to the boxing promoter. To cover the shortage, he sent in the debit part of the branch settlement form in the amount of the unauthorized payment. In effect, the computer was told to transfer funds from another branch to cover the shortage.

Before the ten days were up, the employee made out the credit part of the form using the identification code of another branch. If the credit part had been sent in by itself, the bank's books wouldn't have balanced because the bank had not actually received any money to compensate for the original unauthorized payment. Therefore, at the same time that the credit part was sent in, the employee also sent in the debit part of another branch settlement form. The computer used the amount called for in the debit part to balance the books and again waited ten days for the corresponding credit part.

This process could be repeated indefinitely. Each ten days the employee sent in the credit part of the outstanding settlement form and the debit part of a new one. Actually, many unauthorized payments were made, and their amounts were added to those being "rolled over" every ten days. The scheme continued until, through some slipup, an expected credit part was not received in time. The computer brought the discrepancy to the attention of bank employees, who quickly unraveled the entire scheme.

Some, including the bank itself, claim that the Wells Fargo fraud was not a computer crime. There was no direct tampering with the computer, and roll-over frauds can be perpetrated on noncomputerized systems. Yet many of the earmarks of computer crime were present. The computer processed branch settlements according to certain fixed rules. As long as the rules were followed, the computer processed each settlement routinely without bringing it to human attention. And the identification codes for the branches were used in unauthorized ways to get the computer to accept irregular transactions.

Equity Funding

The Equity Funding Corporation of America went bankrupt in 1973 following the discovery that the company had perpetrated a $2 billion dollar fraud involving the resale of insurance policies to other companies. The fraud involved an accepted practice whereby the insurance company that issues a policy can sell the policy to another insurance company. The company that issues the policy collects the premiums paid by the policyholder and passes them on to the company that bought the policy, retaining only a small percentage as compensation for handling the paperwork. The company that bought the policy pays any claims made by the policyholder.

Equity Funding used its computers to create over 60 thousand bogus insurance policies, which were then sold to other companies. Because no premiums were being paid on the bogus policies, Equity Funding had to pay the premiums itself; to get the money to pay the premiums Equity Funding sold still more phony insurance policies.

Again, there is an argument over whether Equity Funding committed a computer crime. Those who think it was make two points: (1) it would have been impossible to produce over 60 thousand convincingly phony policies without the aid of computer, and (2) the computer was used to deceive auditors, who made the unjustified assumption that whatever was printed by the computer was correct.

The Gambling Teller

A New York bank's head teller, who was addicted to gambling and hoped to win enough to pay back previous embezzlements, used his bank's computer to steal $1.4 million. The money itself he simply took from the bank's vault. To hide the thefts he used teller terminals to reduce the balances in certain accounts. For these accounts, the figures stored in the computer showed a smaller balance than the depositor thought he or she had.

head teller would apologize for a "computer error" and use a teller terminal to transfer money from some other account to that of the complaining customer. Such errors occurred frequently at the head teller's branch, but he blamed them on mistakes made by the tellers under his supervision. He was finally caught when police raided his bookie and became suspicious at finding that a bank teller was betting $30 thousand a day.

Unauthorized Access

Many computer systems are connected to the public telephone network and can be contacted by anyone with a computer, a modem, and a telephone. Some systems, such as many electronic bulletin boards, are intended to be accessible to the general public. Access to most systems, however, is restricted to authorized users. Many systems contain sensitive information, such as medical or credit records. Although connecting systems to the telephone network allows convenient access by authorized users, it also exposes them to unauthorized access by any of the millions of people who own microcomputers and modems.

Unauthorized access is often the work of hackers. A *hacker* is an enthusiastic and compulsive computer user and programmer, someone who spends most of his or her spare time working with computers. Although hackers are sometimes criticized for devoting too much time to computers at the expense of other personal activities, most are inoffensive hobbyists who engage in no illegal activities. But a small minority of hackers (sometimes called *crackers*) specialize in unauthorized access to computer systems. Although a few of these use their skills to commit crimes (such as charging purchases with other people's credit card numbers), most are interested only in the challenge of exploring a computer system and circumventing its security provisions. But even the most well-intentioned intruder can accidentally destroy important data and perhaps even crash (interrupt the operation of) the system. And the ability of hackers to access files containing sensitive information makes a mockery of privacy legislation.

Some hackers are highly skilled in working their way past the security provisions for computer systems. But most unauthorized access is achieved in more obvious ways that involve little technical skill. People entrusted with telephone numbers and passwords of computer systems are often careless about who they provide with this information (as in the Pacific Telephone case). Telephone numbers and passwords are often posted near computer terminals for the convenience of authorized users, a practice that is all too convenient for those contemplating unauthorized access. Authorized users are often allowed to choose their own passwords; unfortunately, many choose passwords that are easily guessed, such as common personal names. Some computer systems will accept passwords such as "test" that were used during system installation and (through oversight) were never removed form the list of valid passwords. Hackers can obtain the phone numbers of computer systems by writing programs that systematically dial different phone numbers and note which calls are answered with data signals.

Electronic bulletin boards are sometimes used to aid unauthorized access and other computer crimes. Just as most hackers are honest, most electronic bulletin boards are used only for legitimate purposes. Some, however, have been used to post illegally obtained information, such as credit card numbers and computer system passwords. A hacker who learns how to access a computer system (perhaps through the carelessness of an authorized user) may post the information on a bulletin board, making it available to the entire hacker community. In a celebrated case, an attempt was made to prosecute a bulletin board operator whose bulletin board was found to contain a telephone credit card number, the publishing of which was prohibited by state law. Charges were eventually dropped, however, because it was questionable whether the bulletin board operator could be held responsible for information posted by others. To avoid this kind of problem, many legitimate bulletin board operators now require users to register with the operator and obtain account numbers, which they must supply to gain access to the bulletin board. The account numbers identify the users and so allow any illegal information to be traced to the person who posted it.

Persons guilty of unauthorized access are being prosecuted under various computer crime laws. But unauthorized access is one of those crimes, like car theft, in which prevention may be more effective than prosecution. If you leave the keys in your car, this does not lessen the guilt of the thief who steals it, but it leaves you looking stupid for not taking the most elementary precautions to protect your property. Many computer systems are almost as accessible as a car with the keys left in it. Improving computer security is the most important step in preventing unauthorized access.

Software Piracy

We seem to be moving inexorably into an information age in which information will be bought, sold, and traded just like such traditional commodities as oil, steel, and grain. A problem with information as a commodity, however, is that it can be duplicated without loss of or damage to the original. People who purchase information can make as many copies as they wish to give away or to sell. Laws and licensing agreements intended to prevent such piracy (unauthorized copying) are difficult to enforce.

Microcomputer software is a case in point. Programs for microcomputers are usually delivered on floppy disks. Most microcomputer operating systems have a command to copy the contents of one disk onto another without in any way harming the original. A person who purchases a program can easily make copies for his or her friends. Often one purchased program is used to make copies for all interested persons in a company, school, or computer club. Pirated copies of software are sometimes stored on electronic bulletin boards, from which they can be downloaded to users' computers. Professional software pirates copy software for resale; this practice is particularly common in some foreign countries. Software producers estimate that half of the existing copies of some programs are pirated.

The response of the software industry has been *copy protection*, which prevents disks from being copied with the standard operating system copy commands. We recall that a disk is organized into circular tracks, each of which is divided into sectors. Before data can be stored on a disk, a special label must be recorded at the beginning of each sector, a process known as formatting. The operating system expects the sectors to be laid out in a standard format—sector 1 followed by sector 2, sector 3, and so on. Copy-protected programs use a nonstandard disk format that the operating system's copying program cannot handle.

Copy protection imposes a severe burden on the user. Floppy disks are easily damaged: a fingerprint on the exposed disk surface or the magnetic field from a ringing telephone are enough to render a floppy disk unusable. Even if disks are protected from damage, they eventually wear out. For that reason computer users are normally advised to make backup copies of all important programs and to store the backup copies in a safe place. Copy protection prevents users from making backup copies. Software companies sometimes provide one backup copy for copy-protected disks, but many users feel safe only with two or three backup copies of important programs. If all copies of a program became damaged, important data processing crucial to the operation of a business might be delayed until new copies could be ordered. And because of the volatility of the software industry, a software company might not even be in existence when backup copies are needed.

In response to the need for backup copies, several companies have deciphered the most popular copy protection schemes and put out programs that will make copies of copy-protected disks. Such programs are sometimes called *bit copiers* because they copy the pattern of bits on each track, making as few assumptions as possible about how the tracks are divided into sectors. Although bit copiers come with warnings that they are to be used only for making backup copies, nothing prevents their use by software pirates. The software industry has responded by inventing new copy protection schemes, but these are quickly broken by the manufacturers of bit copiers. Software makers have attempted to pressure computer magazines into not advertising bit copiers, but such attempts have enjoyed only limited success.

Another drawback of copy-protected software is that it cannot be copied to a hard disk, which is faster and more convenient to use than floppy disks. Generally bit copiers are able to copy only from one floppy to another and cannot copy programs to hard disks.

To avoid some of these problems, many software producers have turned to protection systems based on the use of a *key disk*. The floppy disk on which the software is delivered contains a special code that serves as a key for unlocking the software. The key code is placed on the disk when it is manufactured and cannot be copied by copying programs. For example, the coating on which information is recorded can be destroyed in certain places, creating dead spots in which no information can be stored; the pattern of dead spots constitutes the code. The programs on the disk can be copied to other floppies or to hard disks as the user desires. But to use a program, the user must place the original disk in a designated disk drive. The program will not operate unless it is able to detect the key code on the disk in the designated drive.

The key disk approach allows users to make backup copies of programs and to place programs on hard disks. But users still complain that having to insert the key disk to run their programs is a bother, and they will be unable to run their programs if the key disk becomes so damaged that the key cannot be read. Also, all copy protection methods that use a key code can be broken by locating the points at which the program checks the key code and modifying the program so that the checks are bypassed.

The Association for Data Processing Organizations (ADAPSO) has proposed a copy protection scheme based on hardware keys. Each program would be supplied with a hardware key—a ROM chip containing a key code. Attached to the computer's RS-232 port would be a "key holder" into which the hardware keys for all frequently used programs would be plugged. When a program was executed, it would check the key holder for its hardware key and function only if that key was present. The program itself could be copied or stored on hard disk as desired. On the negative side the key holder would be an added expense to the user, the hardware keys would increase the cost of software, and (as mentioned) all key-based protection schemes can be broken by modifying the program to bypass the key checks.

Software producers have recently sued several companies for unauthorized copying (usually done by employees without the knowledge of the company's management). To avoid such suits, many companies are now clamoring for site licenses, in which the company pays a substantial fee for the right to make as many copies of a program as it needs. Some major software vendors are resisting the movement toward site licensing but in the end will probably be forced to go along with it. Site licensing may be the best solution to the problem of copying within organizations; it does nothing, however, to address the problem of copying by individuals, to whom site licensing is inapplicable and for whom lawsuits are usually impractical. Although some partial solutions to software piracy have emerged, the entire question of unauthorized copying of information remains one of the outstanding unsolved problems of the information age.

Computer Security

Computer security is concerned with protecting the data stored in computers. Positive identifications of users, access controls, and secure operating systems guard against unauthorized access. Encryptation protects data during both storage and transmission. Backup copies protect data from accidental destruction.

Positive Identification of Users

Security is impossible without positive identification to prevent unauthorized users from impersonating authorized ones. Traditionally, a user is identified by an account number, a password, or both. But users are often careless in guarding this information. Allowed to choose their own passwords, users pick words that are easy to remember but also easy to guess. For example, many users choose the name of their spouse or one of their children.

Some of these problems can be avoided if access codes are read from cards similar to credit cards. Because the user does not have to remember the access codes, they can be more complex and so harder to guess. The access card can be stolen, but the access codes will be changed when the authorized user reports the theft. To help guard against stolen cards, the user can be required to enter a personal identification number in addition to the information stored on the card. This method is used with automatic teller machines, but with less success than might be hoped. Most users write down their personal identification numbers and place them in the same wallet or purse as the access card. Thus a pickpocket or purse snatcher gets both the card and the personal identification number.

Another useful security technique is the callback system. When a user calls the system and supplies his or her access codes, the computer hangs up and then calls back the person authorized to use those codes. The return call goes, of course, to the authorized user, not to an unauthorized person calling from a different location.

Other proposed approaches involve using various personal characteristics, such as voice, handwriting, and fingerprints, for identification. Some have even proposed lip-prints, although requiring you to kiss your computer to get it to accept your commands might be going too far. The drawbacks of these proposals are the complexity and expense of the hardware and software needed to measure and analyze each characteristic.

Access Controls

Once a user has been identified, it is the responsibility of the operating system and the database management system to control access to data. The system maintains a table showing what access rights each user has to each file. Generally three access rights are considered: read, write, and execute. Read access means that the user can read the information in a file but not change it. Write access conveys the right to change the contents of the file. Execute access conveys the right to execute a program but not the rights to read or change the program code. The operating system and the database management system consult the access-rights table for each requested data access and deny those requests for which the user does not have the proper rights.

Although access rights are most commonly applied to files, they can also be applied to individual fields within a record. For example, clerical employees at a company might have read and write access to all fields of an employee record except the salary field, access to which would be limited to the payroll department. Even most employees in the payroll department might have only read access to the salary field; only a few trusted employees might have write access, the right to change someone's salary.

Secure Software

User identification and access rights will go for nought if software and hardware access controls can be bypassed. In current systems, security is almost entirely the responsibility of software, with little or no support from the hardware. Operating systems and database management systems are so complex that loopholes are sometimes inadvertently left in their security systems. All too often clever hackers have found ways to do such things as print out a list of users' passwords or give themselves access rights to which they are not entitled.

It is essential that the system be run only under the control of the operating and database management systems that will enforce security provisions. If some other system software were substituted— say, a version of the operating system that had been modified by a hostile user—all bets would be off as far as security was concerned. A related problem is that of *Trojan horse programs*. A programmer writing a program for a trusted user with extensive access privileges might include code that would access sensitive data and pass it to other less privileged users. Privileged users must regard programs given them by others with the same suspicion the citizens of Troy should have applied to the original Trojan horse.

Current microcomputer systems provide little if any security. A hostile user can easily run programs that will bypass any security restrictions imposed by the operating system or a database management system. Utility programs intended for recovering data from damaged disks can usually be used for bypassing security restrictions. The following are the only security options available to most microcomputer users:

☐ Store sensitive data on floppy disks, which can be locked up in conventional filing cabinets and safes when not in use.

☐ Store data on the computer's hard disk and keep the computer system locked when not in use; some computers are provided with a key-operated switch for this purpose. All bets are off if the entire computer is stolen, since any keyswitch is easily bypassed by anyone with the opportunity to work on the machine unobserved.

☐ Use data encryption to store data in a scrambled form meaningless to anyone not having the proper key.

Data Encryption

Data encryption stores data in a scrambled form that can be unscrambled only by those having a special data item called the *key*. An encryption algorithm converts the *plaintext*—the data to be protected—into scrambled *ciphertext*. The scrambling is controlled by the key. Only someone who has the key can use the encryption algorithm in reverse to convert the ciphertext back into plaintext. As with passwords, it is often difficult to keep keys from being stolen or to prevent people from carelessly letting them fall into the wrong hands. Encryption can protect data stored in files as well as protect against wiretapping during data communications.

Backup Copies

Stored data can be lost through fire, theft, natural disaster, or, more commonly, through failure of storage media such as disks and tapes. Most large computer installations periodically copy all their stored data on magnetic tapes and store the tapes in a remote location to prevent their loss in a fire or other disaster. Some organizations maintain (at a different location than the main system) a standby computer system to which they can turn if the primary system is destroyed. Organizations that do not maintain their own standby systems often have contracts with organizations that specialize in supplying computer facilities on short notice.

Wise microcomputer users make backup copies of all disks containing important programs or data. The backup copies protect not only against disk failure but against accidental erasure of files due to operator errors. Copy protection techniques that do not allow backup copies of programs to be made present serious risks to users.

Although hard disks are reasonably reliable, they do fail occasionally, so data stored on hard disks needs to be backed up on floppy disks. Many users are failing to do this. Hidden away inside the computer, the hard disk is out of sight and out of mind; many users are probably unaware that it can fail. Also, backing up all the data on a hard disk is cumbersome and time-consuming, because many boxes of floppy disks are usually needed to store the data from one hard disk.

Summary

Computers have given rise to new forms of crime as well as to new variations on old forms. Traditional crimes such as embezzlement may be even easier with computers, since computer systems will accept any transactions that obey certain formal rules even though the same transactions would look suspicious to a human auditor.

Unauthorized access to computer systems has become much more common since the microcomputers and modems needed to commit this crime have become widely available. Most unauthorized accesses result not from the cleverness of the perpetrators but from poor or nonexistent security. Although persons guilty of unauthorized access are being arrested and prosecuted, improved security techniques are likely to be far more effective than prosecution of offenders.

Software piracy is one of the unsolved problems of the computer age. Users have demonstrated that they will make unauthorized copies of software if not somehow prevented from doing so; unauthorized copying is particularly prevalent in corporations, schools, and computer clubs. Yet most current copy protection techniques present serious risks for honest users. Site licensing, for which many corporations are now clamoring, basically accepts that copying will take place and tries to make the best of it.

Computer security is concerned with protecting data from loss and from unauthorized access or changes. Positive identification of users, access rights, and secure software help control access to data. Encryption can protect stored data as well as that being sent over communications links. Security is poor or nonexistent for most microcomputer systems; measures such as locking up disks in filing cabinets or locking the computer system may be needed to prevent unauthorized access. Backup copies of computer files, preferably kept at a different location than the originals, are essential to guard against data loss due to disaster or failure of data storage media.

Chapter
9

Business

Outline

Objectives

When you finish this chapter, you will be able to do the following:

Language and Study Skills

1. Read and identify the key elements of a case study.
2. Use principles of persuasive communication to write a promotional letter.
3. Work with a group to complete a writing project.

Content Mastery

1. List and describe some basic principles of leadership.
2. Compare the organizational cultures of the United States and Japan.
3. Apply leadership concepts to a case study.
4. Use basic business writing principles.

No matter what your major, someday you will have a job and come into contact with the business world. You may work in a position that requires leadership skills. At some point, you will probably need to write a business letter or memo. These are the topics for this chapter. We look at some typical subjects covered in business classes, specifically principles of leadership and business writing. You will have a chance to experience working with a case study and completing a group writing project, two typical business course assignments.

Important Terms and People

As you listen to the lecture and read the passage for this chapter, note the following important terms and their meanings. When you finish the chapter, you should be able to define each one.

authoritarian/autocratic leader   laissez-faire/free-rein leader
behavioral approach   law of the situation
behavioral style   leadership continuum
case study   leadership
cognitive style   management
conceptual style   Douglas McGregor
contingency-situational approach   William Ouchi
corporate culture   people-oriented/employee-centered leader
Decision Style Inventory   personal tone
democratic/participative leader   Ringi system
directive style   Robert Tannenbaum & Warren Schmidt
doubtful tone   tall organization
flat organization   task-oriented/production-oriented leader
Edwin Ghiselli   Theory X
heterogeneity   Theory Y
homogeneity   Theory Z companies
I-approach   top-down authority system
impersonal tone   traitist approach
Shigeru Kobayashi   you-approach

LECTURE: "CORPORATE CULTURE"

Business organizations have their own distinctive cultures, just as societies do. In this lecture you will hear about the key characteristics of corporate culture and how individuals fit into it. It was given by Dr. James D. Boulgarides of the California State University, Los Angeles, Marketing Department to a group of international students interested in business. This is an example of a lecture that might be given in an introductory management course. Although management courses are not a requirement for students who are not majoring in business, the concepts are useful for anyone who will someday work in a business. The professor will refer to Figure 9.1 during the lecture.

Comprehension Questions

Refer to your notes as needed to answer the following questions.

1. What is a corporate or organizational culture?
2. List and describe four different cognitive styles.
3. How do the cognitive styles of individuals affect how they behave in groups?
4. Compare the United States and Japan in terms of
   a. cognitive style.
   b. organizational structure.
   c. heterogeneity and homogeneity.

Questions for Analysis

1. What kind of corporate culture would you prefer to work in? Why would you prefer this kind of culture?
2. Find an article in a news or business magazine that gives an indication of a corporate culture. Share it with the class.

TOP HALF	ANALYTICAL	CONCEPTUAL
Thinking	Technical	Creative
Executive	Careful	Humanistic
Complex	Hierarchical	Artistic
Ideas	Innovative	Optimistic
	Uses Much Data	Achievement-Oriented
	Uses Insight	Future-Oriented
	Problem Solving	Uses Judgment
	Enjoys Variety	Wants Independence
		Initiates New Ideas
BOTTOM HALF	DIRECTIVE	BEHAVIORAL
Doing	Productive	Supportive
Maintenance	Aggressive	Empathetic
Need for	Verbal	Wants Affiliation
Structure	Acts Rapidly	Communicates Easily
	Uses Rules	Uses Instinct
	Needs Power/Status	Uses Limited Data
	Uses Intuition	Prefers Meetings
	Impatient	Avoids Stress

LEFT BRAIN	RIGHT BRAIN
Task-Oriented	People-Oriented
Technical	Social
Logical	Relational
Verbal	Visual

Figure 9.1. Decision Style Inventory—Characteristics

WORKING WITH A CASE STUDY

Case studies are often used in business courses as a teaching tool. A case study is a story, often true, about a business situation. It generally involves a problem or decision, and often shows how the problem was handled or how a decision was implemented. Readings similar to case studies are included in the Graduate Management Admission Test (GMAT). The following five points to recognize are taken from the points used in GMAT exam questions.

In order to understand a case study, as you read you should look for these things:

1. *Major Objectives* of the case study are the most important goals that need to be met by the people or business in the case.
2. *Major Factors* are important facts about the situation that need to be considered for a successful outcome.
3. *Minor Factors* are facts about the situation that should be taken into account, but which are less important than the major factors.
4. *Major Assumptions* are the unspoken ideas about the situation that people in the case study are taking for granted. Assumptions may be correct or incorrect.
5. *Unimportant Issues* are things that are mentioned in the case study that are not important to consider when analyzing the case.

Practice 1

Review the case study about Kenny at the beginning of the reading passage for this chapter. In order to work on reading comprehension for case studies, use the following two steps.

1. Analyze the passage by finding and marking the five preceding points.
2. Compare your analysis with your classmates, or go over the analysis with your teacher.

The analysis you have just completed is the first step in working with a case study. Usually, specific questions are given that require you to apply concepts from the business course. Generally the questions are answered in a class discussion, although sometimes they form the topics for essays.

Discuss the following questions about the case study (they are from the business textbook).

1. Which of McGregor's assumptions did Kenny hold concerning his people?
2. What if the renegade crew decides not to cooperate with Kenny, and its members continue to be poor performers? Should Kenny continue to be supportive and use his usual leadership style? Why or why not?

Practice 2

This case study (861 words) is taken from a different management textbook, *Management*, by Daniel A. Wren and Dan Voich, Jr. Read the case study to find the major objective, major and minor factors, and any major assumptions made by people in the study. You will answer five practice test questions when you finish.

Case Study: Carol and Her Friends

The Davis Thermometer Company manufactures veterinary and human thermometers. It is a small company, employing about 75 workers. Mr. Davis retired two years ago, leaving Phillip Adams, his son-in-law and partner, in charge of the business. Mr. Adams is 55 years old and one of his major duties is to act as supervisor of production. Mr. Adams, who wants to be called "Phillip" by his workers, is the type of individual who will take very little "back talk" from a worker but will listen to the problems brought to him. Some workers feel that he is too cold-hearted to care about their problems and try to work things out among themselves.

Under the direct supervision of Mr. Adams are five female workers and their 10 machines in the Scaling Department. The thermometers arrive on trays from the Waxing Department. Each "scaler" sets the point of the machine just above a thick painted line on one end of the thermometer, and then lines the gauge up with a line at the other end. When this has been done, a lever is pulled, and the point cuts through the wax and puts the calibrations on the thermometer. The scaler quickly swivels her chair to another machine and repeats the process. The operations are considered "smooth" when the scaler can set one machine before the other has stopped running. The scaler then checks the thermometer to see whether the point has exactly split the painted line. If the calibration is not exact, the scaler takes a hot electric rod and smooths the wax until the marks are removed from the thermometer. When one thermometer is finished, the scaler places it on an empty tray. When a whole tray is completed, the scaler signs her initials to a slip of paper and places it on the tray. This tray is then sent to the Inspection Department.

The scalers are a very close group. Carol is the best known and the best liked among them. She is 40 years old, married, and has been a scaler for four years. Nancy was hired one year later than Carol, and Linda was hired six months after Nancy. The three are the best of friends and share a ride to work.

Early this year, the following incident occurred. Carol suffered a back injury, which required her to miss four weeks of work. When she did return to work, her physical condition made it difficult for her to maintain the production rate set by management. Everyone in the department knew this and helped her out by signing her initials to work they had done. They never told Mr. Adams this, believing that he would not understand. As a result, the production rate for the whole department decreased to below the minimum. Mr. Adams noticed this, but since the scalers displayed the best teamwork of any department in the plant, he decided to transfer another worker into the department to help out. He picked Joan, who was a conscientious and fast worker in the Inspection Department. Joan initially did not like the idea of a transfer but decided to give it a try.

Nancy, who was the fastest worker, was instructed to teach Joan the operations of the machine and the method of production. After an hour of instruction, Joan commented, "Well, this is a lot easier than testing. This job should be a cinch."

The scalers were slow to accept Joan; Linda once commented, "She's always complaining that her machine isn't right. I'll bet she just hasn't got what it takes." Joan did not help matters any. Every day she would eat lunch with her friends in the Inspection Department.

In the following weeks, Linda's comment was proved wrong. Joan increased her production until it substantially surpassed the quota set by management. At this time, the others decided to tell Joan of their practice of sharing the amount of work each produced to help out Carol. Joan listened, but made no comment.

Two days later, Mr. Adams approached the workers and asked how everything was coming along. In the course of the conversation, to the dismay of the others, Joan said, "Phillip, wouldn't you think a worker who has been here the longest should be able to produce more than the rest of us?" After a moment of shocked silence, Carol replied that she had been having trouble with her machine and under those conditions she could not work more quickly. Mr. Adams nodded and walked away. From that point on, the workers avoided speaking to Joan.

As the days passed, tension continued to grow and Joan continued to produce more than the others. She refused to help Carol by giving her finished thermometers. When Joan was not looking, the others would hand several scaled thermometers to Carol.

About two weeks after the incident with Mr. Adams, Linda saw Joan talking to him at the water fountain. After the conversation, Mr. Adams hurried into his office with a worried look on his face. Linda quickly returned to the Scaling Department and told the others of the incident. They all wondered what would happen now.

Test Practice   The following questions are similar to those given in the GMAT test. Mark each question with the letter representing the correct classification.

   a. Major Objective
   b. Major Factor
   c. Minor Factor
   d. Major Assumption
   e. Unimportant Issue

   _____ **1.** Carol's injury.

   _____ **2.** The scalers felt Mr. Adams wouldn't understand Carol's problem.

   _____ **3.** Meeting the Scaling Department quota.

   _____ **4.** Joan always ate lunch with her friends in the Inspection Department.

   _____ **5.** Mr. Adams was the son-in-law of the original business owner.

Discussion   If you were Mr. Adams, what would you do? Consider your answer. Which leadership style is reflected in your decision?

READING EXERCISES: "LEADERSHIP IN ACTION"

Reading Goal   Review and practice the SQ3R method.

The reading passage for this chapter (6,142 words) is excerpted from an introductory management textbook, *Management Concepts and Applications*, by Leon C. Megginson, Donald C. Mosley, and Paul H. Pietri, Jr. There are 20 chapters in the book. The reading is from a chapter that is 31 pages long.

Since the chapter had to be condensed, there are references to theories that are not included in the reading passage. These references are enclosed in brackets to show that they are not discussed in the reading material.

SQ3R Review

When reading, remember to use the SQ3R study-reading method:

   1. Survey the chapter, checking titles, and any special features.
   2. Then write Questions for each heading and subheading.
   3. Read to find answers to your questions.

4. Record the answers you find by writing notes in outline form.

5. Review your notes when you prepare for a test.

Reading Comprehension

Refer to your SQ3R notes to answer the following questions. If you took good notes, they should include most of the answers. The reading comprehension questions labeled with an asterisk (*) have been taken directly from the review questions at the end of the text-book chapter.

* **1.** How would you characterize the leadership style of Kenny in the Opening Case?
* **2.** How would you define (a) autocratic leaders, (b) democratic leaders, and (c) laissez-faire leaders?
* **3.** What is the difference between leadership and management?
* **4.** How would you describe the traitist approach to studying leadership?
* **5.** How would you describe the behavioral approach to studying leadership?
  6. What are the key assumptions in McGregor's two theories?
* **7.** How would you describe the contingency-situational approach to studying leadership?
  8. Tannenbaum and Schmidt published an article in 1958 that has become a classic. How do you account for the popularity of their "Leadership Continuum?"
  9. What are some ways that leadership theory can be applied in daily situations?

Questions for Analysis

* **1.** Should a supervisor use one leadership style with certain workers, another with other workers, and perhaps a third with others? Defend your answer.
* **2.** Which one of the various leadership theories and approaches discussed in this chapter do you think is the most applicable in the real world? Support your position.
  3. Reread Tips 12.1 "Using Effective Leaders as Role Models" in the reading passage. Follow the directions to complete a self-assessment. How do your results compare to other students' answers?

WORD PARTS

Match the words in the list of examples with the correct word part; then write your guess for its meaning. Check your answers with your teacher or the list in Appendix A. Make a point of learning any of the word parts that are new to you.

Root	Meaning	Example
1. scrib, script	_____	_____
2. sens, sent	_____	_____
3. soph	_____	_____
4. spec, spic	_____	_____
5. tact, tang	_____	_____
6. tend, tens, tent	_____	_____
7. therm	_____	_____
8. typ	_____	_____
Prefix		
9. super-, sur-	_____	_____

10. syn-, syl-, _____ _____

     sym-, sys-, sy- _____

11. tele- _____ _____

12. trans- _____ _____

13. ultra-, outr- _____ _____

Suffix

14. -less _____ _____

15. -ly _____ _____

Examples

description	supervision	tension
gentlemanly	sympathy	thermometer
helpless	synchronize	transcendence
philosophy	tactful	typical
sensation	telephone	ultraconservative
spectator		

PRINCIPLES OF BUSINESS WRITING

Introduction

This section is adapted from a business communication textbook, *Communication for Business and the Professions*, by Marla Treece, and includes several lessons on business writing style.

To get an idea of what business writing is about, analyze the following letter. Cover the page below the dotted line so that the bottom of the page is hidden. Discuss this question: What is wrong with the following short letter? (The address, salutation, and closing are purposely omitted.) After you have discussed your ideas, uncover the bottom of the page to see the correct analysis.

> As newly elected membership director of the Junior Chamber of Commerce, I am in charge of recruiting new members. I would like very much for you to join. I am working for a record-making membership this year.
>
> I do not know why you are not a member, anyway; most of the other young business owners in this town are, you know.
>
> Fill out the enclosed application blank and return with your check.

Analysis

First paragraph. Throughout the paragraph, writer benefits are stressed, not those of the reader. Note that "I" is the subject of every sentence.

Second paragraph. Most undiplomatic. Even if readers had been planning to join, this letter is enough to keep them away forever.

Third paragraph. A direct order. Discourteous. No reader benefit.

A Sincere You-Attitude

A sincere you-attitude is important in any business communication. The you-attitude looks at a situation from the viewpoint of the reader or the listener. The you-attitude is sincere. The opposite concept is the *I-attitude.*

To use the you-approach, direct your communication toward the reader. A type of wording that violates the you-approach is shown by the following sentences:

1. Our company is pleased to announce the opening of our new store.
2. We are very happy that the Smith Sporting Goods Company is now expanding.
3. I am very happy to have your order.

Analysis   Each of these sentences, when read alone, seems only to show pride in the employing company, a worthy attitude but not enough. If the reader does not interpret these company actions in the light of personal benefits, the letter has not been written in the complete you-attitude.

Sentences 1 and 2 could be improved by changing to "We are now located in your neighborhood."

Even better would be "You are now only five minutes away from the store that can fill all your sporting goods needs." Notice the focus on the benefit to the reader.

Sentence 3 could be improved by changing it as follows:

"Your order will be shipped tomorrow."

Or better yet:

"You should receive your suit within a week."

The second sentence is better because it contains more specific information about the order and when the customer can expect it.

Practice

Improve the following sentences by using the you-approach.

1. The Scott Appliance company is pleased to announce the opening of our new store, to which all our customers are invited.

_____

_____

2. We are flattered that you want to open a credit account with us.

_____

_____

Personal vs. Impersonal Tone

Almost all letters and memorandums, as well as many reports, are written in what is described as the "personal tone," in which first-person pronouns (*I, we, us, me,* etc.) are used when they seem desirable or necessary. The personal writing style also uses second-person pronouns (*you,* etc.).

This style is preferred for business communication because it sets a tone that seems more directly related to the reader. It is important, however, to choose pronouns carefully. A letter or memorandum filled with *I*'s, *we*'s, and other words that refer to the writer (such as the company name) is not likely to be written with the you-approach.

The "impersonal tone," also described as the "third-person writing style," includes no *I*'s, *we*'s, *you*'s, or other first- or second-person pronouns. The impersonal tone is appropriate for many reports, academic writing, most news stories, and other kinds of written material. A good communicator writes well in both the personal and the impersonal tone and chooses the most appropriate style for the particular material, situation, and readership.

The personal tone: Now you will find a wider choice of merchandise in the greatly enlarged building.

The impersonal tone: The enlarged store building has allowed for a much greater variety of merchandise.

There are times when the impersonal tone and even the I-approach are more appropriate. This usually happens when the message is negative in some way. It is more diplomatic to associate a negative message with the writer or use an impersonal tone.

1. **a.** You must pay $22 for this product. (you-approach)
   b. This product sells for $22. (impersonal tone)
2. **a.** You must pay the full amount of your loan immediately. (you-approach)
   b. We are sorry that we cannot grant a further extension of time on the loan. (I-approach)

Practice

Use the appropriate tone and approach for each message.

1. Do not fail to finish the project by the end of this week.

   _____

   _____

2. It's against company policy, so we must reject your request for sample packages for your customers. You must realize that if we give away merchandise you will have to pay more for what you buy. (From a manufacturer's letter to a retailer.)

   _____

   _____

Emphasize the Positive and Subordinate the Negative

Emphasize the benefits readers or listeners will gain from the product, not difficulties or misfortunes they will avoid.

1. **a.** This plastic dinnerware won't scratch or dent, and it won't melt in your dishwasher. (focus is on the negative)
   b. Because this sturdy dinnerware is highly resistant to heat and pressure, it is completely safe in your dishwasher. It will still be shining and beautiful many years from now. (focus is on the positive)
2. **a.** The odor of this cat food is not offensive. (focus is on the negative)
   b. You'll like the fragrance of Kitty Cuisine almost as much as your cat likes the taste. (focus is on the positive)

Practice

1. This letterhead paper is not the thin, flimsy kind that always comes out looking cheap.

   _____

   _____

2. This scarf won't keep out the wind and the rain, but it's pretty.

   _____

   _____

Don't Mention Weak Points

Some things are better left unsaid. Instead, emphasize strong points.

1. **a.** Unfortunately, I have no business experience. (deficiency)
    b. My courses in business administration at Indiana State University have given me an understanding of the fundamentals of management and supervision. (strong points are emphasized)
2. **a.** My grade average is not good but . . . (weak point)
    b. My leadership skills gained as captain of the Michigan State University football team can be an asset to your company. (strong point)

Practice

1. I have not had any experience except for helping my father in his real estate business.

    _____

    _____

2. I did not have any extracurricular activities in high school because I had to study for the college entrance examination. (from a college application essay)

    _____

    _____

BUSINESS WRITING: A PROMOTIONAL LETTER

Work in groups of two or three. This is a **group** writing project. Group exercises of this kind tend to be assigned more often in business courses than in other classes; however, it is useful to be able to work with others on a written project, regardless of your major.

Writing Topic

Pretend that you are handling the marketing and promotion of the school or program where you are currently studying. Write a letter that will be sent to potential students to encourage them to enroll in your school or program.

Gathering Information

You will need to have information about the following aspects of your school/program in order to write your letter:

curriculum

extracurricular activities

entrance requirements

enrollment dates and procedures

cost

other important or special aspects of your school/program

Since a promotional letter uses persuasive communication, you might want to review the reading and writing sections on persuasion in Chapter 6, in order to get some additional ideas.

Narrowing the Topic

When you write a business letter, you narrow the topic by choosing your message and your method of presenting it. Work with your project group. Discuss the details of the items listed in Gathering Information. Decide which things your message should emphasize, and which might need to be played down or left out.

Choose which persuasive methods you will use to convince prospective students. (You may want to review these in Chapter 6.) For example, will you mention benefits? Will you show how the classes can meet students' needs? Work with your group to plan a persuasive strategy, using the information you have gathered.

Planning the Letter

Business letters follow a different pattern from essays. First of all, you need to use the **personal tone**. In contrast, most academic essays use the **impersonal tone**. The language of a business letter needs to be simple and direct. You will also need to use the other principles discussed in the Business Writing exercise. Following is an outline of a typical persuasive business letter:

I. Introduction
Get the reader's **attention**. You need to make the reader interested enough to read the complete letter.
II. Body
Give persuasive **evidence** that will encourage students to attend your school or program.
III. Conclusion
Tell the reader what **action** to take. In this case, you need to tell the reader how to enroll in the course(s).

Writing the Letter

Since this is a group project, you need to divide the work of writing the letter. There are several ways that the work can be divided. Here is an example: Each member of the group can be assigned to write one part of the letter—the introduction, the body, or the conclusion. When the writers have prepared their sections, they can share them with the group, and make any changes necessary. Then one member of the group can rewrite the letter in its final form.

Follow-up Exercise

Work with your group. Pretend that you are a student overseas who wants to come to the United States to study. Your teacher will give you a copy of one of the promotional letters written by another group. Read the letter and discuss the following question with your group: Would you like to attend the program the letter is promoting? Why or why not?

Leadership in Action

Kenny—An Effective Supervisor

Kenny was a maintenance supervisor in a chemical plant of an international corporation.[1] The plant was suffering from problems caused by the ineffective and autocratic leadership of the former plant manager. This poor management had adversely affected the entire plant, resulting in low morale at all levels and losses from plant operations. However, one crew seemed to have escaped the adverse effects—it had very high morale and productivity. This was the maintenance crew that was under Kenny's supervision.

Kenny was in his early thirties, with a two-year associate degree from a community college. He had a very positive attitude, especially in light of the overall low morale and productivity. In Kenny's mind, the plant was one of the finest places he'd ever worked and the maintenance people had more know-how than any other group he'd worked with. Kenny believed that his crew did twice as much work as other crews, that everyone worked together, and that participative management worked.

Kenny's boss reported that Kenny's crew did not do twice as much work as other crews—actually, it did *more* than twice as much. He claimed that Kenny was the best supervisor he had seen in 22 years in the industry.

Why did the pressure and criticism from the old, autocratic manager seem to have no effect on Kenny's crew? According to the crew members, Kenny had the ability to act as an intermediary and buffer between upper management and the crew. He would get higher management's primary objectives and points across without upsetting his people. As one crew member described it:

> The maintenance supervisors will come back from a "donkey barbecue" session with higher management where they are raising hell about shoddy work, taking too long at coffee breaks, etc., etc. Other supervisors are shook up for a week and give their men hell. But Kenny is cool, calm, and collected. He will call us together and report that nine items were discussed at the meeting, including shoddy work, but that doesn't apply to our crew. Then he will cover the two or four items that are relevant to our getting the job done.

Unfortunately, Kenny did have one real concern. He was being transferred from the highest-producing crew to the lowest-producing one. In fact, it was known as the "Hell's Angels crew." The crew members were considered renegades who were constantly fighting with production people as well as with each other. The previous supervisor had been terminated because he could not cope with the crew members.

After Kenny was assigned to the "Hell's Angels crew," he had to decide on the leadership strategy he would use in dealing with its members. His initial diagnosis was that the crew had the ability to do the work, but lacked the willingness because of a poor attitude.

On his first day with the crew, Kenny called a meeting, shut the door, and conducted a "bull session" that lasted over two hours. Among other things, Kenny told the crew about his leadership philosophy and the way he liked to operate. He especially stressed that he was going to be fair and treat everyone equally. Kenny allowed the crew members to gripe and complain about matters in the plant as long as they liked, and he listened without interrupting. In the course of the session, Kenny

Leadership is the projection of personality—that combination of persuasion, compulsion, and example—that makes other people do what you want them to do. Industry must find the natural leaders, train them in the technique of management, and give them an opportunity to lead.

—FIELD MARSHAL
SIR WILLIAM SLIM

expressed his expectations of the crew. In response, they told him they would do it his way for two weeks to see if he "practiced what he preached."

How do you think Kenny's leadership worked with the new crew? Before the year was out, it was the most productive in the plant.   ■

THIS CASE ILLUSTRATES that effective leadership is found in many levels of our society and not simply with the more glamorous top-level positions. We agree with John W. Gardner that effective leadership is dispersed "from the most lofty levels of our national life down to the school principal, the local union leader, the shop foreman."[2]

On the other hand, there is an unfortunate amount of ineffective leadership in our society. Although no single model of leadership exists that everyone agrees with, this chapter should help you identify the need for leadership and how to nurture and use it.

WHAT IS LEADERSHIP?

It is important to clarify some terms that you'll be reading throughout this chapter. So, let us point out the distinction between management and leadership and define different kinds of leadership characteristics.

Leadership Defined

Like management, *leadership* has been defined in many different ways by many different people. Nevertheless, the central theme running through most of the definitions is that leadership is a process of influencing individual and group activities toward goal setting and goal achievement. As a leader, you work to ensure balance between the goals of the organization, yourself, and your group. In the final analysis, the successful leader is one who succeeds in getting others to follow. A leader has to work effectively with many people, including superiors, peers, and outside groups. But in working with followers, he or she is the spark that lights the fire and keeps it burning.

> *Without Jerry Ayres in the lineup, the City Junior College Wildcats are just another mediocre basketball team. But Jerry makes the team click. Only 5'6", he's not a high-scoring player, but as a leader he's unequaled, and his presence in the game helps his teammates play better. According to his coach, Jerry's playmaking and leadership on the floor are the major factors in the team's 20–6 record, which ranks them in the state's top 10 teams.*

Ways of Classifying Types of Leaders

There are many ways to classify leaders or leadership styles. The two most important, however, are (1) by the approach they use and (2) by their orientation toward getting the job done.

Approach used. One common way of studying leadership is in terms of the basic approaches used by leaders: autocratic, democratic, or laissez-faire.

Autocratic leaders—often called **authoritarian leaders**—make most decisions themselves instead of allowing their followers to make them. These leaders are usually thought of as "pushers," somewhat like the image of a military drill instructor.

Democratic or **participative leaders** involve their followers heavily in the decision process. They use group involvement in setting the group's basic objectives, establishing strategies, and determining job assignments.

Laissez-faire leaders—also called **free-rein leaders**—are "loose" and permissive and let followers do what they want. You might think of this approach as similar to teachers who handle classes loosely, with few homework assignments, class sessions that seem to drift from one issue to another as they arise, and little direction or discipline.

Orientation toward job. Another way to categorize leaders is to examine their attitudes toward getting the job done. Some leaders emphasize the task; others emphasize followers or subordinates; as you will find out later in the chapter, some can emphasize both.

Task-oriented or **production-oriented leaders** focus on the "work" aspects of getting the job done. They emphasize planning, scheduling, and processing the work, and exercise close control of quality. Another term used in describing this approach is *initiating* structure.

People-oriented or **employee-centered leaders** focus on the welfare and feelings of followers, have confidence in themselves, and have a strong need to be accepted by their team members. Other common terms used to describe people-oriented leaders are *relationship centered* and *considerate*.

Leadership Is Not the Same as Management

People often equate management and leadership. Reporters, for example, comment on the U.S. president's "exercise of leadership." They refer to such things as new programs (planning), organizational changes (organizing), quality of advisers (staffing), ability to inspire confidence (leading), and ability to make changes quickly when things go wrong (control). Perhaps one explanation for such a broad interpretation of leadership is that we sometimes use the term *leader* when referring to managers. Although the two are similar, there are some significant differences.

Leadership is the ability a person has to influence others to work toward goals and objectives. **Management** involves leadership, but it also includes the other functions of planning, organizing, staffing, and controlling. Here is an example of outstanding leadership but poor management.

Coach Jones has the most highly motivated, committed group of players in the league. "We'd run through a brick wall if he asked us to," said one of the players. But the team has been very unsuccessful to date. The offense is poorly conceived, consisting of some very simple, fundamental plays, and the defensive system is outdated. Moreover, the recruited players are just not that good. But the players respect the coach and really put out for him. If a "spirit" award were given, the Bay High football team would certainly get it.

Coach Jones may be highly effective in getting commitment from his players and inspiring them—that is, in leading—but his inability to perform the other management functions negates the effectiveness of his leadership skills.

What is your view?

Do you think that the reverse may also be true—that is, that someone may be an effective manager but a poor leader? Explain.

Leading, then, is an important part of management, but it is not the same as management.

Leadership research and theories can be classified as *traitist, behavioral,* and *contingency-situational* approaches. We present these to you chronologically, since they have evolved from studies of leadership that have been emphasized over the years, as follows:

traitist → behavioral → contingency-situational

THE TRAITIST APPROACH

According to the **traitist approach,** leaders possess certain traits or characteristics that cause them to rise above their followers. Lists of such traits could be very long but tended to include one's height, energy, looks, knowledge and intelligence, imagination, self-confidence, integrity, fluency of speech, emotional and mental balance and control, sociability and friendliness, drive, enthusiasm, and courage.

Research on Traits

Most of the early research on leadership attempted to (1) compare the traits of people who became leaders with those who were followers and (2) identify characteristics and traits possessed by effective leaders. Studies comparing the traits of leaders and nonleaders often found that leaders tended to be more intelligent, somewhat taller, more outgoing, and more self-confident than others and to have a greater need for power. But specific combinations of traits have not been found that would distinguish the leader or potential leader from followers. The underlying assumption of the trait researchers seems to have been that *leaders are born, not made.* But research has still *not* shown that certain traits *can* distinguish effective from ineffective leaders. Yet respected research is still being done in this area.

One of the earliest trait researchers was Ralph Stogdill, who was doing such studies during World War II.[3] As late as 1974, Stogdill found several traits to be related to effective leadership. These included social and interpersonal skills, technical skills, administrative skills, and leadership effectiveness.

A later researcher, Edwin Ghiselli, found that certain characteristics do seem to be important to effective leadership.[4] The most important of these are:

1. *Supervisory ability,* or performing the basic functions of management, especially leading and controlling the work of others.

2. *Need for occupational achievement,* including seeking responsibility and desiring success.

3. *Intelligence,* including judgment, reasoning, and reactive thinking.

4. *Decisiveness,* or the ability to make decisions and solve problems capably and competently.

5. *Self-assurance,* or viewing oneself as capable of coping with problems.

6. *Initiative,* or the ability to act independently, develop courses of action not readily apparent to other people, and find new or innovative ways of doing things.

Limitations of the Traitist Approach

There are some obvious limitations to the traitist approach. For example, we know that people such as Alexander the Great, Napoleon, Joan of Arc, Abraham Lincoln, Florence Nightingale, Geronimo, Mahatma Gandhi, Mao Zedong, Adolf Hitler, Winston Churchill, Vince Lombardi, and Martin Luther King, Jr., were somehow different from others. Yet there appear to be no particular leadership traits found in all of them. In fact, some of them, such as Hitler and Lincoln, had quite different traits! Thus, in summary, the traitist approach did not yield significant findings as to what attributes are the hallmark of a leader. Moreover, there are many cases in which a leader is successful in one situation but may not be in another. For example, Winston Churchill was the brilliant World War II leader who led Great Britain to victory over Hitler's German forces. Yet he was defeated for Prime Minister by a relatively unknown politician in the spring of 1945.

Before leaving the traitist approach, you might wish to complete TIPS 12.1, to see what characteristics are found in effective leaders.

TIPS 12.1   Using Effective Leaders as Role Models

Think of two of the most effective leaders you have had direct contact with and who have had an influence in your life. These leaders can be anyone, such as a parent, a teacher, a coach, a boss, a student leader, a religious leader, or a relative or friend.

Write a list of at least six characteristics and/or beliefs that made these people such outstanding leaders. Next, do a self-assessment on a scale of 1 to 5 as to how you measure against their characteristics and beliefs.

1	2	3	4	5
Poor		Average		Excellent

On points where your self-assessment is not 4 or 5, develop an action plan that will improve your self-assessment (1) six months from now, (2) one year from now, and (3) five years from now.

THE BEHAVIORAL APPROACH

It became obvious that the traitist approach could not explain what *caused* effective leadership; thus attention shifted to the **behavioral approach,** which involved studying the behavior of leaders. Behaviorists assume that leaders are not born but developed. There are some important implications of this approach. First, by focusing on what leaders *do*, rather than on what they *are*, it could be assumed that there is a "best" way to lead. Second, although traits are stable—many are in us at birth—behavior is learned. Many of the traits found by Stogdill are not innate, but are learned.

The behavioral approach, considering the orientation or identification of the leader, assumes that the leader will be (1) employee oriented, (2) task or production oriented, or (3) some combination of the two. Thus the behavioral view is that the leadership process must focus not only on the work to be performed but also on the need satisfactions of work group members.

The most popular behavioral research and theories include author Douglas McGregor's Theory X and Theory Y.

**McGregor's
Theory X and
Theory Y**

The leadership strategy of effective use of participative management proposed in Douglas McGregor's classic book, *The Human Side of Enterprise*, has had a tremendous impact on managers.[6] The most publicized concept is McGregor's thesis that leadership strategies are influenced by a leader's *assumptions about human nature.* As a result of his experience as a consultant, McGregor summarized two contrasting sets of assumptions made by managers in industry.

The assumptions of Theory X. According to the first set of assumptions, **Theory X,** managers believe that:

1. The average human being has an inherent dislike of work and will avoid it if possible.

2. Because of this human characteristic, most people must be coerced, controlled, directed, or threatened with punishment to get them to put forth adequate effort to achieve organizational objectives.

3. The average human being prefers to be directed, wishes to avoid responsibility, has relatively little ambition, and wants security above all.

A first-line supervisor in a recent training program said: "My first feeling is that people are lazy, don't like responsibility, and have no ambition. If I didn't really push my group, threaten to put the screws to them, and often do it, nothing would get done around here. I'm sort of like the circus master who gets into the cage with those animals. He's got to really stay on those cats and crack that whip to get them to perform their tasks effectively. If they don't perform, they get popped. That's about how my job as supervisor is. I've got to stay on top of my crew just like that animal trainer does."

The assumptions of Theory Y. Managers who accept **Theory Y** assumptions believe that:

1. The expenditure of physical and mental effort in work is as natural as play or rest, and the average human being, under proper conditions, learns not only to accept but to seek responsibility.

2. People will exercise self-direction and self-control to achieve objectives to which they are committed.

3. The capacity to exercise a relatively high level of imagination, ingenuity, and creativity in the solution of organizational problems is widely, not narrowly, distributed in the population, and the intellectual potentialities of the average human being are only partially utilized under the conditions of modern industrial life.

You can readily see that a leader holding Theory X assumptions would prefer an autocratic style, whereas one holding Theory Y assumptions would prefer a more participative style.

Participants in the Summer Case Workshop at the Harvard Business School in July 1958 heard the late Douglas McGregor say he wished he had never written the two theories, since they had been misunderstood. Most workers did not fit into either the X or the Y category but had some characteristics of each, and the workers' behavior tended to vary from one to the other over periods of time. He said he intended to write "Theory Z," a combination of the two theories. Unfortunately, he died before accomplishing this.

McGregor's concepts have had a significant influence on practicing managers, as the following example shows.

Robert Townsend became president of Avis when it was floundering and had not made a profit for 13 years. He was advised that the top management team was incompetent and should be fired. But three years later the company had grown in sales and had made successive annual profits of $1 million, $3 million, and $5 million. The amazing thing is that this success was achieved with the same management that had been labeled incompetent! Townsend attributes this success to the use of a Theory Y, participative style of leadership and to removing undesirable aspects of bureaucracy.[7]

What is your view?

In the Opening Case, which of these assumptions did Kenny hold concerning his people? What if the renegade crew decides not to cooperate with Kenny and its members continue to be poor performers? Should Kenny continue to be supportive and use his usual leadership style? Why or why not?

Japanese Style Leadership

In 1981, William Ouchi published a book entitled *Theory Z*,[12] which compared Japanese and American industry and concluded that some Japanese corporations can serve as models for American firms. Ouchi felt that Japanese industrial success was a result of better management and that some American companies had characteristics similar to those of Japanese companies. Invariably, it turned out that these were among the best managed in the world; they included IBM, Procter & Gamble, Hewlett-Packard, and Eastman Kodak. Ouchi referred to these organizations as **Theory Z companies.**

It is becoming quite apparent that the Japanese leadership style discussed by Ouchi is one of the most significant factors in their success in the industrial world. Also, experience with this leadership style in the United States, where Japanese managers are responsible for managing American workers, shows that these techniques are as effective here as they are in Japan—and in some instances more effective. (See Chapters 17 and 20 for more detail.)

THE CONTINGENCY-SITUATIONAL APPROACH

Just as the traitist approach was inadequate to explain leadership, so was the behavioral approach. Instead, most researchers today conclude that no one leadership style is right for every manager under all circumstances. Instead, the **contingency-situational approach** prescribes that the style to be used is contingent on factors such as the situation, the people, the task, the organization, and other environmental variables.

Examples of Contingency-Situational Approach

Fortune magazine ran a story on the corporate world's 10 *toughest* bosses.[17] Among the traits these leaders had in common were an overriding dedication to their jobs and an insistence that subordinates be equally dedicated. Among the top 10 were Robert Stone and Robert Abboud. Stone, who was known as "Captain Queeg" when he ran Hertz in the 1970s, was a galley master who, hearing that the rowers would die if the beat was raised to 40, would say, "Make it 45." But during his term at Hertz, profits multiplied fourfold. Abboud, former chairman and chief executive officer of First Chicago Bank, was nicknamed "Idi" (for Idi Amin) because he was so tough. During

Abboud's reign, top managers left the bank in droves, profits dropped 40 percent in 1979, and shortly after the *Fortune* article appeared in April 1980, Abboud was fired by the bank's executive committee.

So you see that although a hard-nosed, tough leadership style may get results in one situation, it may not in another.

The most popular contingency theories to be discussed include Tannenbaum and Schmidt's leadership continuum.

Tannenbaum and Schmidt's Leadership Continuum

In a 1958 issue of *Harvard Business Review*, there appeared an article entitled "How to Choose a Leadership Pattern," by Robert Tannenbaum and Warren Schmidt. The article was so popular with practicing managers that it was reproduced in 1973 as a "classic," along with a retrospective commentary by the authors.[18] The original article had been so well received because it sanctioned a range of behavior instead of offering a choice between two styles of leadership, democratic and authoritarian. It helped managers analyze their own behavior within a context of other alternatives, without labeling any style right or wrong.

What it involves. Tannenbaum and Schmidt's concept is presented as a **leadership continuum,** as shown in Figure 12.5. The continuum is based on Mary Parker Follett's **law of the situation,** which states that there are several alternate paths managers can follow in working with people. Therefore, in making leadership decisions, managers must consider forces in themselves, their subordinates, and the situation.[19] These forces are interrelated and interacting, as shown in Figure 12.6.

Forces in the manager include his or her (1) value system, (2) confidence in subordinates, (3) own leadership inclinations, and (4) feelings of security or insecurity.

Forces in subordinates include (1) their need for independence, (2) their need for increased responsibility, (3) whether they are interested in and have the knowledge to tackle the problem, and (4) their expectations with respect to sharing in decision making.

Forces in the situation include (1) the type of organization, (2) the group's effectiveness, (3) the pressure of time, and (4) the nature of the problem itself. The key point is that the successful manager is the one who has a high batting average in assessing the appropriate behavior for a given situation.

FIGURE 12.5

Continuum of manager-nonmanager behavior.
Reprinted by permission of *Harvard Business Review.* An exhibit from "How to Choose a Leadership Pattern" by Robert Tannenbaum and Warren H. Schmidt, May-June 1973. Copyright © 1973 by the Presidents and Fellows of Harvard College; all rights reserved.

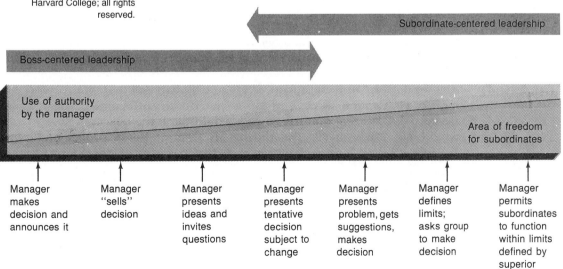

Subordinate-centered leadership

Boss-centered leadership

Use of authority by the manager

Area of freedom for subordinates

| Manager makes decision and announces it | Manager "sells" decision | Manager presents ideas and invites questions | Manager presents tentative decision subject to change | Manager presents problem, gets suggestions, makes decision | Manager defines limits; asks group to make decision | Manager permits subordinates to function within limits defined by superior |

FIGURE 12.6
The relationship among
the leader, subordinates,
and the situation.

Subordinates must understand what is expected of them. An important warning, though, is that a leader must communicate clearly to subordinates just what degree of involvement they will have in a given situation. Will the workers *make* the decision? Does the supervisor only want to *consider* subordinates' inputs before making the final decision? One mistake leaders make is to "fake" a high degree of involvement, already knowing what the decision will be. In other words, the manager thinks, "I know their thinking on this will be identical to mine, so I'll let them feel that I've involved them in my decision." Beware! *You* do not like to feel manipulated, and the leader who plays such a human-relations "game" may eventually be hurt or surprised by it. The leader will find that thinking can be more varied than he or she ever dreamed.

> *The department chairperson called in four of her junior faculty members who were teaching principles of management and said, "It is time for us to change textbooks, and these are the four I would like for us to consider. Since we are the ones teaching the course, we will not involve other members of the department in the decision. Will each of you review each book and write me a report ranking them in order of your recommendation? Your recommendations will be of major importance; so take this assignment seriously."*
>
> *The newest junior faculty member read each book, turned in a list of the pros and cons of each, and made his recommendations. He was surprised when the chairperson adopted the text he had ranked the poorest. He thought, "Hey, I really blew this one. I need to talk with the other instructors and see what I missed in that text she chose."*
>
> *The four faculty members were upset and dismayed to discover that all of them had ranked the adopted text the poorest of the four. They later learned that the chairperson and the author of the adopted text were close friends.*
>
> *Primarily as a result of this incident, three of the four junior faculty members sought and obtained positions at other universities.*

What is your view?

Where on the leadership continuum did the junior faculty *think* they were operating? Where were the junior faculty *actually* operating? What would have been a more appropriate leadership behavior on the chairperson's part?

APPLYING LEADERSHIP THEORY

In discussing leadership, many textbooks present too many theories and not enough summary or nuts-and-bolts usefulness. This section will show how to *apply* leadership theory. We have discussed several leadership theories and shown that no one of them has all the answers. We agree with the contingency theorists that the real challenge for those in leadership positions is to take time to make a thorough diagnosis of the situation and then plan their leadership strategies carefully, based on that situation. Moreover, leadership strategies must be oriented toward carrying out the organization's mission and achieving its objectives.

Some managers ignore ideal leadership models such as 9,9 and System 4. We think that viewpoint is a mistake because there is an increasing number of situations where the appropriate action is to shift toward these leadership styles. More will be said on this point in Chapter 13. Notice in the Opening Case that Kenny dealt with the "Hell's Angels crew" that way.

Inspiring and Developing People

The following are concepts leaders can apply to increase their effectiveness.

Say "thank you." It has been shown that productivity can be drastically increased simply by saying "thank you." "Thank yous" can vary from financial rewards for good performance to simply writing letters of recommendation.[25] One approach is to look for positive contributions and give people feedback on the spot, as recommended in *The One Minute Manager*. The book's authors suggest one-minute techniques such as:

1. Telling people up front that you are going to let them know how they are doing.
2. Praising people immediately.
3. Telling people what they did right—specifically.
4. Telling people how good you feel about what they did right and how it helps the organization and the other people who work there.
5. Stopping for a moment of silence to let them "feel" how good you feel.
6. Encouraging them to do more of the same.
7. Shaking hands or touching people in a way that makes clear that you support their success in the organization.[26]

Expect the best of people. Essential to effective leadership is the awareness that, to bring out the best in people, you must assume the best about them. If you expect the best from people and develop realistic yet difficult performance objectives, your expectations will act as a self-fulfilling prophecy. But you must trust your work team and do what you say you will. A study of school teachers has revealed that having high expectations of students can increase their IQ scores up to 25 points.[27]

What is your view?

As indicated in the Opening Case, Kenny gained the trust of his renegade work team. They gave him two weeks to prove that he would supervise them as he said he would, and he did.

Maintain a positive self-regard. A study of nearly 100 outstanding leaders in different fields revealed that having a good feeling about oneself is one key to effective leadership.[28] We are not talking about cockiness or self-worship, but a sincere self-respect, based on awareness of one's strengths and weaknesses and the desire to improve one's talents.

Develop the entire team. Kenny made a conscious effort to sit down once a month and talk with each member of his crew. But he went beyond focusing on developing individual crew members and developed the entire team by holding regular crew meetings and emphasizing the importance of working together. As a result, the crew thought and acted as a team, helping one another. For example, one team member was afraid of heights; so other members covered for him when there was an assignment involving heights.

Develop the desire to achieve. While the most effective leaders have a strong desire to achieve excellent results, they will be less effective if they become so task oriented that they slight the human-relations aspects of working with people. Kenny did not fall into this pitfall, nor did he go to the opposite extreme of emphasizing human relations at the expense of achievement. For the very reason that he was very achievement oriented, Kenny used a contingency-situational strategy: If his initial approach had not worked, he would have shifted to a more directive style to turn things around.

Chapter
10

Natural Science

Outline

Objectives

When you finish this chapter, you will be able to do the following:

Language and Study Skills

1. Understand the key points of reading material containing technical vocabulary.
2. Explain a graph.
3. Write a laboratory report.
4. Use scientific evidence to support an essay thesis.

Content Mastery

1. Explain the greenhouse effect and its importance to world climate.
2. From various scientific studies, trace the changes in Earth's climate over the last 150,000 years.
3. Give examples of how climatic changes can affect plants and animals.
4. Conduct a climate experiment.

Most undergraduates are required to take a course in natural science, and a popular choice is ecology, the study of how organisms interact with the environment. In this chapter, we take a look at one aspect of ecology: how plants and animals interact with climate. As in any scientific field, the vocabulary is at times quite technical. But many new vocabulary words in the reading passage are not essential to understanding the material (for example, scientific names of plants and animals). For other new words, a general idea of the meaning is enough (for example, plankton = tiny living things).

Important Terms

As you listen to the lecture and read the passage for this chapter, note the following important terms and their meanings. When you finish the chapter, you should be able to define each one.

biological community	Mill Creek culture
boreal forest	nitrous oxide
Cahokia people	overpopulation
carbon dioxide	ozone
carbon monoxide	particulate matter
cellulose	photosynthesis
deciduous forest	plankton
desertification	Pleistocene ice sheets
drought	polar zone
ecology	pollution
ecosystem	respiration
fossil fuels	Russell cycle
glaciation	solar power
greenhouse effect	stratosphere
greenhouse gases	temperate forest
hypothesis	temperate zone
ice age	tree-ring research
interglacial period	tundra
methane	

LECTURE: "THE GREENHOUSE EFFECT"

Is Earth's climate getting hotter? Many scientists predict that gases put into the air by human activity will seriously affect Earth's climate. This lecture explains how this might happen. It was given by Richard J. Vogl, Professor of Biology at California State University, Los Angeles in a guest lecture to a group of international students. It is an example of a lecture you might hear in an ecology class.

Comprehension Questions

Refer to your notes as needed to answer the following questions.

1. What is the greenhouse effect?
2. What gases cause this effect and where do some of them come from?
3. What are two other important factors in the greenhouse effect and what are their sources?
4. According to the professor, what steps can be taken to slow or stop the dangerous changes taking place in our atmosphere?
5. Not all scientists agree that Earth's climate is getting hotter. Outline the three different viewpoints discussed in the lecture.
6. What is the basic global problem underlying the greenhouse effect and many other environmental problems?

Questions For Analysis

1. Reducing emissions that increase the greenhouse effect requires changes in national policies, business practices and people's lifestyles. Industrialized and developing countries are contributing to the problem in different ways and have to make different kinds of adjustments. Discuss ways of involving both developing and industrialized countries fairly in reducing greenhouse gases.

2. Imagine that you are planning a publicity campaign to promote energy conservation. Create a slogan and a one-paragraph advertisement that could be aired nationally on TV, radio, in magazines and newspapers to persuade people to change to a more energy-conserving lifestyle.

3. Find a news article that is related to one of the issues discussed in the lecture. Prepare an oral or written summary of the article, pointing out in what way it is related to the issues in the lecture.

UNDERSTANDING GRAPHS

Graphs are often used in college textbooks. They are also sometimes used as test questions in standardized tests such as the Test of English as a Foreign Language (TOEFL), Scholastic Aptitude Test (SAT) and Graduate Record Examination (GRE). They are included on tests because understanding graphs is a basic academic and business skill. The reading passage for this chapter uses graphs extensively, and two basic examples have been reproduced with comprehension questions in the following Practice activities. You may work in groups to answer the questions.

Practice 1

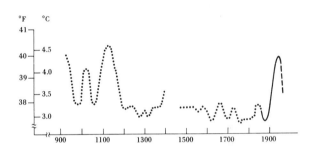

Figure 10.1 A thousand years of Icelandic temperatures. The dotted line shows estimated average temperatures (with the early part of the fifteenth century omitted because of insufficient data). The solid line shows temperatures based on thermometer readings. The dashed line shows the change in recent years for the Northern Hemisphere. (From Bryson and Murray 1977)

1. What does the graph show?
2. What does the X-axis represent? The Y-axis?
3. Around which date was the highest average temperature?
4. About when did the lowest average temperature occur?
5. What is the meaning of the dotted line, the solid line, and the dashed line?

Practice 2

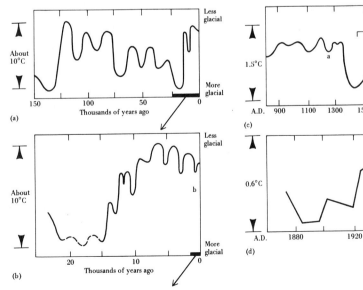

Figure 10.2 Northern Hemisphere temperatures for the past 150,000 years with more detail for recent years. (a) The last 150,000 years as indicated by marine deposits, pollen records, and shoreline changes. (b) The last 25,000 years as indicated by tree rings, pollen records, and glacier records. (c) The last 1,000 years. a, Mill Creek cooling; b, Little Ice Age; c, early twentieth-century warming; (d) The last 100 years, showing the cooling that has occured since 1950. (From Bryson and Murray 1977)

1. What is measured on the X and Y axes of each graph?
2. What is the temperature range for each graph?
3. During what period of time did the "Little Ice Age" occur?
4. Since about 1700, what has been the main trend in temperature?
5. Since about 1950, the average temperature has cooled off a little. About how much cooler has the temperature become?
6. **a.** Based on these graphs, at present are we in a more glacial or less glacial period?
   b. Compare current temperatures to those of the last 150,000 years.
7. Find a trend in these graphs that can be projected to predict future temperatures. You may use a colored pencil to highlight the trend. Compare your answer with those of your classmates.

Group Discussion

Form groups of three or four. Your teacher will assign each group one graph or chart from the reading passage. (There are 9 figures, excluding the two already discussed.) Discuss the meaning of the graph or chart, and then explain it to the class.

REVIEW: GUESSING MEANING FROM CONTEXT

This exercise focuses on technical vocabulary. In the following paragraphs from the reading passage, guess the meanings of the underlined words from the context. Write your guesses next to each word listed below. When you finish, discuss your guesses with your classmates in small groups or as a class. Remember that your guesses do not need to be exactly accurate. In most cases, all you need is a general idea of the meaning, just so that you can continue reading and understand the main point.

Paragraph 1

Fossil pollen studies have proved successful at describing the sequence of plant communities over the past 30,000 years. Because of the Pleistocene ice sheets in the Northern Hemisphere, climatic and vegetational shifts occurred around the globe. Figure 9.3 on page 132 shows the pollen record for Rockyhock Bay in North Carolina, an area of the eastern United States about 500 kilometers south of the line of maximal glacial advance. In this bay about 5 meters of sediment has been deposited over the past 30,000 years. From 30,000 to 21,000 years before the present (B.P.) temperate forests of oaks (*Quercus*), birches (*Betula*), and pines (*Pinus*) occupied the area. From 21,000 to 10,000 B.P., boreal forest was present, with spruce (*Picea*) and northern pines, and the climate was colder and drier than at present. Deciduous forests, with a predominance of oak, replaced the boreal forests about 10,000 B.P. Swamp forests began to develop about 7,000 B.P., featuring blackgum (*Nyassa*), cedar (*Cuppressaceae*), magnolia (*Magnolia*), and red maple (*Acer rubrum*). The swamp forests were essentially modern by 4,000 years ago.

fossil _____

Pleistocene ice sheets _____

sediment _____

temperate _____

B.P. _____

boreal _____

deciduous _____

swamp _____

modern _____

What do the italicized words in parentheses refer to? _____

Paragraph 2

The complex series of <u>ecosystem</u> changes that make up the Russell cycle can be summarized as follows. A <u>plankton</u> community dominated by the chaetognath *Sagitta elegans* was replaced during the 1930s by one dominated by *Sagitta setosa*...[1] At the same time there was a drop in the dissolved <u>phosphate</u> concentration of the seawater. Phosphate is a critical nutrient for <u>phytoplankton</u> in the spring. The abundance of <u>zooplankton</u> dropped at the same time, and the numbers of young fish in the plankton fell dramatically....<u>Herring</u>, which feed on plankton, decreased, and <u>pilchard</u> replaced herring as the dominant pelagic fish in the English Channel....During the 1970s the cycle reversed. *Sagitta elegans* returned to the plankton, pilchard declined, and <u>larval</u> fish became abundant in the plankton. The <u>net</u> result was that by 1980 the English Channel had returned to a stage approximately like that of the 1920s.

[1]Chaetognaths, or arrow worms, are small <u>invertebrates</u>, 1 to 10 millimeters long, that are one of the larger species in the plankton community of the oceans. They feed on smaller crustaceans in the plankton....

ecosystem _____

plankton _____

chaetognath _____

phosphate _____

phytoplankton _____

zooplankton _____

herring _____

pilchard _____

larval _____

net _____

invertebrates _____

crustaceans _____

READING SPEED POSTTEST

You will have 1 minute to read the following passage. Mark the word that you are reading at the end of that time.

18	We grow used to the daily and seasonal changes in weather, and we view these changes as vari-
35	ations within a constant climate. Our faith in the constancy of climate may be shaken by observ-
55	ing that there are wet years and cold years, but we assume that over the long run the apparent devi-
71	ations will all average out. This assumption of climatic constancy is completely wrong. One of the
89	major themes to emerge from the last 30 years of scientific research is that climate changes on all
91	time scales.
107	Evidence of changing climates comes from a variety of sources. Let us start with recent his-
125	tory in which we have a written record of change. Figure 9.1 shows a thousand years of tempera-
141	ture changes from Iceland. Thermometer data go back only 140 years in Iceland and before this
160	one must rely on indirect evidence—reports of drift ice floating by the island. Drift ice is a ther-
176	mometer of the North Atlantic. The earliest reports are from A.D. 825 when Irish monks visited
196	Iceland and found no ice there even in winter. To reach pack ice they had to sail one day's journey

217 to the north. There was no record of drift ice off Iceland for at least 400 years until the 1200s when
234 severe winter pack ice moved south and cut off the old Norse colonies in Greenland, causing them
254 to be abandoned. From about 1500 to 1900 the best years in Iceland were only as good as the worst
269 years the Vikings had experienced during the tenth and eleventh centuries. From about 1890 to
286 1950 a great warming occurred, followed by a cooling during the last 25 years. A message clearly
303 emerges from the Icelandic saga: *The climate of the present century is not typical of the previous*
305 *thousand years.*
321   To extend our vision about climatic change back further, we can use pollen grains trapped in
337 lake sediments. Pollen grains in sediments are fossils of older plant communities. Because differ-
353 ent species of plants have pollen that differ in shape and size, ecologists can reconstruct plant
367 communities back in time. In combination with radiocarbon dating of sediments, we can deter-
376 mine the timing of community changes over the globe.
389   Fossil pollen studies have proved successful at describing the sequence of plant communities
405 over the past 30,000 years. Because of the Pleistocene ice sheets in the Northern Hemisphere, cli-
413 matic and vegetational shifts occurred around the globe. . . .
416   Most of the plant and animal communities of the polar and temperate zones are still recover-
433 ing from the last episode of Pleistocene glaciation that ended about 15,000 years ago. We can look
450 for evidence of climatic fluctuations most easily at the tree line. The present polar limit of trees
466 in northern Canada and Alaska has changed dramatically since the Ice Age ended and is still
480 changing today. . . .These changes have occurred because of slow but systematic changes in the
497 amount of solar energy reaching the surface of the earth. In northern Canada there has been a
514 general shift in the polar limits of trees, which were 200 to 300 kilometers farther north 1000
520 years ago than they are today.

GO ON TO THE COMPREHENSION QUESTIONS

Comprehension Questions

Answer the questions without referring to the passage. Focus on the questions for the lines that you read. You may guess the answers to questions for lines that you didn't have time to read.

1. (18–91) One of the major findings of recent research is that
   a. climate is fairly constant.
   b. climate is always changing.
   c. climate changes a little from year to year but over the long run it stays the same.
   d. climate appears not to vary, but over long periods of time it does change.
2. (107–305) T F The most important point to learn from the evidence from Iceland is that drift ice is like a thermometer of North Atlantic sea temperatures.
3. (321–413) In order to study climatic changes that occurred in the more distant past, scientists can use
   a. fossilized pollen grains.
   b. ice sheets.
   c. carbon.
   d. vegetational shifts.
4. (416–520) T F Evidence from a study of the polar limit of trees shows that many plant and animal communities have been changing since the end of the last Ice Age.

Your Reading Speed

Find the mark you made when the teacher announced that 1 minute had passed. Count the number of words on the line that you didn't have time to read. Subtract this from the number at the beginning of the line. The result is your reading speed in words per minute.

READING EXERCISES: "CLIMATES CHANGE, COMMUNITIES CHANGE"

Reading Goal Survey the chapter to find the beginning of each main section. Read one section carefully to prepare a formal oral summary.

The reading passage for this chapter (3,380 words) is from an ecology textbook, *The Message of Ecology*, by Charles Krebs. The complete chapter (16 pages) is included. The textbook has 10 chapters.

Although this chapter does not have subheadings, there are actually nine sections covering different aspects of the topic. The first section is an introduction to the subject.

1. As you survey the chapter, find and mark with a star (or other small mark in the margin) each of the nine sections of the chapter. You may need to use your skimming skill to quickly go through the chapter and recognize when a new subject is being discussed.
2. Compare your findings with your classmates.

Oral Summaries

Work in small groups. Each group will be assigned a different section of the chapter (one of the sections you found in the preceding exercise). Your job is to read the section and prepare an oral summary to present to the class. Each member of your group will report a part of the summary, so that everyone will have a chance to speak. Meet with your group and prepare the summary as follows:

1. Begin by stating the main topic of the section.
2. Mention important parts of the section; for example, what research method was used, what kind of evidence was found, and so on. Include a brief explanation of any important diagrams or graphs.
3. End by pointing out the significance of the section for the chapter; in other words, explain the way this topic illustrates how climates and communities change.

Once the summaries are prepared, group members will present them. The audience should take notes on the summaries to use later as a study and comprehension aid.

Reading Comprehension

1. How do we know that the climate today is not typical of the climate of historic times (for example, the last thousand years)?
2. Over the past 30,000 years, what climatic changes have affected plant life?
3. How are tree rings used to trace changes in temperature?
4. What evidence is there that the Mill Creek Indian culture disappeared due to climatic changes?
5. What is the possible connection between the disappearance of the Mill Creek culture and that of the Cahokia people?
6. Describe the Russell cycle and its probable cause(s).
7. What evidence seems to show that today's climate is not characteristic of earth's climate, either in the short or long term?
8. What are some reasons why Earth's climate changes?

Questions for Analysis

1. Is it reasonable to use the average temperatures of Iceland to indicate temperature changes for the Northern Hemisphere? Explain your answer.
2. Evidence in the reading passage has been used by scientists to make predictions about future temperature trends.

a. If you were a scientist looking at the evidence presented here, over the long term, the next few thousand years, what would you predict might happen to global temperatures? Point out which evidence you used to make your prediction.

b. If you also considered evidence from the lecture, what would you predict might happen to Earth's climate in the short term, within the next hundred years? What evidence supports your position?

WORD PARTS

Match the words in the list of examples with the correct word part; then write your guess for its meaning. Check your answers with your teacher or the list in Appendix A. Make a point of learning any of the word parts that are new to you.

Root	Meaning	Example
1. vac	_____	_____
2. ven	_____	_____
3. vid, vis	_____	_____
4. vita, viv	_____	_____
5. voc, voke	_____	_____
6. vor	_____	_____

Prefix

7. un-	_____	_____
8. uni-	_____	_____
9. vice-	_____	_____

Suffix

10. -ly	_____	_____
11. -ward(s)	_____	_____
12. -wise	_____	_____
13. -ate, -ify	_____	_____
14. -en	_____	_____
15. -ize, -ise	_____	_____

Examples

broaden	herbivore	upward
convene	nullify	vacuum
counterclockwise	socialize	vice president
courageously	unauthorized	video
equivocation	universe	vitality

LABORATORY EXPERIMENT AND REPORT

The Experiment: Microclimates

Microclimates are the special climates of a particular place. They are influenced by such things as shade, plants or water present, rock or pavement, and other local conditions. In this activity, you will measure the temperature in several locations and observe conditions that could cause temperature to vary between one place and another.

Experiment Setup

1. For this experiment, the class will need a total of four thermometers. (They can be purchased for $1 or less at a school, science, or hobby supply store.)
2. Label the thermometers "A," "B," "C," and "D." Put each thermometer in a different place. For example, one thermometer may be in the classroom, another inside a car, in the parking lot, outside the classroom door, under a tree, and so on.
3. Wait about 15 minutes for the thermometers to measure the temperatures at their locations. While you wait, go over the procedures that follow for reporting a laboratory experiment. Prepare a title page and an experimental data page according to the examples.

Gathering Data   Form four groups. Each group will begin at a different thermometer, and will rotate from one thermometer to the next until each group has checked all four thermometers.

Record your temperature measurements as accurately as possible on the experimental data page. Also record your observations of any local conditions that may affect the temperature reading. These could include shade or sunlight, wind, and so on. You may want to discuss these with group members as you visit each thermometer.

Experiment Follow-up   After collecting data, most science classes require a written report. With your report, you must hand in your *original* data sheet. You cannot change your data, even if your figures disagree with other members of your group. There is always a little variation in measurements for any experiment, and the temperature may have been changing as well. Write your report according to the directions that follow for writing a laboratory report.

Laboratory Report

Write a laboratory report for the "Microclimates" science activity. The report should be written or typed as neatly as you can, using one side of each page. The guidelines for writing the laboratory report were adapted from *Handbook of Technical Writing*, by Charles T. Brusaw, Gerald J. Alred, and Walter E. Oliu.

Report Guidelines   The key sections of a laboratory report are:

1. The **purpose** for the laboratory investigation
   State what you intended to demonstrate, learn, or verify. Generally background information such as a theory or basic principle is also included in an academic report.
2. The **equipment** and **procedures** used (and any problems encountered).
3. The **results** of the test or investigation (the data).
   Present the results clearly; for example, by using a graph or chart.
4. The **conclusions** reached, and a **discussion** about the conclusions.
   For the microclimates experiment, discuss factors that may have influenced the temperature readings at each location.

A laboratory report often places special emphasis on the equipment and the procedures used in the investigation because these two factors can be critical in determining the accuracy of the data obtained.

Present the results of the laboratory investigation clearly and concisely; however, write complete sentences. Sentence fragments are not usually sufficient for clear communication.

When preparing your laboratory report for the "Microclimates" experiment, follow the format of the following example.

EXAMPLE:

Page 1 (title page):

```
                        Chloramine Content of Water
                      Glendale City Public Water Supply

                               Submitted to:
                            Professor Bremburg
                             Chemistry 300A

                               Submitted by:
                                  Jian Do

                         Laboratory Group Members:
                                 Joe Smith
                                 Sue Stone


                              May 24, 1990
```

Page 2 and subsequent pages:

Chloramine Content of Water
Glendale City Public Water Supply

PURPOSE
    The purpose of this test was to determine the amount of monochloramine (NH_2Cl) in the public drinking water supply of Glendale by using a colorimeter.
    Chloramine has recently replaced chlorine as a disinfectant in the Glendale water supply. It is preferred because it lasts longer in water than chlorine, and unlike chlorine it doesn't form dangerous compounds called trihalomethanes (THM). One THM is chloroform, a suspected carcinogen.) Standards for the amount of chloramine are set by the California Department of Health Services based on guidelines recommended by the U.S. Environmental Protection Agency. The current standard specifies 1.5 milligrams chloramine per liter of water; in other words 1.5 parts per million (ppm.).
    The Glendale water supply consists of a combination of water from the Los Angeles Metropolitan Water District (MWD) and water from the city's own wells. The MWD water already contains the standard amount of chloramine, but when it is mixed with the well water, it is diluted, and more chloramine must be added. Glendale drinking water was tested to see whether the city maintained consistent chloramine levels under these conditions.

EQUIPMENT AND PROCEDURES
    The equipment used was a colorimeter, a wet chemistry testing device. N,N-diethyl-p-phenylenediamine (DPD) was used as the reagent. This test is accurate to 0.05 ppm., and can measure chloramine levels from 0.1 to 2.0 ppm.

One milliliter samples of water were taken directly from a cold water tap at two locations in the city of Glendale. One location was a private home, and one was a business. Samples were taken at the same time on two different days.

Sample A: May 22 970 E. Glenoaks Blvd. (home)
Sample B: May 22 500 N. Brand Blvd. (business)
Sample C: May 23 970 E. Glenoaks Blvd.
Sample D: May 23 500 N. Brand Blvd.

RESULTS

Results are shown in Figure 1. The samples varied in chloramine content between 1 and 2 ppm. The variation between locations on the same day was 0.5 ppm. The average variation between samples taken on different days was 0.5 ppm.

Figure 1

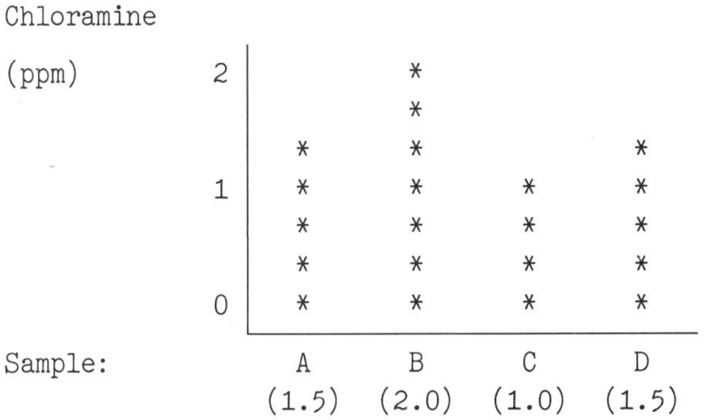

Chloramine

(ppm)   2 | *
               | *
               | *   *   *
             1 | *   *   *   *
               | *   *   *   *
               | *   *   *   *
             0 |_____*_____*_____*_____*____
Sample: A   B   C   D
                   (1.5) (2.0) (1.0) (1.5)

Average chloramine content May 22: 1.75 ppm.
Average chloramine content May 23: 1.25 ppm.

CONCLUSIONS AND DISCUSSION

On the days tested, chloramine content in Glendale drinking water varied between 1 and 2 ppm. At these levels, the water is disinfected without posing any danger to humans from chlorine exposure; however, 1 ppm. may be less effective in disinfecting water. Chloramine is also safe for most pets, such as dogs, cats and birds. This level of chloramine is toxic to fish, however, and appropriate measures should be taken to neutralize the chloramine by adding a reducing agent such as ascorbic acid to tap water before using it in fish tanks.

Final page:

Experimental Data

Sample A: 970 E. Glenoaks Blvd. (home)
        sample taken at 1:00 pm on May 22
        1 ml. cold tap water had 1.5 ppm. chloramine

Sample B: 500 N. Brand Blvd. (business)
        sample taken at 1:30 pm May 22
        1 ml. cold tap water had 2 ppm. chloramine

Sample C: 970 E. Glenoaks Blvd.
        sample taken at 1:00 pm May 23
        1 ml. cold tap water had 1 ppm. chloramine

```
Sample D: 500 N. Brand Blvd.
    sample taken at 1:30 pm May 23
    1 ml. cold tap water had 1.5 ppm. chloramine
```

Follow-up Exercise   Work in pairs or small groups. Exchange lab reports. Compare your reports on the following points, and discuss any differences.

1. *Data:* Did your classmate get the same temperature readings you did? How about the observations?
2. *Diagram:* Are the diagrams the same? Can different diagrams each represent the data accurately?
3. *Theory and Procedure:* Did you and your classmate(s) mention the same key points in this section?
4. *Conclusions and Discussion:* Did you reach the same conclusions?

WRITING: USING SCIENTIFIC EVIDENCE

Writing Topic

Many people take the world's present climate for granted, thinking that it has always been this way and expecting the climate to remain about the same in the future. Using evidence from research studies, show how climate has actually fluctuated widely in the past, and explain some of the causes of climatic change that will probably result in future climatic shifts.

Gathering Information

You will need to carefully review the reading passage and your lecture notes to find research evidence and causes of climatic change. Notice details such as who conducted each study and when and where the research was done. When writing the essay, be sure to describe the evidence in your own words. To ensure this, your teacher may require you to work from memory or notes when you write the essay, rather than letting you refer to the reading passage.

Narrowing the Topic

For this essay, narrowing the topic consists of choosing the best evidence to support your thesis. Several research studies are mentioned in this chapter. You need to select the studies that would be most persuasive for your essay; focusing on a few key studies will be more effective than briefly mentioning many studies. You will also need to choose the causes of climatic change that are most likely to have an effect on future climate. Some theories about the causes of climatic change are more widely accepted than others, and you will need to take this into consideration when deciding which causes to discuss.

Planning the Essay

In this kind of essay, you need to focus on expert sources, rather than relying on your own ideas. Your job is to organize the evidence so that it clearly supports your thesis. Following the general outline below, write an outline for your essay.

I. Introduction
State your thesis and briefly describe what kind of evidence you will use to support it. Define important terms such as "climate."

II. Body
A. Research evidence showing past climatic fluctuations. You will need to discuss each item of evidence with enough detail to satisfy a professor that you under-

stand the research and what it shows about climate. Mention the names of the researchers and the dates of each study. In order to be persuasive, you must relate each piece of evidence to your thesis or argument.

    B. Causes of climatic change likely to influence future climate. Based on your evidence, discuss the causes that you have selected in such a way that a professor can see that you understand the processes that change global climate. Explain how these causes are likely to continue to influence climate in the future.

III. Conclusion

Summarize your evidence and restate your thesis, showing how it is supported by the research.

Follow-up Exercise

Work with a classmate, exchanging essay drafts. Read your classmate's essay and discuss the following with him or her:

1. Find the sentence that states the thesis of the essay. Do you agree with the thesis? Why or why not?
2. What research evidence is used? Does it clearly support the thesis? Why or why not?
3. Are the causes used as an argument for future climatic changes convincing? Do the research studies cited support these causes? Why or why not?
4. Read the conclusion. Do you think a professor would like it? Why or why not?
5. What did you find was the most difficult part of this writing assignment?

Rewrite your essay, paying particular attention to using convincing arguments and evidence to support your thesis.

Climates Change, Communities Change

We grow used to the daily and seasonal changes in weather, and we view these changes as variations within a constant climate. Our faith in the constancy of climate may be shaken by observing that there are wet years and cold years, but we assume that over the long run the apparent deviations will all average out. This assumption of climatic constancy is completely wrong. One of the major themes to emerge from the last 30 years of scientific research is that climate changes on all time scales.

Evidence of changing climates comes from a variety of sources. Let us start with recent history in which we have a written record of change. Figure 9.1 shows a thousand years of temperature changes from Iceland. Thermometer data go back only 140 years in Iceland and before this one must rely on indirect evidence—reports of drift ice floating by the island. Drift ice is a thermometer of the North Atlantic. The earliest reports are from A.D. 825 when Irish monks visited Iceland and found no ice there even in winter. To reach pack ice they had to sail one day's journey to the north. There was no record of drift ice off Iceland for at least 400 years until the 1200s when severe winter pack ice moved south and cut off the old Norse colonies in Greenland, causing them to be abandoned. From about 1500 to 1900 the best years in Iceland were only as good as the worst years the Vikings had experienced during the tenth and eleventh centuries. From about 1890 to 1950 a great

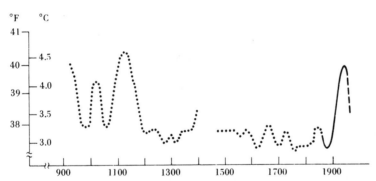

Figure 9.1 A thousand years of Icelandic temperatures. The dotted line shows estimated average temperatures (with the early part of the fifteenth century omitted because of insufficient data). The solid line shows temperatures based on thermometer readings. The dashed line shows the change in recent years for the Northern Hemisphere. (From Bryson and Murray 1977)

warming occurred, followed by a cooling during the last 25 years. A message clearly emerges from this Icelandic saga: *The climate of the present century is not typical of the previous thousand years.*

To extend our vision about climatic change back further, we can use pollen grains trapped in lake sediments. Pollen grains in sediments are fossils of older plant communities. Because different species of plants have pollen that differ in shape and size, ecologists can reconstruct plant communities back in time. In combination with radiocarbon dating of sediments, we can determine the timing of community changes over the globe.

Fossil pollen studies have proved successful at describing the sequence of plant communities over the past 30,000 years. Because of the Pleistocene ice sheets in the Northern Hemisphere, climatic and vegetational shifts occurred around the globe. Figure 9.3 shows the pollen record for

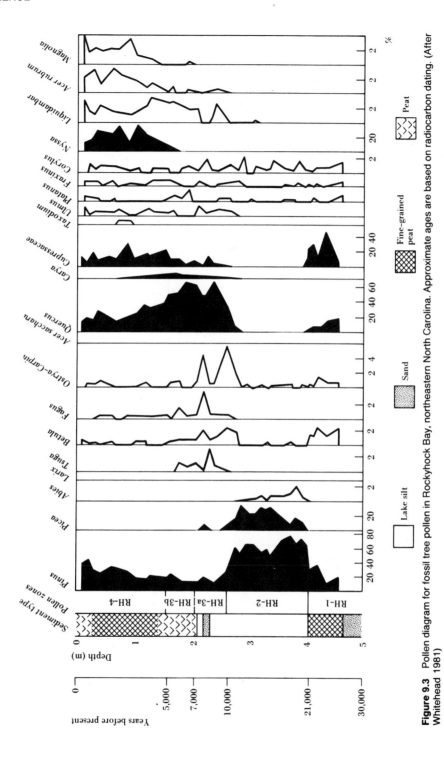

Figure 9.3 Pollen diagram for fossil tree pollen in Rockyhock Bay, northeastern North Carolina. Approximate ages are based on radiocarbon dating. (After Whitehead 1981)

Rockyhock Bay in North Carolina, an area of the eastern United States about 500 kilometers south of the line of maximal glacial advance. In this bay about 5 meters of sediment has been deposited over the past 30,000 years. From 30,000 to 21,000 years before the present (B.P.) temperate forests of oaks *(Quercus),* birches *(Betula),* and pines *(Pinus)* occupied the area. From 21,000 to 10,000 B.P. boreal forest was present, with spruce *(Picea)* and northern pines, and the climate was colder and drier than at present. Deciduous forests, with a predominance of oak, replaced the boreal forests about 10,000 B.P. Swamp forests began to develop about 7,000 B.P., featuring blackgum *(Nyassa),* cedar *(Cuppressaceae),* magnolia *(Magnolia),* and red maple *(Acer rubrum).* The swamp forests were essentially modern by 4,000 years ago.

Most of the plant and animal communities of the polar and temperate zones are still recovering from the last episode of Pleistocene glaciation that

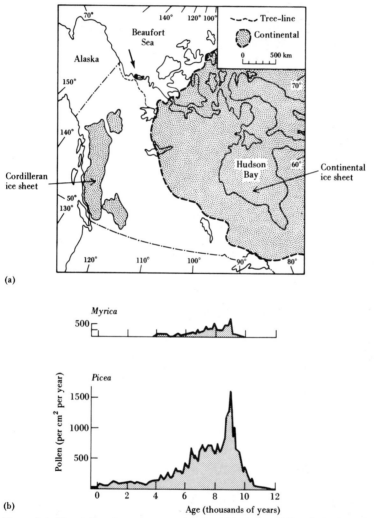

Figure 9.4 Vegetation changes at a tundra site. (a) Location of Sleet Lake (arrow) on the Tuktoyaktuk Peninsula of northwestern Canada. The map shows the approximate position of the large continental ice sheet and the smaller Cordilleran ice sheet 10,000 years ago. Ice sheets began to recede about 14,000 years ago. (b) Pollen deposition rates for two species of boreal forest plants from Sleet Lake. Spruce *(Picea)* forest occupied this site from about 10,000 to 6,000 years ago when the climate was warmer. Bog myrtle *(Myrica)* also occurred there during this period, but is now only found further south. (From Ritchie et al. 1983)

ended about 15,000 years ago. We can look for evidence of climatic fluctuations most easily at the tree line. The present polar limit of trees in northern Canada and Alaska has changed dramatically since the Ice Age ended and is still changing today. Figure 9.4 shows the changes in pollen rain for a small lake that is now surrounded by arctic tundra 70 kilometers north of the present tree line in the Northwest Territories of Canada. Since ice began receding about 14,000 years ago, this area has been occupied by tundra plants, then by boreal forest, and finally by tundra again. These changes have occurred because of slow but systematic changes in the amount of solar energy reaching the surface of the earth. In northern Canada there has been a general shift in the polar limits of trees, which were 200 to 300 kilometers farther north 1000 years ago than they are today.

Another technique employed to trace recent climatic fluctuations is the analysis of tree growth. Trees in the temperate and polar zones are particularly affected by how good the growing season is. Figure 9.5 illustrates how temperature variation from year to year affects the growth of bristlecone pine *(Pinus longaeva)* needles. Trees in the temperate and polar regions lay down annual layers of wood (seen as rings in a cross section). The better the

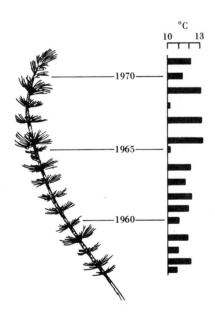

Figure 9.5 Needle length of bristlecone pine *(Pinus longaeva)* at the upper tree line in the White Mountains of California in relation to temperatures in the summer. Needle elongation takes place during the summer. Sequences of unusually cool or unusually warm summers could produce large fluctuations in the total photosynthetic area of a tree. Temperature data are July–August mean maximum temperatures. (From LaMarche 1974)

growing season, the more wood produced and the wider the rings (Figure 9.6). Soil moisture and temperature are both critical for tree growth, but as one approaches timberlines in mountainous regions, temperature becomes the most critical environmental factor affecting growth. By comparing sections of trees of different ages or by using old individual trees, scientists have been able to establish ring-width chronologies going back 8681 years. Much of this work

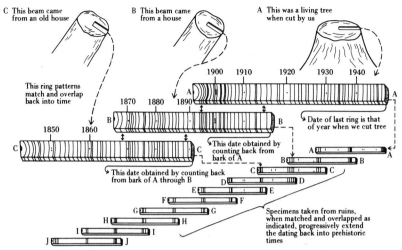

Figure 9.6   Tree-ring analysis. The diagram illustrates how cross-dating is done and how a dated tree-ring chronology is extended backward in time. (From Stallings 1949)

was pioneered at the Laboratory of Tree Ring Research at the University of Arizona founded by A. E. Douglass, who started his work in the early 1900s.

Bristlecone pine has been used extensively in tree-ring research because it grows very slowly near timberline in the mountains of California and thus serves as a good indicator of climate. Individual bristlecone pines may live more than 4600 years and are the oldest living trees. Near timberline, wide tree rings in this pine indicate warm summers and narrow tree rings indicate cool years. Figure 9.7 shows how average ring widths have varied in bristlecone pine during the last 5000 years. Clearly, there is a correlation between poor tree growth and glacier expansion and good tree growth and glacier contraction.

What consequences do these fluctuations in temperature have on animal and plant communities? We can see some of the best evidence on this point by looking at some prehistoric human sites. Stretching across the Great Plains of the United States are the remains of several hundred small Indian villages.

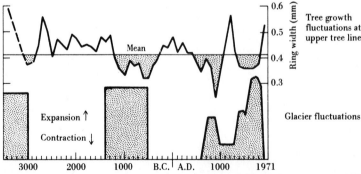

Figure 9.7   Relationship between tree-ring width and glacier fluctuations in the Northern Hemisphere. The upper graph gives the average ring widths of bristlecone pine *(Pinus longaeva)* in the White Mountains of California over the past 5300 years. The lower graph shows periods of expanding and contracting mountain glaciers over the same time period. There is a good correlation between periods of low summer temperatures and periods of growth and advance of glaciers. (From LaMarche 1978)

They were all abandoned by the time European explorers crossed the Great Plains in the sixteenth century. Indians in these villages planted corn in the summer and hunted during the winter. They were replaced by other Indian tribes that were nomadic hunters. What caused all these villages to be abandoned?

Several sites of ghost villages were excavated in northwestern Iowa in the 1930s and were called by archeologists the Mill Creek culture. This part of Iowa now averages 25 inches (63 centimeters) of rain a year, enough to produce good crops of corn and soybeans. But if a drought occurs and rainfall drops 25 percent, the corn crop fails. Is there any evidence that the Mill Creek culture disappeared because of climatic changes like a prolonged drought?

At the Mill Creek sites only a few inches of soil overlies material left by the Indian farmers. Archeologists found most of their informative material in the town dump—bones from animals, broken pottery, ashes from fires, and litter, along with pollen grains that drifted in.

The Mill Creek people ate many types of game animals from fishes and turtles to birds and mammals. Three of the larger animals are of particular interest. Deer and elk are browsing animals and depend on trees for much of

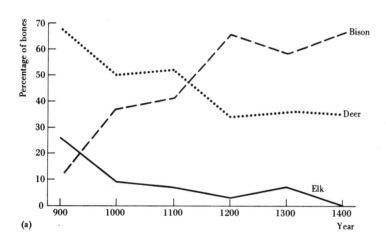

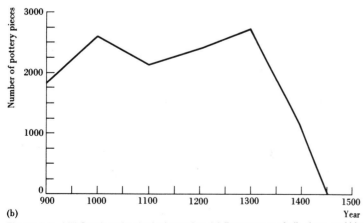

Figure 9.8 Mill Creek archeological remains. (a) Percentage of elk, deer, and bison bones found at one excavation site. (b) Number of pottery pieces found at the same site and used as an index of corn production. (From Bryson and Murray 1977)

their food. Bison are grazing animals characteristic of the short-grass prairies of the western Great Plains. Grasslands are favored by drought and woodlands by abundant rainfall. Consequently, these large mammals are types of climatic indicators. Figure 9.8 shows the proportions of deer, bison, and elk bones found at one Mill Creek excavation site. Older remains are predominately deer. After A.D. 1100 the percentage of deer bones dropped and bison came to predominate. But after 1100 the total number of bones also began to decrease, suggesting that hunting was becoming more difficult after the twelfth century.

As an index to corn production archeologists have used the number of pottery fragments in the deposits, since pottery must be used to store and cook corn. Figure 9.8 shows that the number of pottery fragments dropped off rapidly after 1300. By 1400 the Indians had vanished.

All the evidence from Mill Creek is consistent with the idea that drought, beginning about 1200, reduced both corn yield and game abundance and gradually caused these villages to be abandoned. We have here in all probability a thirteenth-century dust bowl.

Pollen samples from the sediments at the Mill Creek sites help to verify this interpretation. Before about 1200 the tree pollen was dominated by oaks; after that time willows came to predominate. Similar changes toward plants characteristic of drier communities occurred in the prairie plants. Aster and sunflower pollen decreased rapidly around 1200 and were replaced by grass pollen from drought-adapted grass species.

There are other suggestions of the collapse of Indian cultures in North America linked with climatic changes. In southern Illinois, just east of St. Louis, stood a major population center of Indians around A.D. 1000. Within a 10-kilometer radius there were many settlements like the one now called Cahokia, which had a population of perhaps 40,000. By the time European explorers arrived, these Indians were all gone. They left an impressive array of mounds. One, Monks Mound, covers an area 300 by 200 meters and is 30 meters high. The labor that went into such mound building shows that these Indians were highly organized and successful.

The Indians who lived at Cahokia grew corn on the floodplain of the Mississippi River. Beginning about A.D. 600 Cahokia grew for 600 to 700 years and then suddenly began to decline after 1200. No one knows why the mound builders of Cahokia disappeared. Perhaps the drought that made Mill Creek uninhabitable also reached into Illinois. Figure 9.9 shows that years of drought in this century follow a geographical pattern consistent with this explanation—a finger of drought reaches over Cahokia.

The Mill Creek farmers and the Cahokia people were not victims of short-term droughts such as we now see in Africa. The changed climate that brought about the collapse of the Indian corn farmers of the Great Plains lasted for about 200 years from 1200 to 1400. After that time the pattern switched back and the rains returned, but by then the people were gone and their culture lost. Both the Mill Creek and the Cahokia settlements were in existence for a time period longer than the United States has existed.

The historical record from Europe and Asia contains many more examples of how humans have been affected by changing climate. Most of these effects have been described for terrestrial ecosystems. Let us look at one recent

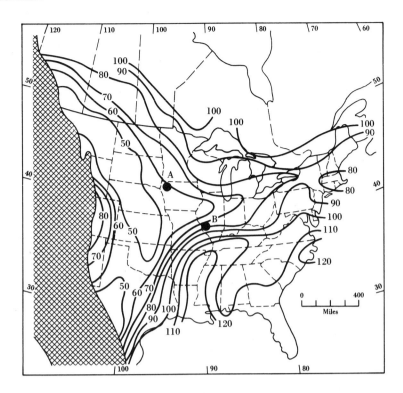

Figure 9.9 Percentage of normal rainfall in average July of major drought years of the 1930s. Note the fingerlike extension of the major drought area into northern Illinois and Indiana to include the Mill Creek sites (A) and the Cahokia sites (B). (Modified from Borchert 1950)

example of a large-scale change in an oceanic ecosystem that has been studied for a long time, the English Channel.

The western part of the English Channel off Plymouth has been studied for more than 75 years and illustrates on a large scale the changes in production and community structure that can occur in aquatic ecosystems. The series of changes that began in the 1920s have now reversed so that a complete cycle can be described. It is called the *Russell cycle* after its principal investigator, the English biologist F. S. Russell.

The complex series of ecosystem changes that make up the Russell cycle can be summarized as follows. A plankton community dominated by the chaetognath *Sagitta elegans* was replaced during the 1930s by one dominated by *Sagitta setosa* (Figure 9.10a).[1] At the same time there was a

---

[1]Chaetognaths, or arrow worms, are small invertebrates, 1 to 10 millimeters long, that are one of the larger species in the plankton community of the oceans. They feed on smaller crustaceans in the plankton (see Figure 6.3).

drop in the dissolved phosphate concentration of the seawater. Phosphate is a critical nutrient for phytoplankton in the spring. The abundance of zooplankton dropped at the same time, and the numbers of young fish in the plankton fell dramatically (Figure 9.10c). Herring, which feed on plankton, decreased, and pilchard replaced herring as the dominant pelagic fish in the English Channel (Figure 9.10b). During the 1970s the cycle reversed. *Sagitta elegans* returned to the plankton, pilchard declined, and larval fish became abundant in the plankton. The net result was that by 1980 the English Channel had returned to a stage approximately like that of the 1920s.

What caused the Russell cycle? Three major hypotheses have been suggested to explain these ecosystem changes: (1) nutrient control, (2) competition, and (3) climatic changes.

The nutrient control hypothesis explains these changes by variations in the flow of deeper oceanic water into the English Channel from the west. An influx of deeper ocean water would increase the amount of critical inorganic nutrients such as phosphate that limit primary production. This theory has been rejected because no change in primary production was measured during the reversal of the cycle from 1964 to 1974, when phosphate levels increased. Also, variations in oceanic currents are usually produced by climatic changes, and any correlation with nutrient changes may thus be secondary effects of climate.

The competition hypothesis states that the community in the English Channel can exist in two alternate stable states—a *Sagitta elegans*–herring community and a *Sagitta setosa*–pilchard community. Pilchard were able to exclude herring and assume dominance in the 1930s, possibly aided by overfishing on herring, according to this hypothesis. But pilchard have now been replaced by mackerel, and herring are still scarce, and the decline of the pilchard cannot be due to overfishing. The competition hypothesis does not explain the changes shown in Figure 9.10 convincingly.

The climatic change hypothesis is generally agreed to be the underlying explanation of the Russell cycle. Figure 9.11 shows the average change in sea surface temperature in the English Channel since 1924. A distinct warming and then cooling trend is seen, which correlates with a general pattern of climatic fluctuation that has been measured in the Northern Hemisphere (see Figure 9.1). Rises and falls in sea temperature may result in sudden switches in the ecosystem at a faunal boundary. Herring, for example, is a cold-water fish near the southern edge of its distribution in the English Channel. Pilchard is a warm-temperate species close to its northern limit. The changes over the Russell cycle are broadly consistent with a temperature control hypothesis, and the apparent stability of marine ecosystems over a short span of years may in fact be part of a long cycle of dynamic change.

One other important aspect of the Russell cycle is the apparent disparity between the biological fluctuations and the physical-chemical changes. Sea temperature has changed only 0.5°C, and phosphate less than 25 percent. But this has resulted in the virtual disappearance of some zooplankton and fish species and a 10-fold change in populations of others. The impact of climatic change on ecosystems cannot be judged by the size of the temperature shift. Small changes may produce enormous effects in ecosystem structure and function.

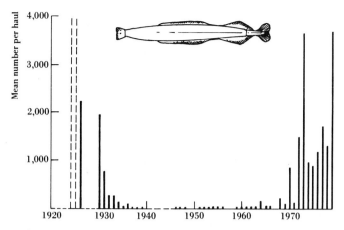

(a) *Sagitta elegans*

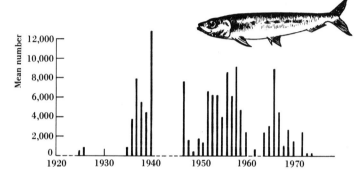

(b) Pilchard eggs

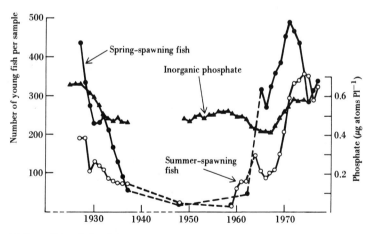

(c) Young fish and phosphate

Figure 9.10 Some of the biological changes in the Russell cycle of the English Channel. These data, taken off Plymouth, are based on weekly sampling near the Eddystone reef. (a) Numbers of the chaetognath *Sagitta elegans* in 5000 cubic meters of water during the summer months. (b) Number of pilchard *(Sardina pilchardus)* eggs per 2-meter net haul during the spawning season. The number of eggs is assumed to be an index of the number of adult pilchards. (c) Mean amount of inorganic phosphate in winter and mean number of small fish in a 2-meter net sample. The small fish are divided into spring spawners and summer spawners. (After Southward 1980)

It is important to remember at this point that not all the changes that occur in biological communities are due to climatic changes. For example, since detailed observations began around 1850, many birds have extended their geographical ranges in northern Europe. The bird communities in southern Finland, for example, contain more species now than they did in the last century. Most of this colonization is not due to climatic amelioration, but to habitat changes resulting from agriculture and forestry. If there has been a climatic component to bird distributional changes during the last few years, it has been dwarfed by the effects that humans have had on the landscape.

One of the difficulties of thinking about climatic changes is that climatic trends show up slowly and we cannot predict the future well. Figure 9.12

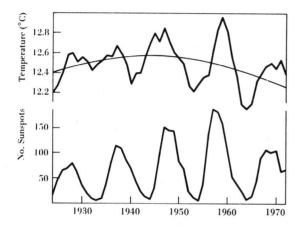

Figure 9.11   Average sea surface temperature in the English Channel compared with mean annual sunspot numbers. The 11-year cycle in sunspot numbers is reflected in sea surface temperatures, but superimposed on this is a global trend in temperature shown by the smooth curve. (After Southward et al. 1975)

shows generalized temperature curves for the Northern Hemisphere, and helps to put the present climate in perspective. Most of the last 150,000 years has been occupied by a glacial period, and to find a time as warm as the last few years, we have to go back about 125,000 years to the last interglacial period.

After the end of the last ice age, about 15,000 years ago, global temperatures began to rise rapidly and during the last 10,000 years they have fluctuated irregularly. We are in an interglacial period. In the past interglacials have occurred about once in every 100,000 years and each has lasted 8,000 to 12,000 years. The present interglacial has already gone on for about 11,000 years.

One thing about climate is certain—the climate we think of as "normal" and the weather office calls "normal" is not typical of the last 1000 years and is much less typical of the last million years. Since 1945 the Northern Hemisphere has cooled about 0.6°C (1°F). Cooling could continue, or temperatures could reverse again. It is impossible to predict which.

Why do climates change? The sun generates our climate, and one possible cause of climatic change could be a change in the output from the sun. The sun does fluctuate in output, as the 11-year sunspot cycle shows (see Figure 9.11), but a changing sun does not seem to be the main cause of climatic changes. A major cause of climatic change is the way the earth's orbit shifts around the sun. The average distance of the earth from the sun varies somewhat, as does the shape of the earth's orbit. And the earth also wobbles slightly on its axis. These orbit variations change regularly in cycles over thousands of years; for example, one complete wobble of the earth's tilt takes 40,000 years. A Yugoslav mathematician, M. Milankovitch, calculated these variations in 1920 and produced a model that correlated the past ice ages with the earth's orbit changes. His calculations match up well with the general pattern of the ice ages, and if his predictions are correct, a new ice age will begin within a few thousand years. These changes in the earth's position relative to the sun are now believed to be the major cause of climatic change.

But there are other ways of changing climate as well. Anything in the air that can affect the net amount of the sun's energy that the earth receives is a potential source for climatic change. Two substances are of major concern, *dust* and *carbon dioxide*.

The concentration of carbon dioxide has increased about 10 percent during the last 80 years because of human activity—burning coal, oil, and wood. Carbon dioxide in the air produces a "greenhouse effect" on the earth. It allows radiation from the sun to reach the earth, but prevents the back radiation of heat, so that the net effect is that the earth is warmed, but the upper atmosphere is cooled.

Dust changes the reflectivity of the atmosphere. It reflects back the sunlight before it reaches the earth's surface and so reduces the mean temperature. Dust ejected from volcanoes has for centuries been recognized as a cause of cold climates. In 1815 a volcanic eruption at Tambora in Indonesia ejected a veil of dust into the upper atmosphere that made 1816 famous as the year that had no summer. Throughout Europe and the United States temperatures averaged 1°C below normal, and some areas had almost continuous rainfall all summer. Crops were killed by frost or failed to ripen. Riots over food occurred in Wales and Ireland.

Volcanic eruptions may have a short-term effect on climate, but they cannot explain major climatic changes. They are important to us because they

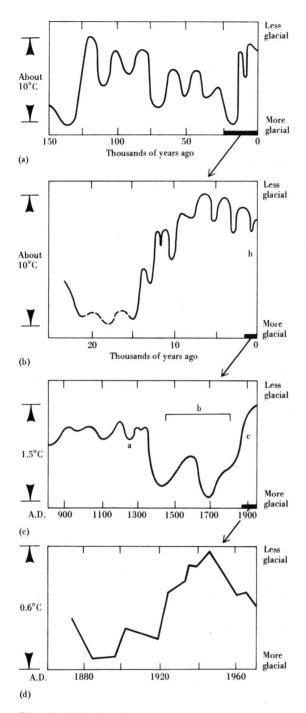

Figure 9.12   Northern Hemisphere temperatures for the past 150,000 years with more detail for recent years. (a) The last 150,000 years as indicated by marine deposits, pollen records, and shoreline changes. (b) The last 25,000 years as indicated by tree rings, pollen records, and glacier records. (c) The last 1,000 years. a, Mill Creek cooling; b, Little Ice Age; c, early twentieth-century warming. (d) The last 100 years, showing the cooling that has occurred since 1950. (From Bryson and Murray 1977)

alert us to the significance of dust to climate. Dust comes from many sources other than volcanoes—industrial smokestacks, wind erosion, and fires. Dust generated by human activities may have an impact on future climatic changes. But there is considerable disagreement on what effect an increase in dust from human activities can do to our global climate. The net effect of dust is to cool, and the net effect of carbon dioxide and greenhouse gases is to warm. Which of these two contrasting effects will predominate in the next 200 years? There is some suggestion that dust is currently winning, and the cooling we have seen since 1950 is a direct result of the increase in dust since 1940. If this is correct, our impact on climate could be the unhappy one of accelerating our return to the ice age. Alternatively, if the greenhouse effect predominates, our climate will warm, and sea level will rise from the melting of the polar ice sheets. Coastal cities would be affected within 50 years if this occurs. Climatic changes caused by human activity will be one of the major problems of the twenty-first century.

To summarize: Biological communities depend on climate, and as climate changes, so must communities. Climatic change may be slow and communities may change gradually, or change may be rapid. Since the last ice age ended, temperate and polar zone animals and plants are still colonizing and recovering in the areas affected by glaciation. Animal and plant communities are never in equilibrium with climate because climate is always changing. We should therefore not view either our present communities or our present climates as constant and everlasting. They are but one frame in a motion picture that never slows. We can see clearly the changes of the past, and they must help us to anticipate the changes the future will certainly bring.

Appendix

A

Word Roots, Prefixes, and Suffixes

Root	Meaning	Example
1. agr	field	agriculture
2. ann, enn	year	annual
3. anthrop	human	anthropology
4. aqua	water	aquarium
5. astro, aster	star	astronomy
6. audi	hear	audience
7. bibli	book	bibliography
8. bio	life	biological
9. capit	head	decapitate
10. celer	fast	decelerate
11. chron	time	chronological
12. clud, clus	close, shut	exclude
13. cosm	world	cosmos
14. crat	rule	autocrat
15. cred	believe	incredible
16. cur, course	run	cursive
17. demo	people	democracy
18. dict	speak	valedictorian
19. duc	lead	conductor
20. fac, fic, fect	make, do	factory
21. flect, flex	bend	reflection
22. frater	brother	fraternity
23. fund, fus	pour	refund
24. gen	race, birth	genetic
25. geo	earth	geography

Root	Meaning	Example
26. gloss, glot	language, tongue	glossary
27. gram, graph	write	grammar
28. gress, grad	step	graduate
29. hydr	water	dehydrate
30. jac, ject	throw	reject
31. jud	judge	judiciary
32. lect, leg, lig	choose, gather	select
33. log	word	monologue
34. loqu, loc	speak	eloquent
35. luc	light	lucid
36. manu	hand	manufacture
37. mar	sea	marine
38. mater	mother	maternity
39. med	middle	mediate
40. min	less, little	minimum
41. mit, miss	send	manumission
42. mort	death	mortal
43. naut	sail	cosmonaut
44. neo	new	neoclassic
45. neuro	nerve	neurosis
46. nomin, nomen	name	nominate
47. nom	law, order	astronomy
48. pater	father	paternal
49. path	feeling, suffering, disease	pathological
50. ped, pod, pus	foot	quadruped
51. pend	hang, weigh	suspend
52. phil	love	philanthropist
53. phob	fear	claustrophobia
54. phon	sound	microphone
55. phot, phos	light	photon
56. plex, plic	fold	application
57. poli	city, state	metropolis
58. poly	many	monopoly
59. port	carry	export
60. pon, pos	place, put	postpone

Root	Meaning	Example
61. psych	mind	psychology
62. reg, rect	rule, right	regulation
63. rupt	break	interrupt
64. scop	look	microscope
65. scrib, script	write	description
66. sens, sent	feel	sensation
67. soph	wise	philosophy
68. spec, spic	look	spectator
69. tact, tang	touch	tactful
70. tend, tens, tent	stretch	tension
71. therm	heat	thermometer
72. typ	image, impression	typical
73. vac	empty	vacuum
74. ven	come	convene
75. vid, vis	see	video
76. vita, viv	life	vitality
77. voc, voke	call	equivocation
78. vor	eat	herbivore

Prefix

79. a-, an-	not, without	apolitical
80. ab-	away from	abnormal
81. ante-	before, in front	antebellum
82. anti-	against, opposite	antisocial
83. arch-	first	architect
84. auto-	self	automatic
85. bene-	well, good	benefit
86. bi-	two	bicycle
87. circum-	around	circumnavigate
88. co-, con-, col-, cor-	with	congress college
89. contra-, counter-	against, opposite	counterclockwise
90. de-	not, away, down	descend
91. dis-, di-, dif-	apart, away, not	disagree
92. e-, ex-	out, away	exhale
93. extra-	outside, beyond	extracurricular

Root	Meaning	Example
94. hetero-	other, different	heterosexual
95. homo-	same	homonym
96. hyper-	above	hypertension
97. hypo-	under	hypodermic
98. il-, in-, im- ir-	not	improper irrational
99. inter-	between	interpersonal
100. intra-	within	intramural
101. mal-	bad, ill, wrong	malformed
102. mega-	large, one million	megabyte
103. micro-	small	microscopic
104. mis-	bad, badly	misunderstand
105. mono-	one, alone	monogram
106. non-	not	nonmaterial
107. peri-	around	peripheral
108. poly-	many	polygamy
109. post-	after	postgraduate
110. pre-	before	prerequisite
111. pro-	forward, before	promote
112. re-	back, again	return
113. retro-	backwards	retroactive
114. se-	apart	secede
115. semi-	half	semiautomatic
116. sub-, suc-, suf-, sug-,	under	submarine suggest
117. super-, sur-	over	supervision
118. syn-, syl-, sym-, sys-,	together	synchronize sympathy
119. tele-	distant	telephone
120. trans-	across	transcendence
121. ultra-, outr-	beyond, excessive	ultraconservative
122. un-	not	unauthorized
123. uni-	one	universe
124. vice-	taking the place	vice president

Root	Meaning	Example
Suffix		
For Nouns		
125. -an, -ian	of, belonging to	American
126. -ant, ent	one who, that which	servant
-ar, -ary		revolutionary
-eer, -er		musketeer
-ess, -ist		bigamist
-or		senator
127. -ance, ence	act, quality	independence
128. -ancy, -ency	state of	infancy
129. -ary, -arium	place where	aviary
-ory, -orium		laboratory
130. -ation	action, institution	nullification
131. -cide	kill	homicide
132. -dom	state, quality	freedom
133. -ee	one who (passive)	employee
134. -hood, -ness	state, quality	hardiness
135. -ion, -tion,	state, quality, act	precision
-ity		civility
136. -ism	quality, doctrine	socialism
137. -logy, -ology	discourse, study	sociology
138. -ment	act, state	commitment
139. -ship	state, quality	kinship
For Adjectives		
140. -able, -ible	able to be	divisible
141. -ac, -al, -an,	like, related to	maniac
-ar, -ative,		stellar
-en, -ent, -ic,		idiotic
-ish, -ive,		directive
-ose, -ous,		comatose
-ious		ambitious
142. -ful	having	plentiful
143. -less	without	helpless
144. -ly	having the quality of	gentlemanly

Root	Meaning	Example
For Adverbs		
145. -ly	in the manner of	courageously
146. -ward(s)	toward	upward
147. -wise	in the manner of	counterclockwise
For Verbs		
148. -ate, -ify	to make, act	nullify
149. -en	make	broaden
150. -ise, -ize	make, act	socialize

References

Claiborne, Robert. *The Roots of English: A Reader's Handbook of Word Origins.* New York: Times Books-Random House, 1989.

Oxford American Dictionary. 1980 ed.

Smith, Robert W. L. *Dictionary of English Word-Roots.* Totowa, New Jersey: Littlefield, Adams & Co., 1966.

Appendix

B

Guide to Writing a Research Paper

THE RESEARCH PAPER: SOME GENERAL GUIDELINES

Subject

College research papers usually answer a *question* or discuss a *problem*. Most often, this is an original question developed by the student that falls within general guidelines set by the instructor. Reports that are merely descriptive or biographical are not as common as reports that address a problem.

The object of most research is for the student to study the literature of a particular subject in depth in order to apply the information to a problem and come up with an original recommendation or conclusion. Freshman research reports generally involve *library* research, not experimental research.

Length

The average length for a freshman-level paper is about 10 typewritten, double-spaced pages. One typewritten double-spaced page equals about two handwritten single-spaced pages, more or less, depending on the size of your handwriting.

Parts

1. Title Page
2. Outline or Table of Contents (not always required)
3. Introduction (about 1/5 of total report)
4. Body (starting on a new page with a separate title)
5. Conclusion (about 1/5 of report, again starting on a new page with title)
6. Endnotes (on a separate page with title)
7. Bibliography (on a separate page with title)

Drawings, charts, and graphs can be included and are placed on the page immediately after the place where they are discussed in the report.

Timing

Expect library research, reading, and taking notes to use up about one-half to two-thirds of the total time allowed to prepare the report.

In order to calculate how much homework time a report represents, you need to allow at least 1 hour per finished page of the report, and most new college students spend 2 to 3 hours per finished page. This rule of thumb applies to the time from start to finish, including planning, library work, reading, writing a first draft, and polishing the final draft of the report. Typing it will require additional time (up to one hour per page for an inexperienced typist).

Amount of Research Needed

Plan to have a minimum of three research notes for each page of the report; more is better.

SAMPLE SCHEDULE FOR A RESEARCH PAPER

This sample schedule is an approximation for college undergraduates. Graduate students are often expected to complete class research papers in a shorter time (sometimes only 2 or 3 weeks!).

1. Choose and narrow a topic, write a preliminary plan, check it with teacher.	1 week
2. Go to library, begin collecting sources.	1 week
3. Read sources, make note cards.	1 week
4. Organize note cards, make detailed outline.	1 week
5. Write rough draft, check with teacher.	1 week
6. Type final draft, hand in report.	1 week
Total time to complete the report:	6 weeks

Exact Schedule

Fill in the blanks with dates based on your teacher's recommendations (or your own plan, if your teacher does not give you a schedule).

Stage of the Report	Date to Be Completed
1. Topic and preliminary outline	_____
2. Sources	_____
3. Note cards	_____
4. Detailed outline	_____
5. Rough draft	_____
6. Final report	_____

Note: It is a good idea to check your topic, outline, and rough draft with your teacher, even if this is not required. In this way you can avoid the possibility of making time-consuming mistakes.

CHOOSING A TOPIC FOR RESEARCH

Choose a topic from one of the general areas covered in this course, from your major, or your teacher may assign a topic. There are many possible topics within each of the following general areas.

Higher Education in the United States

Culture

Psychology

U.S. History/Government

Health

English Communication

Sociology

Technology

Business

Natural Science

Hints on Choosing a Topic

Choose a topic. . .

1. directly related to your college major.
2. that you already know something about.
3. that is currently in the news.
4. that you like or want to know more about.

Don't choose a topic. . .

1. that is very technical (unless you already know a great deal about the subject).
2. that is highly focused on another country (you may not find information about it).
3. that you know nothing about (you may find it too difficult).
4. that doesn't interest you.

Brainstorming

Brainstorming is a popular way of getting ideas. It is not only used in school but also in businesses.

1. On a separate sheet of paper, write as many specific ideas for a research paper as possible. Don't worry if they sound silly or unworkable; just write down any ideas you have.
2. Share your ideas in groups of three or four. Add to your list any new ideas that you get.
3. Choose one idea that you think would be good for your research paper.

Write your idea for a topic here:

_____

PLANNING THE RESEARCH PAPER

After you choose your topic, you need to narrow it down. An easy way to do this is to write a question about your topic and limit your report to answering that question.

Write your question here:

_____

Next, you need a plan for your report, so that you know what information you need to find in the library. The plan consists of a subtopic for the introduction, one for the body, and one for the conclusion. The topic for the body is usually the same as the title of your report. Fill in the outline below with your plan. This plan will be modified as you do your research.

   I. (Introduction) _____

  II. (Body) _____

III. (Conclusion) _____

Very often, the body of a report will be divided into sections. For a report of average size, three sections would be about right. Plan the sections to be included in the body:

II. _____

    A. _____

    B. _____

    C. _____

USING THE INTERVIEW AS A RESEARCH TOOL

A good way to get started on a research paper is to talk to someone who is knowledgeable about your research topic. A teacher of the subject would be a good person to interview, for instance. You can get some basic information about your subject, and the person may even be able to recommend some sources to look for in the library. If you use an interview for part of your research, the following are some guidelines.

1. Choose someone who knows about your topic.
2. Contact the person and make an appointment for the interview. Start this step as soon as possible, because some people are difficult to reach and have busy schedules.
3. Plan your questions and write them down before going to the interview. Some useful questions include:
   a. What do you feel are the most important aspects of . . . (the topic)?
   b. What background information is needed to get a better understanding of . . . (the topic)?
   c. Can you recommend any references for more information on this subject?
4. Arrive at the interview on time, and dress appropriately. Use your best manners. You will get a more helpful response from the person you interview if you show respect for his or her expertise.
5. Ask your planned questions, and take notes on the answers. You may wish to tape-record the interview, but if you do, you must ask permission first.
6. Don't allow the interview to go on too long. About one hour is the maximum interview time, and a shorter time is probably better. Be sure to thank the person for his or her time and help when you end the interview.
7. In your interview notes, include the date, time, person's name, and position. This information is needed when you write the endnotes and bibliography.

USING THE LIBRARY

You will probably be doing most of your research in the library. This section will introduce you to the most commonly used library resources: encyclopedias, periodicals (magazines), and books.

There are many other library resources, such as newspapers, government publications, and technical journals, to name a few. When you work in the library, don't hesitate to ask the librarian for help in using these and other resources.

Using Encyclopedias

Almost every library has a set of general encyclopedias. These books have short articles giving basic information about a variety of subjects. The encyclopedia should be one of the first places you look to find general or background information for your research paper. Not only will you find important terms and different aspects of your topic, but some encyclopedia entries also include a bibliography (a list of other books or articles to read for more information).

Exercise   Visit your local school or city library. Find information about your research topic in the encyclopedia. To do this, check the index, usually the last volume of the encyclopedia. The index will list the encyclopedia volume and page number where information about a topic can be found. Look for your topic, and you will probably also find other related topics listed. These related topics can help you focus your research if you are not sure about your exact topic yet.

When you find information about your topic, check it quickly to be sure it is what you need. Then make a photocopy of it. Write the encyclopedia title, edition, volume, and title of entry on the back of the photocopy. In junior high and high schools, this information can be used when you write your research endnotes and bibliography. In college, many teachers forbid using encyclopedias as bibliographic entries, but they are still a useful starting place for your research.

Periodicals: *The Readers' Guide*

The Readers' Guide is an index of articles published in the major periodicals (magazines and journals) in the United States. It can be found in most larger libraries, and is an important tool to use when doing general academic research. If you want up-to-date information on a subject—for example, U.S. policy on space weapons—the *Readers' Guide* will have a list of articles written on the topic.

Technical information, however, such as the latest developments in computer engineering, cannot generally be found by using the *Readers' Guide*. There are technical indexes for each field that list articles published in scientific and professional journals. These can be found in most university libraries. If you are majoring in a technical field, you should familiarize yourself with these special indexes. The librarian can help you.

Exercise   Use the sample *Readers' Guide* page to answer the following questions. A list of common abbreviations and an explanation of a typical entry are included for reference.

1. What is one main subject heading found on this page?
2. What is the subheading under the heading "Art, Modern"?
3. Find the article about the high cost of museum exhibitions.
   a. What is the title?
   b. Who is the author?
   c. In which periodical is it published?
   d. What issue?
   e. On what page will you find the article?
4. Under what other heading can you find information about Art Nouveau?
5. Pretend you are writing a report about Native American art. Which article(s) might be useful?
6. The article entry about artistry in metal includes the letters "bibl." What does this mean? Why might it be useful?
7. Each volume of the *Readers' Guide* is for a particular year. The volume that the sample page is from is for which year? How do you know?

The Card Catalog

You may wish to use books as you do your research. Books are especially useful for background and general information, but usually libraries do not have the most up-to-date ones. For this reason, it is wise not to rely only on books when preparing a research paper.

ART, EUROPEAN—*cont.*
Exhibitions
See also
Royal Ontario Museum. Samuel European Galleries
ART, HISPANIC AMERICAN
Exhibitions
See also
Museum of International Folk Art (Santa Fe, N.M.).
Hispanic Heritage Wing
ART, INDIAN (AMERICAN) *See* Indians of North America—Art
ART, ISRAELI
Exhibitions
In the shadow of conflict: Israeli art 1980-1989: Jewish
Museum. H. A. Weinberg. il *Art News* 88:205 O '89
Romancing the stones. M. Ronnen. il *Art News* 88:224
O '89
ART, JEWISH
See also
Art, Israeli
ART, LATIN AMERICAN
See also
Art, Pre-Columbian
ART, MODERN
See also
Art deco
Cubism
Impressionism (Art)
Performance art
Exhibitions
See also
Canadian Biennial of Contemporary Art
Instituto Valenciano de Arte Moderno (Spain)
Magiciens de la Terre (Exhibition)
Museum of Modern Art (New York, N.Y.)
The '80s: stop making sense [Los Angeles Museum of
Contemporary Art's exhibition A forest of signs; cover
story] H. Drohojowska. il *Art News* 88:146-51 O '89
In the shadow of conflict: Israeli art 1980-1989: Jewish
Museum. H. A. Weinberg. il *Art News* 88:205 O '89
Moscow and the Hudson [exhibition of American painting
in Moscow] K. Larson. il *New York* 22:79-80 O 16
'89
ART, PRE-COLUMBIAN
Rightful owners [court decisions involving Cypriot mosaics
and Peruvian pre-Columbian art] R. W. Walker and
L. Nilson. il *Art News* 88:51+ O '89
ART, PRIMITIVE
See also
Art, Pre-Columbian
ART, VICTORIAN
See also
Pre-Raphaelites
ART AND ARCHITECTURE
The great outdoors. M. Malone. il *Newsweek* 114:76+
O 23 '89
ART AND CHILDREN
See also
Children's art
ART AND INDUSTRY
See also
Advertising art
ART AND MASS MEDIA *See* Mass media and art
ART AND PHOTOGRAPHY
See also
Photography, Artistic
ART AND SCIENCE
See also
Chaos (Science) in art
Images of pain: headache art lends a hand to science
[cover story] I. Wickelgren. il *Science News* 136:136-7
Ag 26 '89
ART AND STATE
See also
National Endowment for the Arts
Public art
Austria
Double departure [resignation of directors] F. Protzman.
Art News 88:77 O '89
ART APPRECIATION *See* Art—Appreciation
ART AS A PROFESSION
He upped and quit [sculptor P. Tadlock] W. P. Barrett.
il pors *Forbes* 144:282+ O 16 '89
ART CENTERS
Ohio
See also
Wexner Center for the Visual Arts (Columbus, Ohio)
ART DECO
Think architecture is boring? Take a shot at Miami
Beach's art deco district. L. Dennis. il *Popular
Photography* 96:32-3 O '89

ART EXHIBITIONS *See* Art—Exhibitions
ART FAIRS *See* Art—Exhibitions
ART GALLERIES AND MUSEUMS
Acquisitions
Unanswered questions [Museum of Modern Art's private
deal to obtain van Gogh's Portrait of Joseph Roulin]
T. McGhee. il *Art News* 88:56+ O '89
Architecture
Kimbell times two [addition designed by R. Giurgola]
J. Kutner. il *Art News* 88:56 O '89
Museum roof as flying carpet [Newport Beach Art
Museum] il *Architectural Record* 177:53 O '89
Finance
Will high costs curtail museum exhibitions? D. Grant.
il *American Artist* 53:10+ O '89
Austria
See also
Kunsthistorisches Museum (Vienna, Austria)
Museum Moderner Kunst (Vienna, Austria)
California
See also
Newport Harbor Art Museum (Newport Beach, Calif.)
Connecticut
See also
Yale University. Art Gallery
New Mexico
See also
Museum of International Folk Art (Santa Fe, N.M.)
New York (State)
See also
Galerie St. Etienne
Metropolitan Museum of Art (New York, N.Y.)
Whitney Museum of American Art
Ontario
See also
Thomson Gallery (Toronto, Ont.)
Rhode Island
See also
Redwood Library and Athenaeum (Newport, R.I.)
Spain
See also
Instituto Valenciano de Arte Moderno (Spain)
Texas
See also
Kimbell Art Museum
ART HISTORIANS
See also
Daulte, François, 1928-
ART IN THE HOME
Honoring their Cherokee heritage [Kay and Ron Hendricks' log house in north Georgia] C. Engle. il *Southern
Living* 24:90-2 O '89
ART MARKET *See* Art trade
ART METAL WORK
Dirk van Erp: artistry in metal. B. E. Johnson. bibl
f il *Antiques & Collecting Hobbies* 94:32-3+ O '89
ART MUSEUMS *See* Art galleries and museums
ART NOUVEAU
See also
Art deco
ART OBJECTS
See also
Art in the home
ART OF LIVING *See* Conduct of life
ART PATRONAGE
The Force behind the Whitney [J. Force] A. Berman.
il pors *American Heritage* 40:102-13 S/O '89
ART SALES *See* Art trade
ART SHOWS *See* Art—Exhibitions
ART THEFTS
Litigators of the lost art [Cypriot mosaics] S. Mannheimer.
il *The Saturday Evening Post* 261:62-8 O '89
ART TRADE
See also
Art galleries and museums
Ethical aspects
Litigators of the lost art [Cypriot mosaics] S. Mannheimer.
il *The Saturday Evening Post* 261:62-8 O '89
Rightful owners [court decisions involving Cypriot mosaics
and Peruvian pre-Columbian art] R. W. Walker and
L. Nilson. il *Art News* 88:51+ O '89
ART TREASURES, PROTECTION OF *See* Cultural
property—Protection
ARTERIES
Diseases
See also
Arteriosclerosis
Therapy
See also
Blood vessels—Surgery

Figure B.1. Sample Page

ABBREVIATIONS

+	continued on later pages of same issue	Ltd	Limited
		m	monthly
Ag	August	Mr	March
ann	annual	My	May
Ap	April		
Assn	Association	N	November
Aut	Autumn	no	number
Ave	Avenue		
		O	October
bi-m	bimonthly		
bi-w	biweekly	p	page
bibl	bibliography	por	portrait
bibl f	bibliographical footnotes	pt	part
bldg	building		
		q	quarterly
Co	Company		
cont	continued	rev	revised
Corp	Corporation		
		S	September
D	December	semi-m	semimonthly
Dept	Department	Spr	Spring
		Sr	Senior
ed	edited, edition, editor	St	Street
		Summ	Summer
F	February	supp	supplement
f	footnotes		
		tr	translated, translation, translator
il	illustration,-s		
Inc	Incorporated	v	volume
introd	introduction, introductory		
		w	weekly
Ja	January	Wint	Winter
Je	June		
Jl	July	yr	year
Jr	Junior		
jt auth	joint author		

For those unfamiliar with forms of reference used in the entries, the following explanation is given.

Sample subject entry:	**Horse racing** A woman of substance [jockey J. Krone] G. Maranto. il pors *Sports Illus* 67:62+ Ag 24 '87
Explanation:	An article on the subject **Horse racing** entitled "A woman of substance," by Gina Maranto, will be found, with illustrations, in the periodical *Sports Illustrated*, volume 67, page 62 (continued on later pages of the same issue) in the August 24, 1987 issue. A title enhancement, "jockey J. Krone," has been added by the indexer to clarify the meaning of the title. Square brackets are used to indicate these editorial interpolations.
Sample name entry:	**Meese, Edwin, III** The law of the Constitution. il *Natl Rev* 39:30-3 Jl 17 '87 *about* The resilient loyalist. E. Shannon. il por *Time* 130:15 Ag 3 '87
Explanation:	An article *by* Edwin Meese will be found in *National Review*, volume 39, pages 30-33, in the July 17, 1987 issue. An article *about* Edwin Meese by Elaine Shannon will be found in *Time*, volume 130, page 15, in the August 3, 1987 issue.

Figure B.2. and B.3 Abbreviations

Libraries have thousands of books. To find a book, you need to use a catalog. Some libraries have a computerized catalog system for locating books. The title, author, subject, and other information about each book is stored in a computer file called a data base. To use a computerized catalog system, you need to go to the library's computer terminal. Instructions for using the computer are usually posted near the terminal. If you need help, a librarian can give you instructions. Books can be found by their subject, title, or author. A computer system can be faster to use than a manual catalog system, but sometimes not all books in the library have been entered into the computer data base. For this reason, if you can't find the book you need with the computer, be sure to check with the librarian. Don't assume the book isn't in the library.

In addition to or instead of a computerized catalog system, a library will have a card catalog. In the card catalog, each book has three catalog cards: a title card, an author card, and a subject card. This means that you can look for a book by its title, author, or subject. Usually you look for a book by subject, because often you don't know the author or title. All the cards are organized alphabetically, but when you go to the book stacks to actually get the book, you will need to know its "call number," a number listed on the book's catalog card. The following exercise will help you understand catalog cards.

Exercise   Pretend that you are writing a research paper about solar energy. Use the catalog cards that follow to answer the following questions.

1. What is the title and author(s) of each book?
2. Which book is most up-to-date?
3. What is the call number of the book that has information about designing solar heating systems?
4. In which book could you find information about the cost of solar houses?
5. In which book(s) could you find examples of solar homes?
6. Which book(s) include a bibliography?
7. Alphabetize the cards by subject in the order you would find them in the card catalog. Write a number "1" on the card that would be first, a "2" on the second card, and so on.

PREPARING A LIST OF WORKS CITED

It is very important to record the sources of your information. For each article, book, interview, etc., you should keep a record of the pertinent information outlined below. This record is commonly kept on 3-by-5-inch index cards.

Information Needed

Books

Author(s), book title, publisher, city of publisher, copyright date.

Magazines and Journals

Author(s), article title, magazine title, volume number, date (day, month, and year, if the information is available), page numbers on which the article begins and ends.

Newspapers

Author (if given), title of article, name of newspaper, city or state of newspaper, date (day, month, year), section, page, and column numbers.

```
                    SOLAR HEATING.
      f             Watson, Donald, 1937-
      TH                Designing & building a solar house
      7413            Your place in the sun / by Donald
      W37             Watson -- Charlotte, Vt.  :  Garden Way
                      Pub., c 1977.
                          vi, 281 p.  :  ill. ;  29 cm.

                          Includes index.
                          Bibliography: p.  207-209.
                          ISBN 0-88266-086-1 :  $12.95.
                      ISBN 0-88266-085-3 pbk.  :  $6.95

                          1.  Solar  heating.  2.  Solar houses
                      --Design and construction.  I.  Title.

      SU               770807            CLS
      817213                             76-53830
                                         BJ
      TH7413.W37
```

```
                    SOLAR ENERGY.

      TJ
      810
      S4883            Solar energy application in buildings
                           edited by A. A. M. Sayigh  ;
                           contributors, Mehdi N. Bahadori ...
                           [et al.] . -- New York : Academic
                           Press, 1979.
                           xvi, 444 p. : ill.  ; 24 cm.
                           Bibliography: p.  423-433.
                           Includes index.

                           1. Solar energy. 2. Solar heating.
                           3. Solar air conditioning. I. Sayih,
                           A. A. M.  II. Bahadori, Mehdi N.
      CLS        21 APR 80 BJ         CLAMsc           76-67882
```

Figure B.4. Sample Catalog Cards

Reference Works (encyclopedias, dictionaries, etc.)

Title of reference book, edition number if any, title of the entry (word, subject, etc., that you looked up). Page numbers are not necessary for reference works.

Government and Other Official Documents

Government agency and/or individual authors, as listed in documents, publication number if any, title of document, city, publisher (such as Government Printing Office), date.

SOLAR HOUSES--UNITED STATES--FINANCE.

HD
7287.5
B36
    Barrett, David, 1941-
        Financing the solar home :
understanding and improving mortgage-
market receptivity to energy conservation
and housing innovation/David Barrett, Peter
Epstein, Charles M. Haar. Lexington, Mass. :
Lexington Books, c 1977.
        xiv, 201 p. : ill. ; 24 cm.   Includes index

        1. Solar houses--United States--
Finance. 2. Housing--United States
Finance. I. Epstein, Peter, 1941-
joint author.   II. Harr, Charles
Monroe, 1921-   joint author.

CLS   21 FEB 78 BJ   CLAMsc   77-3855

SOLAR HOUSES--NORTH AMERICA.

TH
7414
S48
    Shurcliff, William A.
        Solar heated buildings of North
America : 120 outstanding examples /
William A. Shurcliff. Harisville, N.H.
: Brick House Pub. Co., c 1978.
        xv, 295 p. : ill. ; 28 cm.

        1. Solar houses--North America.
   2. Solar heating.   I. Title

Figure B.5.

Nonprint Sources (interviews, TV programs, etc.)

Television/radio programs

Title of program; writer, director, producer, narrator, based on available information;
television/radio station, date (day, month, year).

Interviews

Specify personal or telephone interview, name of interviewee, title of interviewee if
relevant, date (day, month, year).

RESEARCH NOTES

When you read material for your research paper, avoid starting at the beginning of each article and reading through it completely. Instead, use skimming and scanning to locate information that is pertinent to your report. When you find useful information, take notes on index cards, recording the information, the source and the page(s) where you found the material.

Why Use Index Cards?

Writing research notes on index cards is useful for several reasons.

    a. When you write your report, writing from notes instead of the article will help you avoid accidentally plagiarizing material.

    b. It is much easier to sort and organize index cards than to use sheets of notebook paper or to highlight the articles themselves, which would require constant shuffling of pages to find information you need when you write.

    c. For longer research projects with many sources, it becomes much more difficult to work with the articles themselves, since there might be ten or twenty of them. Often, an article might yield only one or two pieces of useful information, so the index cards would provide a neat and efficient way of keeping track of this information.

General Guidelines for Using Index Cards

Each card should have just one specific point. It is better to have many cards, each with one point, than to list several kinds of information on one card, because you may not use the different points in the same place in your report. Refer to the sample note cards as you read these guidelines.

    1. At the top of each card, indicate in which part of the report the information will be used.

    2. Also at the top of the card, list the author or other information that will remind you what article the information is from.

    3. Use quotation, paraphrase and summary when taking notes, and indicate which of these you used by writing "quotation," etc., at the bottom of each note card.

    4. Write the page number on which you found the information at the bottom of each card. This is *very important*.

When you finish taking notes, arrange your note cards in the order in which you plan to use them in your report. Number the note cards so that if they get mixed up you can easily put them back in the correct order.

PREPARING A DETAILED OUTLINE OF THE REPORT

Once you have most of your research and note cards finished, it's time to start making a more detailed plan of the report. You can use the plan you made at the beginning as a guide. Your note cards provide the support for your own points, which are the topic sentences.

In this exercise you will prepare an outline that contains the topic sentences for each paragraph in the report. The following abbreviated sample outline will give you an idea of what is commonly included in each part of the report.

    I. Title for the Introduction

        A. Topic sentence (TS) for paragraph 1.

           This paragraph is normally a very basic introduction to your subject.

Quotation

Gun Control - Can it work?   *Intro* **IB**

Statistics

Time, Hays Gorey "Why Wait a Week to Kill?"
    "The N.R.A. invariably goes to war against any
    attempt to limit the avalanche of handguns
    that are used to kill 21,000 Americans
    annually."

                                    quotation p. 26

Paraphrase

Gun Control - can it work?   *Intro* **IB**

Statistics

Time, Gorey
    Logical arguments didn't influence Congress to
    approve the gun control measure because the
    NRA lobby paid congressmen $1,167,908 over
    the past 5 years. Although 70% of Americans
    support gun control, this group is not as generous
    in giving money to congressmen.

                                    Paraphrase p. 26

Figure B.6. Sample Note Cards

    B. TS for paragraph 2.
       This paragraph often begins to discuss the importance of the topic. Some common ways to do this are to give historical background, the extent of the problem (perhaps with statistics), or an incident that illustrates the problem. This part of the introduction may include several paragraphs.
    C. TS for paragraph 3.
       This may be a continuation of the material described in paragraph B. Definitions of important terms are usually included in the introductory paragraphs.
    D. TS for the final paragraph of the introduction.
       The final paragraph states the thesis and focus of the research paper.

Summary

> *The Trade Deficit - causes*   *Section IIA causes*
>
> *Time, Stephen Koepp "Good News on Trade - But Beware"*
> *The trade deficit has recently been reduced, but it is*
> *questionable how much more progress can be made. U.S. factories*
> *are operating at 83.7% capacity, and cannot produce much more*
> *or much faster. Also, U.S. Producers have given up some*
> *products, such as consumer electronics, so these must be imported,*
> *limiting how low the deficit can be reached.*
>
> *Summary p. 59*

Your Own Idea

> *The Trade Deficit*   *Conclusion IIB*
> *(Mine)*   *Solutions*
>
> *Since U.S. Factories can't produce much*
> *more to increase exports, we must somehow reduce imports,*
> *The best way to do this is to make U.S. products of*
> *superior quality, so people will buy American.*

Figure B.7.

II. Title for the Body of the Report
(generally the same as the title of the research paper)
   A. Topic of the first main part of the body. The body information is usually organized into parts, although the parts are not marked in the final report.
      1. TS for first paragraph of the body. Very often, the body of a report begins with a more detailed description of the subject. Detailed definitions, statistics, and similar information are often included.
      2. TS for second paragraph.
         Discuss the topic of the first main part of the body.
      3. TS for the third paragraph, etc.

B. Topic for the second main part of the body.
   1. TS for first paragraph about this topic.
      At the beginning of this paragraph, it is important to include a transition from the previous subject to the subject of this part of the body.
   2. TS for second paragraph about this subject, etc.
C. Topic for the third main part of the body. Generally the body of a report has no more than three parts, although for longer reports (perhaps 20 pages or more), there may be more areas covered.
   1. TS for first paragraph about this topic.
      Be sure to begin with a transition from the previous subject to this subject.
   2. TS for the second paragraph about this topic, etc.

III. Title for the Conclusion
   A. TS for the first paragraph of the conclusion.
      Conclusions usually begin with a summary of the report. The summary contains the key points discussed in the body, and may be several paragraphs in length.
   B. TS for the next paragraph in the conclusion.
      Conclusions generally include your own analysis and recommendations in regard to the subject. Based on your research (as shown in the body of the report), what do you conclude? This may take the form of proposed solutions to a problem, predictions of future trends, judgments of the successfulness of actions documented in the body, and so on. This information may take up several paragraphs.
   C. TS for the final paragraph of the conclusion.
      The final paragraph relates to the thesis of your paper, and makes some conclusive statement about it.

USING NOTE CARDS TO WRITE THE RESEARCH PAPER

Now that you have a detailed outline for your report, you need to decide exactly where you will use each piece of information from your note cards. Then you will be ready to begin writing the rough draft.

1. Use the outline you prepared in the previous step.
2. For each main idea in the outline, choose a note card or cards that contain support for that point.
3. Write numbers on the note cards based on the order in which you will use them, and write the number next to the corresponding main idea sentence on your outline.
4. Remember, main idea sentences represent *your* ideas. Use notes from your cards to *support* your own ideas.
5. At this point, students often discover that they need to do additional research because they need more information to support their points. If this is the case for you, finish the research, make note cards, and add the new note card numbers before going on.

Now you are ready to begin writing the rough draft.

WRITING THE ROUGH DRAFT

1. As you write, use the main idea sentences from your outline. Use your note cards for the support within each paragraph. You may choose to quote, paraphrase, or summarize information from your research, based on your notes.
2. Put the number of each card at the end of any sentence(s) you write containing information from that card.

3. Especially in the introduction and conclusion, you can also use your own ideas or experience as support.
4. After you finish the paper, prepare notes as described in the next exercise.

NOTES

Footnotes and endnotes show the sources of your information. The difference between them is that a footnote appears at the bottom of a page, whereas endnotes appear together on a separate page at the end of your report. Most reports use one or the other exclusively. Endnotes tend to be the more popular choice because they make typing easier, so we will focus on these. The rules for writing notes and citing sources are quite technical. The guidelines here follow those in the *MLA Handbook for Writers of Research Papers*, 3rd Edition, by Joseph Gibaldi and Walter S. Achtert (New York: The Modern Language Association of America, 1988). This is an excellent reference book for humanities research papers, but does not include scientific or technical styles.

Every item of support that comes from a research source (and probably was on a note card) must be noted, regardless of whether you paraphrase, summarize, or quote the material. Notes are numbered consecutively throughout your report. For a 10-page research paper, for example, note numbers may go from 1 to 30.

Put note numbers into the text of your report according to the following example.

Statistics on the extent of the nursing shortage show that there are 3,000 nursing positions vacant.[1]

Notice that the note number comes at the end of the sentence containing material from your source, and that it is a half-space above the line. There are several different styles of making notes, but this style is commonly used.

On a separate sheet of paper, write endnotes in order, preceded by the numbers you have assigned them. In the final draft, they will be typed on a separate page titled "Notes" at the end of the report. You should look carefully at the following examples, noting the order of information and the punctuation.

1. John Smith, "The Crisis in Nursing," *American Medical Journal* 102 (May 1988): 89.
2. Jacob Bronowski, *The Ascent of Man* (Boston: Little, Brown, 1973) 57–67.
3. Smith 90.

When you have several notes from the same source, it is not necessary to repeat all the source information every time. Instead, for subsequent references write the new note number, the author's last name (or title, if there is no author), and the page number.

THE FINAL LIST OF WORKS CITED

In addition to notes, most teachers require a list of works cited, which is a list of all the sources you mention in your report. A list of works cited is different from endnotes in that the sources are not numbered and they each appear only once, in alphabetical order. You may want to review "Preparing a List of Works Cited" earlier in this guide to see what information must be included. Study the following examples carefully, noticing what information is included, in what order, and with what punctuation.

Hetherington, Tony. "Plastic Flight of Fancy." *Los Angeles Times* 8 June 1986: 63.
Merwin, John. "How the Smart Crooks Use Plastic." *Forbes* 9 Sept. 1985: 88–91.
Whitney, Eleanor Noss. *Nutrition: Concepts and Controversies*. 3rd ed. St. Paul, Minnesota: West Publishing Co., 1985.

TYPING THE REPORT

All academic assignments should be typed. Use white typing paper (not lined paper), and type on only one side of each page. Double-space your text, and allow at least a one-inch margin on all sides, including top and bottom. Titles are almost always centered between the left and right sides of the page. The completed report should be put in a report folder. The following list shows the pages of a research paper.

1. *Title page.* This page just has the title of your report, your name, date, and the course.
2. *Outline.* Reports usually include either an outline or a table of contents. Include the title "Outline" at the top center of the page.
3. *Introduction.* The introduction starts on a new page, with its own title at the top center of the page.
4. *Body.* The body starts on a new page with a new title, usually the same title as on the title page. Unless the report is long, subheadings should not be used. Instead, use transition sentences and topic sentences to introduce new subjects within the body. Illustrations, charts, diagrams, and other material can be included within the report, following the page on which they are referred to. Alternatively, they can be placed at the end of the report.
5. *Conclusion.* The conclusion begins on a new page with its own title.
6. *Notes.* Endnotes are placed after the conclusion and after any visual aids. They are typed according to the form described in "Notes" in this guide.
7. *List of Works Cited.* This is also known as a bibliography. Type the list according to the instructions for "The Final List of Works Cited" in this guide. Many teachers require both notes *and* a list of works cited.

Skills Inventory

Skill	1	2	3	4	5	6	7	8	9	10	A	B
Reading Skills												
Checking Reading Speed	x			x			x			x		
Finding Main Ideas	x						x					
Guessing Meaning from Context		x			x			x		x		
Marking a Text	x											
Outlining a Reading Assignment		x										
Recognizing Facts and Opinions							x					
Recognizing Word Parts	x	x	x	x	x	x	x	x	x	x	x	
Skimming and Scanning					x			x				
Studying Vocabulary			x					x				
Understanding Essay Questions					x							
Understanding Graphs										x		
Using the SQ3R Method			x						x			
Working with a Case Study									x			
Critical Thinking Skills												
Analyzing a Persuasive Message						x						
Analyzing Data		x					x	x		x		
Applying a Theory							x			x		
Evaluating Evidence				x						x		
Forming Hypotheses		x										
Recognizing Facts and Opinions							x					
Recognizing Inductive and Deductive Reasoning						x						
Recognizing Logical Fallacies						x						
Working with a Case Study									x			
Writing Skills												
Analyzing a Persuasive Message						x						
Answering Essay Test Questions					x							
Applying a Theory							x			x		
Business Writing									x			
Comparing and Contrasting			x									
Defining Terms			x									
Evaluating Evidence				x						x		
Illustrating Concepts		x										
Outlining	x	x	x	x	x	x	x	x				x
Quoting and Paraphrasing							x	x	x			
Stating a Thesis and Focus		x										
Summarizing				x		x	x	x				

Skill	1	2	3	4	5	6	7	8	9	10	A	B
Writing a College Application Essay	x											
Writing a Laboratory Report										x		
Writing a Promotional Letter									x			
Writing About Cause and Effect								x		x		
Writing Topic Sentences				x								
Oral Skills												
Debating						x						
Defining Terms			x					x				
Discussing in Small Groups	x	x	x			x	x	x		x		
Explaining a Graph										x		
Giving an Oral Presentation				x						x		
Interviewing												x
Participating in Class Discussions		x	x									
Presenting Data		x							x			
Summarizing							x			x		
Conducting a Survey							x	x				
Other Academic Skills												
Managing Time					x							
Notetaking for Lectures	x	x	x	x	x	x	x	x	x	x		
Preparing for Tests					x							
Taking Tests					x							
Using Organization Charts				x								
Using a Word Processor									x			
Conducting an Experiment			x							x		
Observing Classroom Norms	x											
Conducting a Field Study		x										
Completing a Group Project									x			
Research Skills												
Choosing a Topic												x
Planning the Report												x
Interviewing												x
Using the Library												x
Encyclopedias												x
Periodicals												x
Card Catalog												x
Preparing a List of Works Cited												x
Taking Research Notes												x
Using Index Cards												x
Preparing an Outline												x
Using Research Notes												x
Writing Endnotes												x
Typing the Report												x

Index